I F P

For Frankie,
Love the Truth,

THE ART OF
PROFILING

READING PEOPLE RIGHT THE FIRST TIME

ALSO BY

DAN KOREM

SUBURBAN GANGS—THE AFFLUENT REBELS

STREETWISE PARENTS, FOOLPROOF KIDS (2D ED.)

THE ART OF
PROFILING

READING PEOPLE RIGHT THE FIRST TIME

DAN KOREM

INTERNATIONAL FOCUS PRESS

RICHARDSON, TEXAS

Published by
International Focus Press
P.O. Box 1587
Richardson, Texas 75083

ISBN 0-9639103-3-7

Library of Congress Catalog Number: 97-093267

For quantity purchases, please write
International Focus Press
at the address provided above.

Printed in the United States of America
First Printing June 1997.

—For my Sandy,
You read me from the beginning,
And showed me how to love.
Twenty-four years . . .

Contents

Foreword

This book is a rare find.

I know of no other text that is even remotely similar.

As a twenty-five-year veteran of the FBI, a former assistant unit chief of the Bureau's Behavioral Sciences Unit, and a criminal personality profiler for a time, I always encouraged new and in-service recruits to try to "read" people in a more accurate way. I was never able, however, to tell them how to do this; I believed it came with some "natural ability" and years of experience.

In *The Art of Profiling—Reading People Right the First Time*, Dan Korem demonstrates that while natural ability and experience may be useful, they are not necessary ingredients. This is a masterful text which proves one does not need a degree in psychology to gain an almost immediate sense of how a person prefers to communicate, perform on the job, and make decisions. The Korem Profiling System offers a simple, direct, and structured system for an activity we find ourselves doing hundreds of times a day—reading people.

While there are others who "profile," they are unable to pass these critical profiling skills to others. Thus the importance of this book. It provides you with necessary information and practice sessions to insure success. Learning the Korem Profiling System will separate you from the masses when it comes to reading people right the first time. Dan has lectured on profiling at the FBI Academy to the toughest audience possible, an assembly of the best police psychologists in the country.

This book will serve as a mile-marker for those interested in improving communication skills, exploring and fine-tuning business relationships, gaining better parenting and/or teaching skills, increasing sales, insuring confident hiring, and more. Profiling is a skill everyone needs and yet very few have. The information in this book allows you to avoid making erroneous assumptions about people—looking beyond their facades to become a better judge of character, a better predictor of behavior, and a better communicator.

Dan provides you with a "compass" and a "map" for your journey into the art of profiling. This insures that you will always know where you are and where you are going. The end result of reading this book and following the instructions provided by Dan will result in your being able to do "Snapshot reads," "Fine-tuned reads," and/or "Comprehensive Profiles."

This method of profiling has been presented to educators, financial institutions, medical doctors, psychologists, law enforcement personnel, and representatives of major corporations. Without exception, its acceptance was immediate and its application proven.

Now you can learn the same skills and techniques used by some of the most effective people and corporations in the world, the Korem Profiling System. It's your next step to a better understanding of people and increased success.

Dr. James T. Reese
Woodbridge, VA
April 14, 1997

CHAPTER 1

Profiling: A Powerful Tool

Imagine within just a few minutes of interaction being able to accurately predict how someone is likely to:

- **Communicate**
- **Perform on the job**
- **Make decisions**

These are three of the most valuable pieces of information most people would like to learn about others in almost any professional environment. Assessing this kind of valuable information about someone is called *profiling*.

Profiling is the ability to assess a comprehensive amount of information about a person's personality.

The term *profiling* is used in various professions to identify many kinds of information. In law enforcement, a *criminal profile* might identify how and when a felon is likely to commit his next crime. In newspapers and magazines, reporters do *background profiles* as a part of feature stories in which they detail a person's past history.

In this book, the term profiling is used to specify a person's *comprehensive profile*, which identifies how a person prefers to communicate, perform on the job, and make decisions.

The ability to use a reliable profiling system should be in everyone's professional toolbox. With refined profiling skills, we can more effectively:

- Teach and educate
- Manage teams
- Sell and close

- Sharpen communication skills
- Consult with clients
- Conduct interviews
- Prepare and deliver presentations
- Hire and develop personnel
- Diffuse confrontations
- Negotiate

In our *personal* lives, profiling can help us:

- Sensitively respond to and meet the needs of spouses, friends, and others
- Reduce conflict
- Understand those whom we love and care about
- Nurture and discipline our children to help them reach their potential

With two to three months of practice, you too will be able to profile most people within just a few minutes of interaction. In fact, you will learn how to assess a profile *without* ever meeting someone.

For those who travel abroad or work with culturally diverse groups, you will learn how to profile people from a different culture, even if you *cannot* speak their language.

And, just by answering two questions about a person, you will learn how to quickly profile the *Random Actor*—one of the most dangerous types of deceivers—and what to do if you have to engage this person. This is especially valuable for managers, teachers, law enforcement officers, and others as many dangerous individuals, such as perpetrators of workplace violence and cult leaders, are often Random Actors. The ability to profile this person quickly is considered an important breakthrough by many of these concerned professionals in the US and Europe.

The profiling concepts taught in this text, which comprise the Korem Profiling System, have been carefully developed over a period of six years. Based upon sound science, the system is constructed so that it provides a comprehensive amount of data for those who do not have the advantage of a behavioral science background. All that is required is a willingness to practice the system.

Previous attempts to provide a profiling system for nonbehavioral science professionals typically supplied a limited amount of information—just a few short descriptors—for each profile. Not enough information was supplied to make them useful across a broad spectrum of applications and professional environments. The Korem Profiling System not only provides a comprehensive amount of data, but proficiency can be developed and applied by virtually anyone.

VERSATILE WITH MANY APPLICATIONS

If you interact with others, profiling skills are a vital necessity in our global marketplace where speed in decision-making is paramount. The Korem Profiling System was constructed so that an entire organization could put it to use. Human resource personnel to sales management to auditors can all use the *same* profiling system to meet their unique and individual needs.

In the past, profiling skills were only acquired by those with a unique professional need, such as FBI agents, who track serial killers or terrorists, or human resource managers, who make hiring and personnel development decisions. Profiling, however, can benefit anyone.

Most people, though, never develop profiling skills because they lack a simple and direct system. Even in the human resource arena, most professionals do *not* have a system for profiling people on the spot without the use of a written personality test. (When I surveyed attendees at one of the largest human resource conferences in the US, over 91% indicated that they did not have a system for profiling others without the use of a written test.)

For some, developing profiling skills seems too "fuzzy" to be easily learned. Be assured that, even if you are someone who has a tough time reading others, with practice, the system presented in this book will enable you to increase your current people-reading skills by at least 25%—and by as much as 50–100% in just twelve weeks.

If you are blessed with keen intuitive insight, you may ask: *Why do I need to learn to profile? I can already read people pretty effectively.*

Here are three questions to consider:

1. Can you teach others in your organization how to develop the same refined skill so that they will have systematic accuracy?
2. Do you know with precision how to quantifiably sharpen and increase your intuitive sense of others?
3. When you misread someone, can you identify precisely what you misread so that you do not repeat the same mistake?

If you answered with a negative to two of the three questions, you have your answer: You need a dependable profiling system.

Here are some typical applications for a wide range of professional responsibilities in which profiling is an indispensable tool.

Human Resource Management

Hiring—Profiling without the use of a written self-assessment test provides an excellent check on written self-assessment tests. (Chapter 13 describes a helpful method for reducing the screening process for applicants.)

Team Management—Aid those with diverse personalities and needs to interact effectively with one another while at the same time reducing unstated biases against specific personality types—"those who are different from us." This enables team players to broaden the range of personality types with whom they can effectively cooperate.

Personnel Development—Identify those in an organization best equipped to take on new responsibilities.

Educators and Counselors

Instruction—Teachers, pastors, medical professionals, and social workers can quickly identify an individual's or a group's needs so that curriculum achieves maximum comprehension and retention.

Identify Allies—Teachers, counselors, and probation officers who interact with at-risk youths can better assess whether a specific parent, guardian, or caregiver will effectively assist in the disciplining and nurturing of a youth.

Avoid and Diffuse Conflict—Recognize how you are perceived so that you can quickly adapt to difficult environments.

Executive Needs

Negotiations—Predict and adapt to the communication and decision-making styles of those across the table.

Senior Level Interactions—Efficiently work with a hard-to-read or difficult partner/colleague.

Visionary and Bottom-line Expectations—Tailor the promotion of one's vision and bottom-line expectations to those with different profiles, increasing productivity (a skill often attained by leading athletic coaches, but often neglected by corporate decision-makers).

Law Enforcement and Security

Confrontations—Quickly identify how to confront different personality types and diffuse potential threats.

Investigations—Better predict criminal strategies and obtain information during interviews.

Sales and Communicators

Closes—Determine whether a person makes decisions confidently or out of fear, and how to sell and bring closure to interactions with either type of individual.

Sharpen Presentations—Predict when one should present more or fewer options to a client or audience.

Office Management

Reduce Cancellations—Appointment secretaries can better predict who is and is not likely to keep appointments (Chapter 7).

Temporary Help—Quickly identify strengths and weaknesses to optimize performance.

Customer Relations—Quickly modify one's language to reduce customer dissatisfaction.

Interviewing Skills

Confrontational Interviews—Auditors, law enforcement, and security can work quickly and effectively when data must be collected in a confrontational environment without inciting hostile retaliation.

Nonconfrontational Fact-gathering—Auditors, journalists, financial analysts, and doctoral students can increase the precision and scope of information gathered during interviews.

Medical Personnel

Structured Follow-up—Identify patients who need more or less structure and guidance to adhere to follow-up recommendations, such as remembering when to take medications, following rehabilitation regimens, etc. (Chapter 7).

Personal Use

Social Contacts—Shorten the time required to establish relationships.
Respecting One's Spouse—Understand and more effectively communicate with your spouse and adapt to his or her weaknesses and strengths.
Child Rearing—Direct and instruct children based upon their unique personalities.

These are just a few of the many practical applications in which the Korem Profiling System has been put to effective use. What follows are some actual cases in which profiling was the difference between success and failure. (Each case will be expanded later in the text. Because this text is designed for an international audience, the male pronoun will be applied when appropriate as this is the accepted convention, although examples will employ both male and female gender.)

Case #1—An outside consultant is working with a creative work group in the audit industry. Every time the consultant makes a proposal that the staff wants to initiate, the group's manager throws up illogical roadblocks that nearly derail the project. What course of action did the consultant take to save the project?

Case #2—Frank and his staff are pursuing a lucrative contract with XYZ Inc., a Fortune 1000 company. However, Frank encounters an unusual challenge. The CFO of XYZ requests an exploratory meeting with his staff beforehand. He tells Frank, though, that under no conditions can any of Frank's staff make contact with anyone at XYZ before the first meeting. Then, the day of the meeting, the CFO slams the boardroom door shut and screams at his subordinates, while Frank and his staff stand outside the door within earshot of the CFO's loud barks. What action did Frank take, based upon the CFO's actions, that increased his company's chances of securing a future contract?

Case #3—In Zurich, Switzerland, several doctors use the Korem Profiling System to identify more accurately those patients who require more or less regimen for follow-up to treatments, taking medicine, etc. What did the doctors and their nurses profile in each patient that enabled them to uniquely meet the needs of each patient ?

Case #4—The leader of a cult-like group, who has a criminal record including kidnapping and robbery, knows that police are likely to arrest him on a stolen guns charge. He has threatened to kill others and himself if he is apprehended, reminiscent of Jim Jones and David Koresh. There is only one opportunity to engage this individual tactically so that a bloody siege does not take place. What key element was addressed during the confrontation which enabled this dangerous individual to be successfully apprehended and a confession obtained?

THE PROFILER'S EQUIPMENT: A COMPASS AND A MAP

When people say that they want to be able to profile others to interact and solve problems successfully, they are really asking for *two* useful pieces of information.

First, they want to identify someone's profile, such as how a person is likely to communicate and perform and make decisions in a given situation. Second, they want to know what to do with this information; that is, they want to know how to operate with each specific profile.

The Korem Profiling System will provide you with a compass and a map that will help you accomplish both of these tasks.

The Compass—A compass points a backpacker in the direction that he should hike. The Korem Profiling System provides you with four questions that will be your profiling compass. After you answer these four questions about someone, you will know his/her profile. You won't ask someone these four questions, rather you will answer these questions in your own mind. And these questions are not complicated. Anyone can answer them without specialized training.

They are as simple as: "Does this person typically control or express his emotions when he communicates?" For example, Queen Elizabeth is a person who typically controls her emotions when she communicates, while actor/comic Robin Williams expresses his emotions when he communicates. With a little bit of practice, you will be able to read which way most people tilt—even those who are hard to read. Once you have answered these four questions, you will know a person's COMPREHENSIVE PROFILE.

How much information will the COMPREHENSIVE PROFILE provide?

Just take a quick look at pages 155 and 156 which details the profile of a person who is called a Sergeant/Manager. This is how much information can be assessed by just answering these four questions—and *without* ignoring proven scientific techniques, engaging in inaccurate stereotyping, or simply relying on reading "body language."

The Map—When backpacking, you not only need to know which *direction* to hike, but you also need to know the best *route* to take toward your final destination. You need a reliable map that helps you gauge distances and points out natural obstacles to avoid, such as swamps and impassable gorges. When profiling, you need a map that will identify the typical strengths, weaknesses, and tendencies of each person's profile. Your profiling map is the COMPREHENSIVE PROFILE. All sixteen profiles are provided in Chapter 11 and include strengths, shortcomings, and interaction suggestions such as how to sell and present ideas/products or how to diffuse a confrontation. Graphically, the relationship between your profiling compass and map is shown below.

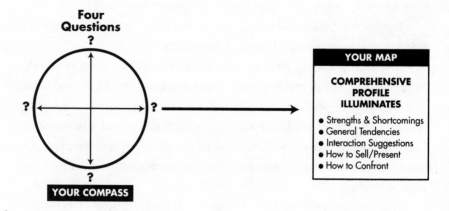

Four Questions

YOUR MAP

COMPREHENSIVE PROFILE ILLUMINATES

- Strengths & Shortcomings
- General Tendencies
- Interaction Suggestions
- How to Sell/Present
- How to Confront

YOUR COMPASS

TALK VERSUS THE WALK

In addition to providing you with a map and a compass, the Korem Profiling System breaks down each profile into two parts: (1) a person's *talk*—how he prefers to communicate; (2) a person's *walk*—how he prefers to perform in a given situation and make decisions.

All of us have been fooled by the salesman who can sell us a dream, but when called upon to act and make the dream a reality, he operates out of fear and doesn't deliver. His *talk* looks and sounds great, but his *walk* is something completely different. It is the *talk* part of his profile that misleads us. Similarly, it is easy to be fooled by someone whose *talk* is shy and retiring, but when called upon to perform, his *walk* is ironclad, predictable, and dependable.

Unless you can separately profile a person's *talk* from his *walk* you will ineffectively operate with people. The Korem Profiling System will always differentiate for you a person's *talk* from his *walk* so that you can make wise decisions.

PROFILE INFORMATION PROVIDED:
THREE CHOICES

You will have three choices of how much information you can access with the Korem Profiling System. They are:

Snapshot Read—A short two-line description, useful in many short-term, noncritical interactions. Proficiency is attainable in about 4–6 weeks.

Fine-tuned Read—Here you will be able to identify specific positive and negative actions, which is useful in most critical long-term interactions. Proficiency is attainable in about 6–8 weeks.

Comprehensive Profile—As previously noted, a full sheet of data is provided that includes general strengths, weaknesses, tendencies, and suggestions for interaction. It is useful for long- and short-term interactions. Proficiency is attainable in about 8–10 weeks.

SELF-ASSESSMENT TESTS AND
ON-THE-SPOT PROFILING

One way to read and profile people more accurately than just using our gut instinct is to use a written personality self-assessment test. Organizations often use these tests when hiring personnel. They are called self-assessment tests because an individual answers, to the best of his ability, a battery of anywhere from twenty to over two hundred questions.

These scientifically developed profiles are usually quite reliable, provided they are administered and interpreted by a qualified professional. Some of the best known are: 16PF, the Minnesota Multiphasic Personality Inventory, the California Psychological Inventory, the Myers-Briggs Type Indicator, the Guilford-Zimmerman Temperament Scale, the Edwards Personality Profile Scale, and the DF Opinion Survey. Some of these tests are not available to the general public, which decreases the likelihood that most untrained professionals will find an accurate, easy-to-use testing system that provides a comprehensive amount of data.

And written tests have limitations.

First, in order to obtain an accurate profile using a written test you must depend upon a person truthfully answering the test questions. Some people, however, have learned how to deliberately distort their answers in order to match a desired profile, rendering a test invalid.

Second, if a person is going through a life-changing circumstance, his traits may be exaggerated or concealed due to uncharacteristic stress. Because of the dramatic increase in social deterioration over the past thirty years, more people are going through life-changing events, which can translate into decreased test accuracy.

For example, one might be able to identify how a person is operating on the day of a test, but when a person's crisis passes, his actual profile can emerge—a profile that may not be suited for a specific work responsibility. In light of this instability factor, a perceived need has developed amongst human resource managers for an on-the-spot profiling system that can be used as a check on written tests.

For these reasons, a profiling system that does not rely upon a written test is an invaluable tool. By using the Korem Profiling System, you won't have to depend on someone accurately answering test questions in order to obtain an accurate profile.

For those who do use written tests when hiring or developing personnel, the Korem Profiling System can be an effective check on self-assessment tests. The combination of using *both* written tests (quantitative information) and interviews or observations (qualitative information) will only help increase the reliability of one's decisions. For those who have acquired behavioral interviewing techniques and strategies, the Korem Profiling System provides a stable and comprehensive platform from which to apply these useful tools.

PROFILING WHEN TESTS ARE NOT APPROPRIATE

Finally, there is one obvious limitation that written tests present: They aren't appropriate in most professional interactions. You can't ask competitors, purchasing agents, students, upper-level managers, or others to just fill one out.

Can you imagine starting a meeting by requesting: "Mr. Johnson, before we negotiate this contract, I want you to fill out this test truthfully so that I will have an accurate bead on your personality type." Or, "Ms. Dean, we haven't met, so before we start this audit evaluation, would you mind filling out this test so that I can identify your profile?" Asking someone to take a written test in most professional and personal situations would be interpreted as assaultive and insensitive.

While written tests are valuable in the right context, they are like a train in their ability to deliver useful information.

Trains can effectively carry cargo and people from one location to another. But trains are dependent upon a track. They can't go where track isn't laid. Trains can deliver goods to a city, but they can't drop cargo off at someone's doorstep. Also, trains have to follow schedules. Engineers can't transport goods at any time they want or collisions would result.

Like trains, written tests can be powerfully used, but their use is limited. You can't just use them anytime you want. Written tests are best administered in situations such as hiring and personnel development. But there are many more daily needs for accurate profiling, which is why there has been a perceived need in most professional environments for a reliable impromptu, on-the-spot profiling system.

The Korem Profiling System fulfills this need.

It is like a car or truck, which can deliver goods or people to any specific location and at any time.

You control *when* and *where* you want to profile someone. You don't have to ask for permission or rely upon truthful answers to test questions. You simply answer four questions in your mind about the person you want to profile. Once you have completed the lessons in the following chapters, you will be able to profile most people at anytime *you* want and on *your* schedule.

HOW THE SYSTEM WAS DEVELOPED

During the early and mid-1980s, as an independent investigative journalist, I investigated a number of individuals and groups that posed a criminal threat. They ranged from youth gangs to cults to sophisticated con artists. I preferred to focus on long-term issues, rather than the latest scam.

Often, I would find myself in a critical situation, needing guidance and reassurance that I was profiling each person or group with pinpoint accuracy. In many situations if I had taken inappropriate action because of a misread, I would have put myself or others in harm's way. In fact, several times law enforcement followed my lead because of the unique nature of the individuals or groups I was investigating. The two people I most relied upon for guidance were Hugh Aynesworth and Margaret Singer, Ph.D. They were my profiling mentors.

In 1981, Hugh, a five-time Pulitzer Prize nominee, agreed to help me with my first investigative documentary. He had just finished coauthoring *The Only Living Witness*, in which he detailed how serial killer Ted Bundy murdered over thirty women. It was one of the first confessions of a serial killer and his interview tapes are archived at the FBI's Behavioral Sciences Unit.

Hugh helped me investigate a cult-like individual, James Hydrick from Salt Lake City, who had the same background profile as Waco cult leader David Koresh. Like Koresh, Hydrick was from an abusive home, was obsessed with weapons, threatened to kill others and himself, embraced a contrived religious dogma, and was a pedophile. The investigation culminated in the only known confession of a cult-like leader. Hydrick detailed how he deceived millions of people into believing that he had powers and how others wanted to use him to control people. During the eighteen-month investigation, Hugh helped me refine my interviewing skills.

Three years later, Margaret Singer, internationally respected for her knowledge of sociopathic behavior, thought reform techniques, and interviewing skills, continued where Hugh left off, further shaping my concepts of profiling. If I could only place one call to one person in a potentially life-threatening situation, Margaret would get the call. She has never failed to provide concise, reliable, and easily digested guidance.

During one harrowing investigation in a small logging town in upstate Washington in 1987, my film crew, feeling the pressure, fled. They were spooked by threats made by a couple of former Vietnam vets who had a history of instability. (I didn't have time to prescreen the crew as I hired them with only one day's notice.) Alone, I called Margaret for advice on how to engage the volatile and unstable group. With razor precision, she helped me tailor each interview question so that it would uniquely relate to both the scoundrels, the victims, and the heroes that I interviewed. After hiring a new crew, not only did we successfully film the story without incident, but as important, no one was hurt *after* the interviews—when volatile individuals had time to mull over what I had asked. Margaret's profiling insight was what provided me with the tools that enabled me to help others safely.

During these years in the early to mid-1980s, my perspective toward profiling skills was shaped by the unique demands of investigative journalism. Profiling needs during investigations are very different than profiling needs when hiring personnel. During an investigation you have to do as much profiling as possible *from a distance, before meeting someone*, relying upon the observations of others, your own unobtrusive observations, past history, and so on. The better prepared you are, the greater the chance of illuminating a dangerous issue.

Traditional profiling applications, such as hiring and development of personnel, however, can be approached with unwritten, accepted rules: Someone agrees to submit his work history, come in for an interview, take a self-assessment test, and answer questions during an interview. There is an expected exchange of information so that the employer can make effective hiring decisions. There is also an expectation that a certain amount of "people reading" will naturally take place by both the candidate and the interviewer.

When talking to victims of crimes, however, it's best to assess their profiles *before* meeting for an interview, so that questions can be sensitively asked. Or, when this isn't possible, you do your best to profile people on the spot.

When investigating criminals, profiling *before* beginning an investigation or attempting an interview is essential. Having knowledge of a criminal's profile only increases the safety factor for the journalist and for those who might be harmed by the criminal. This means selectively relying upon people's observations of a criminal's past history and how he handled specific situations in the past. Obtaining this information is essential because most criminals will not voluntarily divulge needed information.

Taken together, these kinds of diverse needs—both investigative as well as hiring dependable staff—helped shape my concepts about how to profile people accurately, whether on the spot or before meeting someone.

Then, in the late 1980s, I was challenged by several members of the Young Presidents Organization to develop a system for profiling people in the corporate arena, a system that would extend beyond just truth detection and potential criminal behavior. This led to consultation through the early 1990s with a number of behavioral science experts. I examined many different behavioral gauges commonly used to read and profile others. It was from four well-accepted gauges that the core of the Korem Profiling System was developed in 1992—a system which could be used to profile people on the spot or before interaction takes place.

From 1992 to 1995 the system was refined and taught to virtually every kind of professional work group in the US and Europe, including human resource, audit, sales, law enforcement, and educators. Transferability issues were refined to insure that anyone could learn and use the system. Then, in January of 1995, I presented the system to over ninety of the leading police psychologists from the US and Europe at the invitation of the FBI's Behavioral Science Unit to flesh out any structural flaws. None were found. The system is structurally, culturally, and instructionally sound.

WHAT TO EXPECT

You will need to invest about an hour or two a week for about the next twelve weeks to complete a number of assignments. It usually takes about four to eight weeks, depending upon your background, before you will begin to feel comfortable with your newly developed profiling skills—a small investment to develop a critical *lifetime* skill. (In a workshop environment this can be shortened to one day, moving the average participant from 25% accuracy at the beginning of the day to about 75% at the end. The teaching process, however, is rather sophisticated, employing interactive technology.

Participants are shown carefully selected video clips of real people in real situations, and they enter what they believe is each person's profile on their interactive response pad. Responses are then instantly tabulated by a computer and the results are projected onto a screen so that each person can see how they are progressing comparison to the rest of the class. Although solely using this text takes a little bit longer, you can learn to profile just as effectively by following the suggested assignments within the time guidelines suggested.)

The instructional process, which is uncomplicated and direct, is as follows:

1. You will learn how to answer and use the four questions—the compass—that reveal a person's profile (Chapters 3, 4, and 7).

2. You will learn how to combine the four questions so that you can identify the sixteen different comprehensive profiles—your map—which provides detailed suggestions for using each profile (Chapter 11).

3. You will complete about a dozen and a half exercises, each requiring between thirty minutes and two hours, over the next several weeks.

4. Helpful tips are provided in Chapters 6, 10, 13, and 14 to insure that your reads are accurate, avoiding common mistakes. When specific ideas are noted that will be explained in a later chapter, the chapter is noted for easy reference. Important concepts covered in *previous* chapters will, when needed, also include the chapter in which it was first presented.

5. Additional concepts are detailed throughout the text, including:
   - Profiling in a foreign country (Chapter 13).
   - How to profile *before* interacting with someone (Chapter 13).
   - How to profile and interact with the potentially dangerous Random Actor profile (Chapters 8 and 13).
   - *Team Profiling*—A powerful concept in which colleagues in the same work group share their reads of others so that profiles can be developed before interacting with someone in order to achieve targeted objectives (Chapter 13). Applications are unlimited, including: consultant and strategic sales, educators meeting with concerned parents, preparing for negotiations, and investigators conducting fact-gathering interviews.

Throughout the book, I will "lift the hood" and show you how the profiling engine works. You will never be in doubt about how the different parts are at work for you. You will always know *why* the system works. In fact, you will even gain insight into how written self-assessment tests work. (For additional information on profiling, be sure to consult IFP's Internet website for new and useful profiling tips and refinements at IFPINC.COM.)

Once you have completed the learning process, profiling people with pinpoint accuracy will become an instinctive skill that you will be able to use anytime, anywhere.

A word of caution.

Do not skip any of the exercises or work faster than the time requirements suggested. Remember, you are learning a *lifetime* skill. Do not jeopardize a future, critical situation simply because of excessive eagerness. It takes a little time for each idea to be digested. The time allocations suggested to successfully complete each lesson have been carefully selected to help you develop a thorough knowledge of each component without becoming overwhelmed with new information. As you will be studying the system over a period of several weeks, core concepts are regularly repeated throughout the book so that you won't forget them.

Also, it is recommended, when possible, that you select a partner with whom you can learn the system and practice the suggested exercises. A partner can be a useful sounding board and keep you accountable for finishing the recommended assignments.

Lastly, the foundation of this book is rooted in the idea of treating others like you would like to be treated. This means working to understand the other person and trying to meet them at least halfway. When it comes to using profiling skills, our attitude should be:

I know who you are.
Good for me, better for you.

This isn't just another clever saying. It's an attitude about life.

Now let's look at four rules for profiling that promote *systematic accuracy*.

CHAPTER 2

Systematic Accuracy

READING OTHERS:
IT STARTS AS A NATURAL REACTION

Reading people is a *natural* reaction that none of us can avoid. We all spend time reading and interpreting people's actions, trying to predict how they will act in the future. We ask ourselves questions, like:

- What will he do next?
- Have I effectively designed this presentation to meet her needs?
- Is he reliable?
- How can I best communicate with him?
- Why am I not getting through to this student?
- Why is she misreading me?
- How does he make decisions?

We want to know what makes people "tick."

Each time we make an observation that answers one of these questions, we have made a *read*. When we compile several *reads* together, we identify a *profile*, which provides a more complete picture of a person.

In this short chapter are detailed the four simple and direct rules that will help you develop *systematic accuracy* when profiling. The rules aren't complicated. Many will seem like common sense—and they are. Most people, however, fail to achieve systematic accuracy because they fail to abide by these four bedrock concepts. For this reason, they will regularly be referred to throughout the text.

THE FOUR RULES OF SYSTEMATIC ACCURACY

The four rules reviewed in this chapter that will help you attain systematic accuracy are:

1. People typically act in consistent, similar ways called *traits*. When two or more traits are combined together, we have what are called *types*. Combine two or more types together and you get a *profile*.
2. We must always measure different people's traits with the same gauges or questions.
3. Anything that is worth measuring is worth measuring at least twice.
4. The best questions or gauges focus on actions that are related to what you are trying to predict.

RULE #1

People typically act in consistent, similar ways called <u>traits</u>. When two or more traits are combined together, we have what are called <u>types</u>. Combine two or more types together and you get a <u>profile</u>.

ACTIONS AND TRAITS

When initially sizing up people, the first thing that we usually do is *read* their actions. If we are negotiating, for example, we might try to read whether a person prefers to dominate a conversation or be more in the background. Or a school counselor might try and read a student's desire for predictability during a career counseling session.

Throughout the text, the word *read* will be used when we are trying to identify a *specific* action. We will use the word *action* to specify observable actions as well as speech, attire, nonverbal reactions (popularly called "body language"), and past actions. Even the tone and content of a memo could be interpreted as an *action*, if the memo helps reveal how a person prefers to communicate or perform in a specific situation.

Rule #1 acknowledges that most people's *actions* are typically consistent over the long haul. The key word is *typical*. On a given day we may act out of character or in a way that is unique, but day in and day out we will typically act and respond in the same way. For example, if Joe usually expresses his emotions when he communicates with others, we can count on the fact that on most days he will follow this pattern.

When several similar actions are observed that follow a pattern and can be grouped together, we call this a *trait*. So if Joe displays the group of actions listed below, we could say that he has a *trait* that allows him to EXPRESS his emotions.

- Outgoing at a party.
- Expressive during a sales presentation.
- Easily expresses emotion when talking with new acquaintances.
- Jubilantly cheers on teammates while playing softball.

If Mary displays the group of actions noted below, we could say that she possesses a trait that allows her to CONTROL her emotions.

- Stoic in most conversations.
- Emotionally restrained.
- Calmly and efficiently interacts with her colleagues.

Categorizing groups of actions into *traits* provides a convenient method of identifying a consistent, patterned feature of a person's actions. Traits can identify many kinds of actions, such as whether a person is *confident* or *fearful* when making decisions or *conventional* or *unconventional* in his/her daily actions. Traits are the first building block of a profile. Beginning in the next chapter, you will learn how to quickly and easily combine traits together in order to identify someone's profile.

TRAITS REVEAL TYPES

In the same way that actions can be grouped together to identify traits, traits can be grouped together to identify what are called *types*.

For example, if Joe EXPRESSES his emotions *and* prefers to be directive and TELL others what he thinks when he communicates, we can say that Joe is a specific *type* of person. One label that could be used to describe Joe's combination of traits could be a SALESMAN type—he can tell others what he thinks while expressing his emotions to generate enthusiasm for his product or idea. Another identifying label that might be applied to Joe could be a COMMUNICATOR type, as good communicators often possess these two traits.

Identifying Joe's type doesn't mean that in *every* situation he will *always* be directive or express his emotions when he communicates. We can obtain, however, a basic idea of the way he prefers to interact with others.

A graphic depiction of combining traits to reveal a type is shown below. To summarize, when two *traits* are combined together, you can identify a *type* of person. *Types* are the second building block which enables us to profile people.

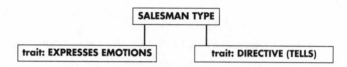

TYPES REVEAL PROFILES

When we can combine two *types* together, we can identify someone's *profile*.

Mary, as earlier noted, is a person who CONTROLS her emotions. Let's assume that she also prefers to be directive or TELL others what she thinks when she communicates. Because she possesses both a CONTROL and a TELL trait, we can say that Mary is a SERGEANT or COMMANDER type when she communicates—someone who can easily direct others while maintaining emotional control.

Imagine that Mary also has two other traits: she is CONFIDENT when making decisions and PREDICTABLE (conventional) in her day-to-day actions. These two traits when combined together would yield a MANAGER type—someone who is CONFIDENT when making decisions and PRE-DICTABLE in her actions.

Thus, Mary is a SERGEANT type when she communicates (the *talk* part of her profile), and she is a MANAGER type when she has to perform on the job (the *walk* part of her profile).

When we *combine* the SERGEANT and MANAGER types together, we get a complete picture or a *comprehensive profile* of Mary. The *comprehensive profile* of a SERGEANT/MANAGER, which was referenced in Chapter 1, can be found on pages 155 and 156. A diagrammatic representation of a SERGEANT/MANAGER is shown in **ILLUSTRATION 1**.

ILLUSTRATION 1

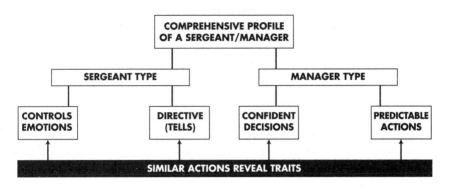

Traits and types are the two building blocks of a profile. If the relationships between actions, traits, types, and profiles aren't completely clear now, don't worry. In just a few short chapters they will be. Right now, all that is necessary for you to grasp is that:

1. Similar ACTIONS reveal a TRAIT.
2. Combine two TRAITS together and you get a TYPE of person.
3. Combine two TYPES together and you get a COMPREHENSIVE PROFILE of a person.

In graphical form, Rule #1 is shown in **ILLUSTRATION 2.**

ILLUSTRATION 2

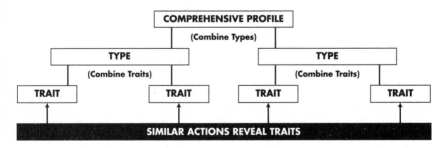

TYPES, NOT STEREOTYPES

The ancient Greeks were some of the first who tried to type people. They characterized people based on what they observed about people.

They believed that a person who had a ruddy complexion and appeared warm and outgoing had higher than normal levels of blood in his system. They labeled this person as a "sanguine." Similarly, those who appeared slow were thought to have excessive phlegm in their throats and were called "phlegmatic." The Greeks also believed that sad, "melancholy" people had excessive black bile, while reactive types had too much yellow bile and were accordingly labeled "choleric."

In addition to their mythical body fluids theory, one of the Greeks' greatest errors was that they believed that there was no differentiation between people who had the same type. All *sanguine* people, for example, were all thought to be virtually identical.

Today, this tendency to overgeneralize is called *stereotyping*, which only leads to ineffective profiling.

To stereotype a SERGEANT type, for example, is to say that: (1) all SERGEANTS have the *exact same set of actions*, and (2) all SERGEANTS use their actions with the *same degree of intensity*.

Some positive and negative actions that we do commonly see in SERGEANTS, as further detailed in Chapter 5, are: strong, confident, overbearing, unsympathetic, outgoing, egotistical, and directive. Not every SERGEANT, however, will have the same number of actions. SERGEANT #1 may display every one of these actions, while SERGEANT #2 may only have half of these actions operative in his life. The actions for both individuals, though, come from a defined list of actions that are common to SERGEANTS *and* are distinct from other personality types.

Additionally, not every SERGEANT will use his actions with the same degree of intensity. For example, two SERGEANTS might both be outgoing, but one may be more outgoing than the other.

When the term *type* is used in this book, we are acknowledging, as in the case of SERGEANTS, that:

1. A SERGEANT type is likely to operate out of a list of actions—both positive and negative—that is distinct from another personality type.

2. Not every person who is a SERGEANT type will have the exact same set of actions in his/her life.

3. Each SERGEANT will use his/her actions with an intensity that may differ from other SERGEANTS.

RULE #2

**Always measure different people with the
same gauges or questions.**

When we ask, "What is the temperature outside?" meteorologists use an accurate gauge, called a thermometer, to measure the temperature. They could try to estimate how cold it is outside by observing what people are wearing, but this wouldn't be as accurate as looking at a thermometer. One person may wear a coat when it's 50 degrees outside while another may only wear a sweater. Attire isn't a consistent or systematic measure of temperature.

For consistent accuracy, meteorologists use the same thermometer (because thermometers can vary) and place it in the same location each day. This gives them a method for achieving systematic accuracy.

We will apply the same principle to profile people accurately. We will use the same gauges for everyone.

When identifying a specific trait, such as whether a person CONTROLS or EXPRESSES his emotions, we will use the same reliable gauge for *everyone*. This will insure that our profiling accuracy will be more precise than solely relying upon our "gut feeling" or natural instincts—which can fluctuate daily due to anything from personal circumstances to stress.

If we don't use the same gauge for everyone, our profiling skills will tend to be biased.

Think of it logically. Would you want someone to profile you with a different gauge than he uses to profile everyone else? Even if you don't like an individual, profiling someone solely by instinct is in no one's best interest. The very best thing we can do is read people accurately and then operate with them based upon their *actual* profile, rather than upon our own slanted read.

The four gauges that you will use to profile are four questions that will be explained in Chapters 3, 4, and 7. You will use these same four questions for everyone. As explained in Chapter 1, you will answer these questions in your own mind about the person you are profiling. You won't have to ask someone to answer these four questions. And, in many cases, you will be able to answer these four questions without ever meeting the person you are profiling (a concept further described in Chapter 13).

RULE #3

**Anything that is worth measuring
is worth measuring at least twice.**

Everyone can make mistakes, that's why Rule #3 emphasizes that we recheck our initial reads.

Most people meet someone, make a quick assessment of that person, and then look for information that will confirm their initial hunches. Research on interviewing has demonstrated that this error, which is called *gatekeeping*, is one of the single greatest mistakes made by interviewers.

People also commonly make quick, impulsive, and emotional reads and then try to back them up with logic. This is when you can get into real trouble. The perspective toward profiling that you will adopt is just the opposite.

Skilled profilers accept the fact that some of their reads will be inaccurate.

To help you address the potential for inaccuracy, you will learn how to develop a read and then apply various strategies to test the accuracy of your reads. This will help you resist the natural temptation of attempting to justify your first impression. You won't be asked to shelve your intuitive ability, but rather to test it. In fact, those who have sharp intuitive skills will gain greater insight into why their intuition works and how to sharpen their intuitive ability.

RULE #4

**The best questions or gauges focus on actions
that are related to what you are trying to predict.**

The system presented in this book is designed to help you identify the three pieces of information that most people want to know about others. How someone prefers to: communicate, perform on the job, and make decisions.

There are many other questions/gauges that can be incorporated into a profiling system. Other questions/gauges can identify traits, such as whether a person is or isn't creative. The four specific questions/gauges used in the Korem Profiling System were selected because they identify the profile information that most people would like to know about someone else which can be practically applied in most professional and personal environments.

In most situations, you will be able to assess this information within just a few minutes of interaction. From a scientific perspective, the questions/gauges were selected because they are dependable. They were derived from some of the most current research that identifies that human personality is made up of five core traits. Four of the five traits were adapted for the Korem Profiling System.[1]

RECAP OF SYSTEMATIC ACCURACY

1. Similar actions when combined together reveal traits; traits when combined together reveal types; types when combined together reveal a profile.
2. Just like the meteorologist who uses the same thermometer to read the temperature, we must always use the same "unbiased" questions/gauges for everyone we profile.
3. We must verify our first impressions by always using our questions/gauges more than once, testing our reads.
4. We must select easy-to-use questions/gauges that will provide us with information that we can use.

Because our natural tendencies and prejudices can derail our profiling efforts, you will be reminded of these four rules of *systematic accuracy* throughout the text. Although simple in concept, these rules or principles will each take on a richer meaning as you develop your profiling skills.

Now let's take a look at the first question—your first gauge—that will enable you to profile.

The First Question: Control or Express?

CONTROL-EXPRESS

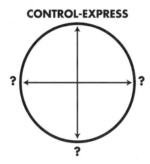

In this chapter you will learn how to use the first point on your profiling compass—the first question that will enable you to identify someone's profile.

This first question/gauge answers the question: *Does this person control or express his emotions when he communicates?*[1]

Specifically, this question, and the one reviewed in the next chapter, will help you determine how a person *communicates*. Think of this question as a *gauge* that will help you identify just one *trait*. Remember, a trait is a pattern of consistent or repeated actions that we are likely to see a person perform, such as controlling or expressing emotions.

In this chapter you will learn how to answer this first question/gauge. In the next chapter you will learn the second question/gauge. The remaining two questions/gauges, covered in Chapter 7, will help you assess how a person *performs* on the job or in a specific situation and makes decisions.

We will spend a little more time on these first two gauges, the *communication* gauges, to be certain that you understand how these gauges work. Once you learn how to use these two gauges you will have completed half the process necessary to profile someone.

QUESTION/GAUGE #1
CONTROL OR EXPRESS EMOTIONS?
Does this person <u>control</u> or <u>express</u> his/her emotions?

One of the first questions we want to answer when we first meet some-one is the question posed above. We want to know:

"Is he outgoing or quiet?"

"Is she expressive or controlled?"

It's instinctive for us to want to identify this trait in others so that we are pointed in the right direction when we communicate and listen to people

Collectively, these questions ask: "Does this person control or express his emotions?"

Or put another way: "Does this person openly express or control his feelings when he *communicates?*"

For example, when we compare the stage personality of actor Robin Williams and the character of Spock in Star Trek, we can easily say that Robin Williams *expresses* his emotions while Spock *controls* his emotions. Another similar contrast would be a person who is the life-of-the-party, who express-es his emotions, while Queen Elizabeth stoically controls her emotions.

The trait that Question #1 measures is *how much* we express our emo-tions. This is why we refer to this question—and Questions 2, 3, and 4—as a *gauge.* At one extreme, people are extremely outgoing and expressive, such as Robin Williams or the life-of-the-party, and at the other extreme, people are extremely reserved and controlled, such as Spock or Queen Elizabeth. Because Question #1 identifies whether a person typically controls or expresses his emotions, we call this the CONTROL-EXPRESS gauge, shown in **ILLUSTRATION 1.**

ILLUSTRATION 1

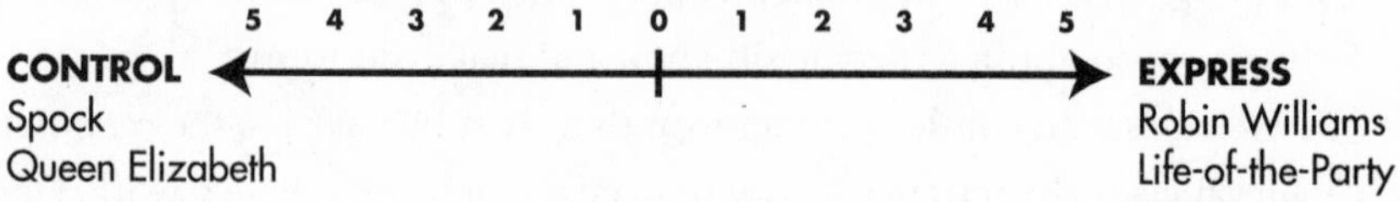

	5	4	3	2	1	0	1	2	3	4	5	

CONTROL ⟵————————————————⟶ **EXPRESS**
Spock   Robin Williams
Queen Elizabeth   Life-of-the-Party

The endpoints on the gauge, represented by the number 5, show the two *extremes* of how people manage their emotions: extremely expressive and extremely controlled. (Number 1 on the gauge, of course, represents low EXPRESS or CONTROL.)

Few people fit the extremes, such as Robin Williams and Spock. Most of us typically express or control our emotions to a lesser degree than Robin Williams or Spock. If we plotted ourselves, most of us are somewhere between 1 and 4 on the EXPRESS or CONTROL side of the gauge. In the example below, **POINT A** represents a person who is medium CONTROL, while **POINT B** plots a person who is high EXPRESS.

ILLUSTRATION 2

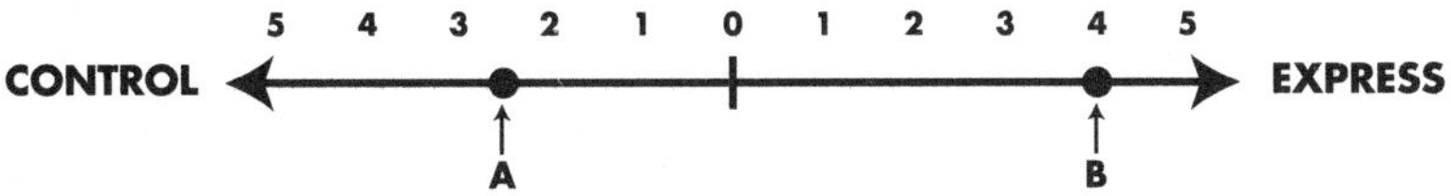

```
        5   4   3   2   1   0   1   2   3   4   5
CONTROL ◄────────────●───────┼───────────●────────► EXPRESS
                     ↑                    ↑
                     A                    B
```

In order to identify on which side of the gauge someone should be plotted, we simply take a look at his or her actions. Below are the typical positive and negative actions associated with people who control or express their emotions.

TABLE 1

People Who CONTROL Emotions: Private, controlled, introverted, quiet, suspicious, introspective, indifferent, detailed, thoughtful, and pensive

People Who EXPRESS Emotions: Outgoing, emotional, sensitive, fiery, explosive, passionate, short-fused, dramatic, extroverted, and expressive

Not everybody who controls or expresses his/her emotions will necessarily display all of the actions listed for each trait. We do know, however, that a person's specific actions will typically come from either the CONTROL or EXPRESS pool of actions—and not both. (There are, however, a small minority of people who can operate out of both pools of actions, and we will examine how to profile these unique people, who are called *combination types*, in Chapter 5.)

For example, one person who is CONTROL, may display all the positive actions of CONTROL, but only one negative action, such as *suspicious*. Or another CONTROL person may only display the positive actions of *private* and *detailed* and the negative actions of *indifferent* and *suspicious*. (This should sound familiar. As discussed in Chapter 2, we can avoid stereotyping by recognizing that we each have a unique set of actions.)

What's important is that regardless of the number of actions that a specific person may display from each action list, we *can* predict that the majority of his actions will reflect the trait that he possesses. From a scientific perspective, psychology has established that when people are under *pressure* they usually display the actions with which they are the most comfortable. This is one reason why we can predict a person's *possible* actions, and we will look more closely at this concept in Chapter 6.

POSITIVE AND NEGATIVE
EXTREMES OF THE CONTROL-EXPRESS GAUGE

Carefully review **ILLUSTRATION 3**. The following examples illustrate individuals and fictional characters, both contemporary and from history, who use their CONTROL and EXPRESS traits to the *extreme*—represented by a 5 plot point. Remember, there are positive and negative actions associated with each side of the CONTROL-EXPRESS gauge. To help you visualize both positive and negative examples of each extreme, examples are provided.

Also, consider that when people EXPRESS or CONTROL their emotions when communicating, they can do this through spoken or written words as well as visible actions. We are all unique and have our own unique blend of how we communicate.

One EXPRESS person may infuse emotion in the *way* he emphasizes words, using the tone of his voice. Another may use broad sweeps of his hand. While a third EXPRESS person may choose specific words or phrases in order to express emotion, such as: "I *feel* that this is the right decision."

Counterpoint this with a CONTROL person who says: "I *think* that this is the right decision." While another CONTROL person might say, "I feel this is the right decision," but in a tone of voice that does not betray any emotion.

Each of the people selected in **ILLUSTRATION 3** all have their own unique way of expressing their CONTROL or EXPRESS trait. And, it will vary from day to day. What is important is that the sum total of how they choose to CONTROL or EXPRESS themselves reveals extreme actions such as *extremely outgoing* or *introverted, quiet* or *expressive*.

ILLUSTRATION 3

EXAMPLES OF THE EXTREMES
FOR THE CONTROL–EXPRESS GAUGE

Positive Extreme CONTROL

• **Spock**

• **Queen Elizabeth II**
(Monarch noted for her stoic composure)

• **Dick Cavett**
(Reserved talk show host)

• **Hugh Downs**
(Straight-forward news commentator)

Positive Extreme EXPRESS

• **Robin Williams**

• **Lou Holtz**
(Former Notre Dame football coach noted for his fiery lockerroom talks)

• **Bill Cosby**
(Stage persona in the 60s and 70s for his stand-up routines)

• **Phyllis Diller**
(Comedienne noted for her wild laugh)

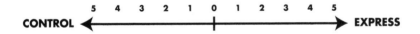

| 5 | 4 | 3 | 2 | 1 | 0 | 1 | 2 | 3 | 4 | 5 |

CONTROL ←——————————————→ **EXPRESS**

Negative Extreme CONTROL

• **Himmler**
(Hitler's coldly indifferent henchman)

• **A Recluse**

• **President Richard Nixon**
(A complex person, his suspicious, dark side is referenced here)

• **Godfather**
(Marlon Brando's quiet but ruthless portrayal of a mafioso)

Negative Extreme EXPRESS

• **John McEnroe**
(Tennis pro noted for screaming at referees)

• **Tammy Faye Baker**
(Female evangelist crying on her TV show when appealing for money)

• **Howard Stern**
(Abrasive and brash radio talk show host)

• **Nikita Khrushchev**
(Former Soviet leader banging his shoe on the table during negotiations)

IS ONE SIDE OF THE CONTROL-EXPRESS GAUGE INHERENTLY GOOD OR BAD?

Neither side of the CONTROL-EXPRESS gauge is inherently good or bad. This is because people can use their traits positively or negatively.

For example, one person who *expresses* his emotions might use his trait to motivate those who work for him, while another person might display his EXPRESS trait when screaming at subordinates.

Each person in **ILLUSTRATION 3** was selected to provide you with a simple, visual "snapshot" of each *extreme* end of the CONTROL-EXPRESS gauge. Both positive and negative examples of each extreme are provided so that you will remember that people can use their trait positively or negatively.

Effective profilers never forget that which side of the CONTROL-EXPRESS gauge that a person is plotted on isn't inherently good or bad. When we regularly recognize this fact, we can reduce some of our built-in prejudices against others.

How?

Imagine that John had a father who regularly beat his mother. Added to this, John's father was at the extreme end of EXPRESS. His father's actions were regularly explosive, revealed by a short-fused temper. As a result of John's experience with his father, John is uncomfortable in a close relationship with *anyone* who is EXPRESS because he associates people who express their emotions with his father.

When John recognizes, however, that people can use their traits *both* positively and negatively, he can learn to work and interact with a broader scope of people. In his personal life, John can become more intimate and develop more long-lasting relationships by respecting the positive differences in others. With time, by focusing on the good actions he sees in EXPRESS people, John can learn to diffuse his built-in prejudice against those who EXPRESS their emotions. For some people, this is one of the greatest benefits of learning how to profile; and in the workplace, this can be a powerful catalyst for developing cohesive and productive teams.

PERSONALIZING YOUR CONTROL-EXPRESS GAUGE

After you have studied the list of personalities in **ILLUSTRATION 3**, personalize your own CONTROL-EXPRESS gauge, provided in **ILLUSTRATION 4**.

You do this by writing the names of people who best represent for you the positive and negative *extreme* of each end of the gauge in the blanks provided. You can choose to use someone from the examples provided, another famous person whom you can easily visualize, or you can select someone you personally know. If you do select someone who isn't on the lists provided, be certain that this person displays his/her traits with the *same extreme degree* of intensity as the examples provided. You should select people who:

1. Help you quickly visualize the extreme *differences* of the endpoints.

2. Are easy to remember and whose actions you can easily visualize.

Pointed-eared Spock and his stoic manner is easy to visualize as extreme positive CONTROL. John McEnroe screaming at a referee is also easy to remember as extreme negative EXPRESS.

Don't select someone who is *almost* as extreme as the examples provided! Be certain that they are at least as extreme as the examples. Remember, you will use this gauge every time you profile someone. If you choose nonextreme examples for the extreme ends of your gauge, you will increase the chance for error and not attain systematic accuracy.

ILLUSTRATION 4

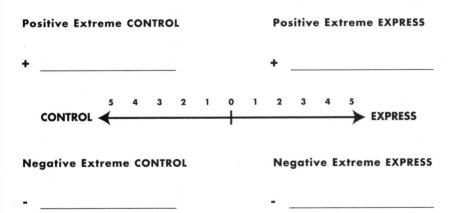

Positive Extreme CONTROL   **Positive Extreme EXPRESS**

+ _____   + _____

CONTROL 5 4 3 2 1 0 1 2 3 4 5 EXPRESS

Negative Extreme CONTROL   **Negative Extreme EXPRESS**

- _____   - _____

Now plot yourself on the gauge in comparison to the two extremes. First, select whether you are CONTROL or EXPRESS. Then, try to approximate the strength of your trait by selecting a 1–5 plot point. Remember 5 is the strongest and 1 is the weakest. Do not compare yourself to anyone else, except the two extremes. If you do, you may incorrectly plot yourself.

If you are inclined to plot yourself in the center, think carefully, as few people have a plot point of 1 or less. While you may not always control or express your emotions in every situation, most people lean toward the left or right of the midpoint. If you have difficulty selecting which end of the gauge you tilt toward, ask yourself honestly: Am I more like the CONTROL or the EXPRESS actions on a *typical* day when I *communicate*?

Resist what is called the "Barnum Effect," thinking that you possess more actions than you really do—that you operate strongly on both sides of the CONTROL-EXPRESS gauge, which is very uncommon. (This psychological observation is one factor which helps horoscopes "work." On most days, one can usually find *several* of the forecasts for the different "signs" that might apply.) One of the most humorous incidents of personal misreading that I observed occurred when a participant in a profiling workshop insisted, in an almost monotone voice, that he was EXPRESS. One person in the class whispered, "Not unless he's comparing himself to a land slug!"

Remember, all you are trying to determine is which side of the gauge you tilt toward on a *typical* day. Anyone can express emotion on an *atypical* day, such as the day when your daughter gets married or when receiving recognition for an act of heroism. Or, one might be able to temporarily restrain any show of emotion during the signing of a long sought after contract. The key word is *typical*. How do you prefer to *communicate* on a typical day?

If you are still struggling a little bit, take a look again at the list of actions for CONTROL and EXPRESS in **TABLE 1** on page 31. The following questions may also be helpful.

HELPFUL CONTROL-EXPRESS QUESTIONS

1. Am I outgoing? (EXPRESS)
2. Do I control my reactions? (CONTROL)
3. Do I easily express my emotions? (EXPRESS)
4. Do I prefer to conceal my feelings? (CONTROL)
5. Is it easy for me to be sensitive about how others feel? (EXPRESS)
6. Am I more stoic about how others feel? (CONTROL)

Which side of the gauge did you select? Are you more expressive, or do you lean toward being more controlled? Where did you specifically plot yourself? For example, did you plot yourself as a CONTROL at about 2 or did you plot yourself as an EXPRESS at about 4?

If you're still uncertain about whether you are CONTROL or EXPRESS or you can't select an approximate point, ask a few trusted friends for help. Ask them to tell you some specific examples of *actions* they have seen from you. Their consensus should help resolve your uncertainty. Be sure to choose wisely when asking someone to assist. Don't ask someone to help you who may try to take advantage of your candid discussion or who lacks keen insight into others.

You may also want to plot yourself based upon your actions when you are at work or at home. For example, some people, who show very little emotion in the workplace, find it easier to express their emotions at home or amongst their family and friends. The shift may not be significant, but it may help you develop a broader picture of your actual inventory of actions for your trait (more on this in Chapter 6).

If you do plot two different points, one for home and one for work, be careful. Make sure that you are really being honest with yourself. Most studies of human personality indicate that our basic traits are quite ingrained in our behavior. While most people are able to make some adjustments in the intensity of a specific trait, like expressing emotion, it is a rare person who can actually move from one extreme end of the gauge to the other. What is common, however, is that a person's actions will vary around his/her point on the gauge. This is called a *range* of actions.

RANGE OF ACTIONS

After you have plotted yourself on the CONTROL-EXPRESS gauge, you now have at least three reference points: yourself and two people on each end of the gauge, who represent the positive and negative extremes. This helps you visualize where you are in relationship to the two extreme ends of the CONTROL-EXPRESS gauge. Your personal plot point on the line also provides a reference point regarding your own *range* of actions on a typical day (what psychologists refer to as *dimensions* of behavior).

We know by common sense that no one uses his traits with the exact same strength on a given day or in a given situation. We do, however, operate within a predictable range.

For example, let's assume that you plotted yourself at **POINT A** as in **ILLUS-TRATION 5**. We can then predict that on a given day the strength of your expressive actions will vary somewhere around that point, as indicated by the parentheses. The average person's range will extend anywhere from 1/2 to 1 full point in each direction. So in the example below, we know that this person's range is probably about 2–4.

ILLUSTRATION 5

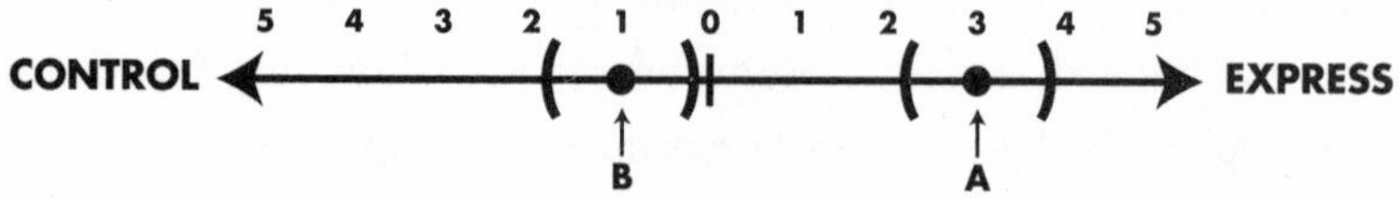

Plotting a specific point is extremely useful because it helps us predict the *range* of intensity of a person's actions or responses. So in the example above, this person, who is near the middle of the EXPRESS side of the gauge, will typically operate between being very expressive and moderately expressive.

If, however, a person is plotted at **POINT B**, we can expect that how a person controls his emotions will range from being just *slightly* controlled to moderately controlled. We can rule out that on a typical day he will react to a situation by extremely controlling his emotions when he communicates with others.

In addition to predicting a range of likely actions, the idea of approximate points on the line also helps us avoid stereotyping people. It prevents us from saying "She always does that," because people don't always act or respond to situations with the same degree of intensity.

A person who is plotted at **POINT C**, as noted in **ILLUSTRATION 6** indicates a person who can operate on *both* sides of the gauge.

ILLUSTRATION 6

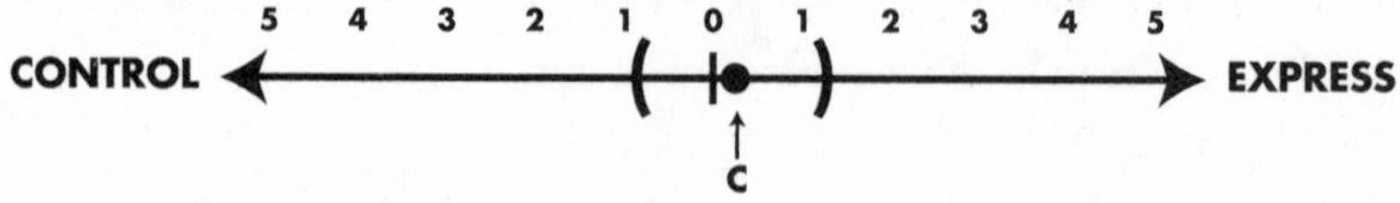

Although not common, this person's actions extend to both sides of the gauge because of his *range*. This person will display both CONTROL and EXPRESS actions, albeit rather weak actions. For some people, however, whose range extends more than a point in each direction, their actions can be much stronger, which is commonly seen in entrepreneurs who must wear many hats and draw upon a broader range of actions. Those whose range extends more than one point in each direction, however, comprise only a small percentage of the population. (The concept of a person whose range extends to both sides of a gauge will be examined in greater detail in Chapter 5, when reviewing the concept of someone who is a *combination type*.)

To summarize the concept of a *range* of actions, a plot point provides us with an idea of the approximate range of intensity that a trait will be displayed, and, in some cases, indicates that a person can operate on both sides of the gauge.

EXTREME AND NONEXTREME EXAMPLES

To help you visualize both extreme and nonextreme examples of people who control or express their emotions, some additional examples are provided in **TABLE 2**. People who represent nonextreme examples are plotted around 2 or 3 on the CONTROL or EXPRESS side of the gauge, while extreme examples are plotted at 5.

TABLE 2
EXTREME EXAMPLES

Positive CONTROL:	People who control their emotions during a volatile crisis and provide stability to a group.
Negative CONTROL:	The cold and suspicious recluse who refuses to help others for fear of having to express his feelings.
Positive EXPRESS:	Coach firing up his team in the locker room.
Negative EXPRESS:	People with short tempers who explode at inappropriate times.

NONEXTREME EXAMPLES

Positive CONTROL:	The usually quiet aunt or uncle who takes it all in and is full of wisdom.

Negative CONTROL:　　Reserved corporate manager who, at times, is indifferent to the feelings of others.

Positive EXPRESS:　　Genuinely warm salesperson who makes you feel at home.

Negative EXPRESS:　　Philanthropists who occasionally let their emotions reject wise counsel.

To summarize, when using the CONTROL-EXPRESS question/gauge, we first identify on which side of the gauge a person should be plotted. Second, the plot point helps us identify the approximate strength of someone's plot point. And third, a plot point helps us identify someone's *range* of actions.

ASSIGNMENT #1

Goal: Learn to use the CONTROL-EXPRESS gauge.

Time Required: 30 minutes.

You have just learned the heart of the Korem Profiling System: plotting someone in relationship to the two extremes of a gauge that identifies someone's trait.

This may seem new to you, but with just a little practice you will be able to plot almost anyone. The key is to observe a person's *actions* and plot them based upon those actions. If a person seems to reveal more of the EXPRESS actions when he communicates, plot him on that side. If he seems to reveal more of the CONTROL actions, plot him on the CONTROL side.

Now for your first assignment.

First, go back to the gauge you personalized, **ILLUSTRATION 4**, review the names you recorded, and modify if necessary. Remember, if you are not reading people in comparison to the extreme ends of the gauge, your profiling skills will be limited. You must avoid reading someone simply based on how you feel on a given day.

Rule #2 that promotes systematic accuracy reminds us: *We must <u>always</u> measure different people's traits with the same gauges/questions.* If you don't discipline yourself to read people with a gauge that has permanently fixed extremes, your profiling will be random and inexact.

Top-gun pilots are taught to trust their instrumentation. Not the horizon or anything else which can deceive them. In the same way, when plotting someone do the following:

1. Compare the person's *overall persona* to your extreme examples at the ends of the gauge, such as Spock and Robin Williams. Ask yourself: *When this person communicates, does he seem to control or express his emotions more like Spock or Robin Williams?* For now, you simply want to identify which side of the CONTROL-EXPRESS gauge that a person tilts toward. (Later, in Chapters 6 and 10 we will look at how to read people with more precision as well as avoid common pitfalls.)

2. If you are still unsure which side of the gauge a person should be plotted, read the list of actions for CONTROL and EXPRESS. Ask yourself: *When this person communicates, which set of actions seems to better fit this person—the CONTROL or EXPRESS actions?* In the beginning, some people will fool you, but you should be able to plot a good number of the people that you know. Like the top-gun pilot, trust that your gauges and your list of actions will direct you toward the right trait.

3. Now write the names of six people you know in the spaces provided in **ILLUSTRATION 7**. Plot them on the CONTROL-EXPRESS gauge. Write CONTROL or EXPRESS in the space provided. Refer to the list of CONTROL and EXPRESS actions in **TABLE 1** and your three reference points—yourself and the two extremes—to help you make a decision.

ILLUSTRATION 7

Name	CONTROL or EXPRESS	Plot Point

#1 _____

#2 _____

#3 _____

#4 _____

#5 _____

#6 _____

4. Next, assign a numerical plot point from 1–5 for each person, measuring the strength of each person's trait. Don't worry if some of your
estimates are off or if you struggle with an exact numerical plot point.
This exercise is intended to help you become acquainted with comparing people to the two extremes of the gauge. With practice, you will
find that your accuracy will steadily improve. It is not uncommon
when first learning to profile to have some difficulty plotting someone
to whom we are close, such as a spouse or best friend. The reason for
this is that even though a person controls his emotions, we may
remember those few instances when this person did express emotion,
such as at a surprise party, at his daughter's wedding, and so on. Most
everyone will express some emotion at some time in their life, even if
they are high CONTROL. The key is to step back and ask yourself:
Does he express or control his emotions when he <u>*communicates*</u> *with people on a typical day?* This should help you develop a more objective
read.

5. Finally, put a plus or negative next to each name, indicating whether
you think they typically express their trait positively or negatively.
This will re-inforce the idea that traits can be used positively and negatively, helping you avert unwanted biases against a particular trait.

Once you've completed this assignment, you are now ready to tackle the
next question/gauge.

CHAPTER 4

The Second Question: Ask or Tell?

In the last chapter you learned the first point on the profiling compass: *Does this person control or express his/her emotions?*

Now you are ready for the second point on your compass—the second question which reveals how a person prefers to communicate.

QUESTION/GAUGE #2
ASK OR TELL?

Does this person prefer to <u>tell</u> others what he thinks, or does he prefer to be more indirect and <u>ask</u> others what they think first?

This second question/gauge identifies whether or not someone prefers to dominate a dialogue when he communicates. It identifies whether a person typically "ASKS" or "TELLS" others what to do or what he thinks. When using the ASK-TELL gauge, we want to identify how a person engages others when he *communicates*. Another way of stating this is: "Does this person prefer to be directive or assertive and lead a conversation, or does he prefer to be more indirect and ask others what they think first?"

This gauge/question does *not* try to identify whether or not a person asks questions. Pushy, dominant people—like some tabloid reporters—can ask questions. What we are looking for is the *style* of how people ask questions, make statements, and carry on conversations.

For example, someone who is polite and has a strong TELL trait might ask a question as follows: "*Tell* me, what do you think of this situation?"

The tone is directive and naturally seeks control of the conversation— *Tell* me…

An ASK person might ask the same question as follows: "So John, may I ask you what you think of the situation?"

Note the softer, less directive way of seeking input from someone.

If Louis, a TELL person, makes a statement, he might sound like this: *I have reviewed the situation and this is what I think we should do.*

If Alex, an ASK person, makes a similar statement, he might phrase his remark like this: *After reviewing the situation, it seems that we should take a different direction.*

Louis (TELL) is more direct, to the point, and uses stronger language. Alex (ASK) is more indirect and laid back, using a softer tone.

Two examples of people who possess the ASK and TELL traits to the extreme and use their traits positively are Mr. Rogers (ASK), the host of the PBS television educational children's program, and General Norman Schwarzkopf (TELL), the American general who defeated Saddam Hussein in Desert Storm. Both are fine men, but they have radically different ways of communicating. Mr. Rogers, who has nurtured millions of kids, gently beckons youngsters with his soft, welcoming signature line, "Won't you be my neighbor?" General Schwarzkopf, the hero of Desert Storm, is also a fine person who used his strong directive trait when leading troops into battle.

Other examples of people who are ASK and TELL are Mother Theresa (ASK) and Margaret Thatcher (TELL). Mother Theresa is world-renowned for her work with over 500 orphanages, homes for the poor, and other charity centers around the world. While she confidently makes decisions, her manner of *communicating* with others is considerate, and not dominating. Margaret Thatcher, the former British Prime Minister, is also a much admired world leader for her direct and forceful way in which she consistently communicates her position.

One common misconception regarding the ASK-TELL gauge is that a person who is ASK doesn't like to talk and engage in conversation while a person who is TELL always likes to talk. The ASK-TELL gauge doesn't identify whether or not a person enjoys being engaged in conversation. Either an ASK or TELL person can enjoy a discussion. What we are looking for is *how* the person prefers to participate in a discussion or conversation. The ASK person's dialogue will typically have a more laid back and indirect flavor. The TELL person's dialogue will be more directive, forceful, or assertive. Both Mother Theresa and Margaret Thatcher would no doubt enjoy a lengthy dialogue together, but Mother Theresa would probably be more altruistic and curious in her dialogue, while former Prime Minister Thatcher would be more directive and forceful. Two engaging people. Two different communication styles.

The ASK-TELL gauge is shown below with examples of the extremes provided—people with a 5 plot point.

ILLUSTRATION 1

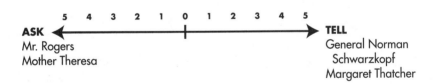

TABLE 3 that follows, provides both positive and negative actions associated with those who are ASK and TELL. Remember, ASK and TELL actions only identify actions that people might display when they *communicate.*

For example, *confident,* a positive action for a TELL person, doesn't mean this person is necessarily confident when making decisions. It only means that he is confident when he communicates—the *talk* part of his life.

Additionally, as noted in Chapter 3, people can express their traits many ways—through the tone of of their voice (being *forceful* v. *laid back*), their words (*Tell* me what you think . . . v. *May* I ask you . . .), their actions (forcefully pointing a finger v. a placid expression), and so forth.

TABLE 3

People Who ASK: Inquisitive, curious, appear uninformed or naive, agreeable, nonassertive, altruistic, weak, indirect, and laid back

People Who TELL: Strong, confident, overbearing, assertive, outgoing, unsympathetic, egotistical, directive, and forceful

ILLUSTRATION 2 provides positive and negative *extreme* examples on the ASK-TELL gauge—people with a 5 plot point. While other famous people are ASK or TELL, such as General Colin Powell (about 4 TELL), they are not included because their plot point is not a 5, such as Martin Luther King.

ILLUSTRATION 2

Positive Extreme ASK

- **Mr. Rogers**
  (The gentle children's educator)

- **Mother Theresa**
  (Known for firm resolve, but gentle demeanor when reaching out to others)

- **Bob Newhart**
  (Famous comedian noted for his laid-back wit and soft demeanor)

- **Columbo**
  (The questioning TV detective whose probing is nonintrusive and indirect)

Positive Extreme TELL

- **General Schwarzkopf**
  (Strong leader of Desert Storm)

- **Martin Luther King**
  (Inspiring orator)

- **Margaret Thatcher**
  (Forceful former British Prime Minister)

- **Captain Kirk**
  (Commander in the Star Trek series)

- **Winston Churchill**
  (Known for fiery oratory)

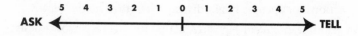

ASK   5 4 3 2 1 0 1 2 3 4 5   TELL

Negative Extreme ASK

- **Neville Chamberlain**
  (Please see discussion of negative ASK)

- **Entrenched Bureaucrat**
  (Never offers an opinion and appears weak and naive)

Negative Extreme TELL

- **Hitler**
  (Ruthless Nazi leader)

- **Howard Stern**
  (Brash radio talk show host)

- **Saddam Hussein**
  (Arrogant Iraqi dictator)

NEGATIVE EXTREME ASK

Most of the examples are self-explanatory, but amplification is necessary for the negative extreme of ASK.

Try and think of famous person who is *extremely* weak, naive, and uninformed. Not just a little weak, uninformed, and naive. But to the extreme.

Don't be surprised if no one comes to mind.

Virtually no one in this century who possesses the negative actions of ASK to the *extreme* has distinguished himself. Logically, who could distinguish himself on the world stage by being weak, uninformed, and naive to the *extreme*? Especially in a media driven age, people who have ASK actions to the negative extreme are unlikely to rise to prominence on the world stage.

After four years of inquiry, I was able to identify only one person in this century who could even qualify as a recognizable candidate. His name? Neville Chamberlain, the former British Prime Minister who preceded Churchill. He was the archetype of a negative extreme ASK person who distinguished himself in this century.

When Chamberlain gave away Czechoslovakia in his negotiations at the Munich Conference with Hitler in 1938, his extreme negative ASK actions were displayed. He appeared extremely weak, uninformed, and naive.

A more common example of a person who is negative ASK to the extreme is an entrenched bureaucrat, who is usually not given to celebrity. Obviously, not all bureaucrats are ASK or possess the ASK trait to the negative extreme. But we all have dealt with those who are. Especially at places such as the local drivers license bureau, a social security office, an institutional firm layered with unproductive managers, or some postal offices.

HELPFUL ASK-TELL QUESTIONS

Here are some questions that will help you decide whether you or someone you are trying to profile is ASK or TELL.

1. Do I use mostly direct, forceful sentences and questions, such as: "I think…"; or "I believe…"; or "This is…"; or "Tell me…"; "Tell me, what do you think…?" (TELL)

2. Is my tone softer and more indirect when making statements or posing questions, such as: "It seems…"; or "Perhaps this idea…"; or "It might be…"; "May I ask you what you think about…?" (ASK)

EXTREME AND NON-EXTREME EXAMPLES OF ASK-TELL

To help you visualize the spectrum of people who are ASK or TELL, here are positive and negative examples of those who have extreme and non-extreme ASK and TELL traits.

TABLE 4
EXTREME EXAMPLES

Positive ASK: Doctor with a carefully refined bedside manner who always asks his patients how they feel.

Negative ASK: The office "brown nose" who obsessively asks about everything to "score" points.

Positive TELL: General Norman Schwarzkopf who led US troops during Operation Desert Storm.

Negative TELL: A cult leader or dictator, such as David Koresh or Adolph Hitler, who tells and directs others with evil intent.

NON-EXTREME EXAMPLES

Positive ASK: Truth-seeking reporter who asks questions but doesn't inject his/her own opinion into the story.

Negative ASK: Office subordinate who occasionally hesitates before offering an opinion when candor is needed.

Positive TELL: A salesperson who delivers a presentation that successfully matches his product or service with the client's needs and desires.

Negative TELL: The CEO who has occasional lapses of sensitivity when giving directives.

ASSIGNMENT #2

Goal: Learn to use the ASK-TELL gauge.

Time Required: 30 minutes.

Caution: Of the four gauges, the ASK-TELL gauge is typically the most difficult to master. Be patient. After using the gauge over a period of time, plotting people won't be difficult. Also, resist the temptation to skip this short assignment or any of the others throughout the book. Even if you think you understand a concept, work through each assignment as recommended, as this will accelerate your profiling comprehension *and* accuracy.

1. Personalize the ASK-TELL gauge provided in **ILLUSTRATION 3** with your choice of positive and negative *extreme* examples. You may select someone listed in **ILLUSTRATION 2** or you may select someone you personally know. Choose carefully. You will compare everyone else to these examples. If you choose people you know, be certain that they use their traits with the same intensity as the examples provided.

2. Plot yourself on the gauge in **ILLUSTRATION 3**. As before, if you are uncertain, seek the opinion of a friend or two for examples of specific actions they have seen from you.

ILLUSTRATION 3

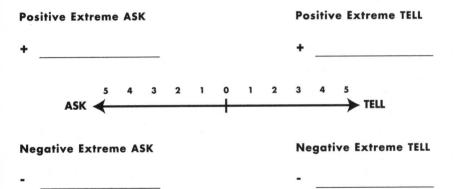

Positive Extreme ASK   **Positive Extreme TELL**

+ _____   + _____

          5   4   3   2   1   0   1   2   3   4   5

ASK ⟵———————————————⟶ **TELL**

Negative Extreme ASK   **Negative Extreme TELL**

- _____   - _____

3. Select six people you know and write their names in the spaces provided in **ILLUSTRATION 4**. Now decide whether each person is ASK or TELL by comparing the specific actions you have observed in their behavior with the list of actions in **TABLE 3**. Then estimate their 1–5 plot point and record.

    You may use the same six people you plotted from your first assignment, or you can select six others. And don't be shy about asking a friend you have plotted if he/she thinks you are correct. Most people will be more than willing to help. While we are not yet achieving systematic accuracy, you will find that within a short period of time that this approach to placing someone on the first two gauges is quite easy and reliable.

ILLUSTRATION 4

Name	ASK or TELL	Plot Point
#1		
#2		
#3		
#4		
#5		
#6		

BRIEF RECAP

1. The first two questions/gauges that you must answer to profile someone are: CONTROL-EXPRESS and ASK-TELL.
2. You have learned how to plot someone in relationship to the two ends of each gauge.
3. You have acknowledged the first part of Rule #1 for achieving systematic accuracy: *People typically act in consistent, similar ways called traits.*
4. We recognize that people can use their traits positively and negatively.
5. A plot point identifies a *range* in which people will use their trait.

USING THE ASK-TELL AND CONTROL-EXPRESS GAUGES IN EVERYDAY SITUATIONS

While the COMPREHENSIVE PROFILES provided in Chapter 11 provide a wealth of information, identifying whether a person is ASK or TELL, CONTROL or EXPRESS can be put to immediate practical use. Here are some guidelines that can be helpful when communicating with people. This does not mean that each suggestion will work in every situation and with every person who possesses the trait noted, but these common sense ideas will help you better meet most peoples' needs.

Also, please use these suggestions cautiously as your profiling skills are in the development stage. You will misread people with greater frequency until you have more experience. People are to be respected and cherished, so proceed carefully. (In Chapter 10 you will learn how to avoid some of the most common reasons for misreading others.)

When a Person Is ASK and . . .
1. You need to be directive, use a TELL person or an ASK whose ASK plot point is closer to the TELL side.
2. You are asking him an important question, use an ASK person (or a TELL person who can modify his style of inquiry so it is not as directive).

When a Person Is TELL and . . .
1. You must be directive, use a TELL person whose TELL trait is stronger, or you will risk the possibility of a confrontation.
2. You must make an inquiry, use concrete language such as, "Tell me what you think about..." rather than being indirect.

When a Person Is CONTROL and . . .
1. You must be directive, use a CONTROL person for most crucial situations, otherwise one's directive might be discounted because of the use of emotions.
2. You must make a factual inquiry, use a CONTROL person. When inquiring about a subjective issue, use someone who is more EXPRESS to help stimulate the person's subjective thought process.

When a Person Is EXPRESS and . . .
You are inquiring about facts, use a CONTROL person. When inquiring about a subjective issue, use a person who is higher EXPRESS.

ASSIGNMENT #3
You are now ready for your first major assignment.
Goal: Learn to plot people on both gauges at the same time.
Time Required: One hour over a one-week period.
You have already learned how to plot people on each gauge. Now you will practice plotting people on both gauges simultaneously.
1. Take a week and plot thirty people, six people from each of the following groups on both the CONTROL-EXPRESS and ASK-TELL gauges.

- Family
- Close friends
- Social acquaintances
- Work—people you work with in your organization
- Work—people outside of your organization

First identify on which side of each gauge each person should be plotted. Then estimate each person's 1–5 plot point. Right now your main focus is to estimate on which side of the gauge a person should be plotted. Refinement of your plot point will come with practice.

Be sure that your thirty selections include people whom you like and get along with as well as those who are not "favorites." This will prevent inadvertent stereotyping in your mind that one trait is better than another. Then ask two or three people whom you trust and respect for their insight to help assess your accuracy. As recommended in Chapter 1, when possible, work with another person who is also learning to profile so that you can sharpen one another.

Take your time with this assignment. Take a *full* week. It takes time to absorb the idea of plotting people against the extremes of more than one gauge at a time. Remember, like a pilot, trust your instrumentation—the list of actions for each trait and the extreme ends of each gauge. If a person's actions do not seem to fit with the side of the gauge you selected, reevaluate the person's daily actions against the list of actions for each trait.

2. Commit to memory the four rules for promoting systematic accuracy noted in Chapter 2. They are the anchors that will enable you to thoroughly trust your gauges as you read others.

Cautionary Note: The theatrical examples that are provided throughout the text, such as Spock and Robin Williams, refer to a character or actor's *public* persona. Some actors or public figures, however, may appear to display one trait on television or in the cinema, but are really another trait in their private lives. Therefore, exercise caution when profiling these kinds of people. Also, be careful if you practice your profiling skills by reading the personalities of TV fictional characters in your favorite series. Good writers maintain trait continuity in their characters. Poor writers, however, can place their characters all over the trait landscape to add artificial dimensions to their characters. So if you practice profiling on TV characters, be sure and pick those that don't seem to change much in how they approach daily situations.

After you have completed this last assignment, the shaded areas of **ILLUS-TRATION 5** show how many of the steps you have learned in order to develop someone's profile. You only have to answer two more questions and you will be able to profile. First, however, we will review in Chapter 5 how to assemble the CONTROL-EXPRESS and ASK-TELL gauges together to identify someone's *talk*—their COMMUNICATION type.

ILLUSTRATION 5

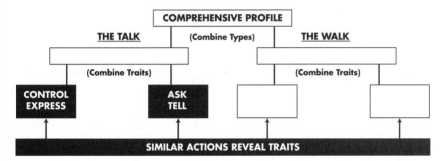

Identifying Communication Types

As you will recall, Rule #1 to achieve systematic accuracy states:

People typically act in consistent, similar ways called <u>traits</u>. When two or more traits are combined together, we have what are called <u>types</u>. Combine two or more types together and you get a <u>profile</u>.

Rule #1 also states the three steps for profiling. First, identify a person's four traits. Second, combine the traits together to reveal a person's two types. Third, combine a person's two types together to obtain a comprehensive profile.

In Chapters 3 and 4 you used two questions/gauges to identify the first two traits: CONTROL-EXPRESS and ASK-TELL. In effect, once you have plotted someone on these two gauges, you have actually completed half of the work necessary to develop someone's comprehensive profile. The next step, combining these two traits together to reveal a person's COMMUNICATION type, has already been done for you, as detailed in this chapter.

You will learn how to combine the CONTROL-EXPRESS and ASK-TELL traits together to assess how a person prefers to communicate. We call this a person's COMMUNICATION type because it identifies the *talk* part of a person's life.

COMMUNICATION TYPES

Types provide a more complete description of a person than a single trait because types show us what happens when two traits interact with one another. They summarize how different traits work together, giving us a richer and broader summary of a person's likely actions. Types also show us how people differ who may even have one trait in common.

For example, let's assume that Bob is CONTROL and ASK while Sherry is CONTROL and TELL. While both CONTROL their emotions, Sherry will tend to dominate Bob when they communicate because Sherry's TELL trait suggests that she is more likely to be forceful, strong, and outgoing.

Identifying a person's COMMUNICATION type, can help you:

- Predict with greater accuracy the likely actions you will see in a person when he/she interacts with others.
- Interact more efficiently and sensitively with people based upon their unique communication style.

To get an idea of how much information we can access about a person when we combine the CONTROL-EXPRESS and ASK-TELL gauges together, look at the list of possible actions for the SERGEANT type on page 63. You will note that like traits, there are potential positive and negative actions for a SERGEANT, as well as "other tendencies" which can be used either in a positive or negative manner.

Combining the two gauges together to obtain a person's COMMUNICATION type is simple and direct because the work has essentially already been done for you.

COMBINING THE GAUGES

In order to combine the CONTROL-EXPRESS and ASK-TELL gauges together, we just turn one gauge on its end as shown in **ILLUSTRATION 1**. Instead of reading both gauges as horizontal lines, the CONTROL-EXPRESS gauge is turned to the vertical, like a thermometer.

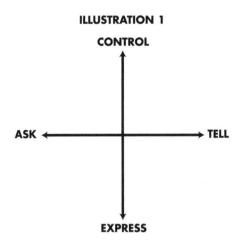

ILLUSTRATION 1

Nothing else has really changed. You still use the same process to plot people on each gauge. When we combine the two gauges together, however, four quadrants are created. Each quadrant represents the combination of two traits, and each of these combinations is called a *type*.[1]

So that the four combinations are easy to remember and visualize, we label each combination as seen in **ILLUSTRATION 2**.

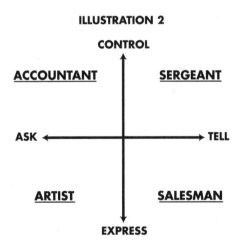

ILLUSTRATION 2

(If the four-quadrant illustration looks similar to other two-gauge schematics, it should. Remember, the system is based upon established principles for profiling. The key difference is that the Korem Profiling System is designed to deliver a comprehensive amount of data *without* relying upon a written test.)

A brief summary of the traits associated with each type are:

SERGEANT	CONTROL and TELL
SALESMAN	EXPRESS and TELL
ACCOUNTANT	CONTROL and ASK
ARTIST	EXPRESS and ASK

FOUR HELPFUL LABELS

The following four labels, SERGEANT, SALESMAN, ACCOUNTANT, and ARTIST, are easy-to-remember picture-labels that were carefully selected so that people from almost any cultural background can quickly visualize each type and its associated traits. Additional options for labels are also provided to help promote a broader understanding of each label.

SERGEANT—A CONTROL/TELL person is labeled a SERGEANT because it is easy to imagine sergeants in the army controlling their emotions while giving orders. The SERGEANT label provides a visual picture of a person who is CONTROL/TELL. This doesn't mean that every sergeant in the army will possess these traits, but it is typically easier for most people to visualize a "sergeant" possessing these traits than a clerk. Other suitable substitutes for a SERGEANT might be a *Leader* or *Commander*.

SALESMAN—An EXPRESS/TELL person is labeled a SALESMAN because it is easy to visualize a salesman telling you about his product as he conveys enthusiasm through his emotions. Another possible label for this type of person is *Communicator* or *Presenter*.

ACCOUNTANT—A CONTROL/ASK person is labeled an ACCOUNTANT because it is easy to imagine an accountant maintaining his emotional composure as he makes inquiries. Other possible labels that might be used for this type of person are *Investigator* or *Detailer*.

ARTIST—An EXPRESS/ASK person is labeled an ARTIST because one can visualize this person taking in all kinds of thoughts, experiences, and ideas from others (ASK) and then putting his emotions into his work. Another possible label for this person is a *Counselor* or *Sensor.*

HOW TO PLOT A TYPE

ILLUSTRATION 3 shows how to plot a SERGEANT type of person who CONTROLS and TELLS. As shown, **POINT A** is the CONTROL-EXPRESS plot point, and **POINT B** is the ASK-TELL plot point. If you draw a perpendicular line out from each point, they will intersect at **POINT C**, forming a rectangle or square. This shows us that this person, a SERGEANT type, operates in the CONTROL/TELL area when he communicates.

ILLUSTRATION 3

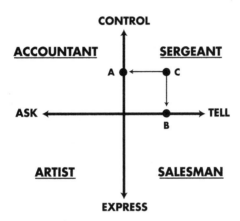

To plot any of the other three types, you simply identify the plot points and extend them until they intersect. **ILLUSTRATION 4** shows how an ARTIST type is plotted who has a strong EXPRESS trait and a moderate ASK trait.

ILLUSTRATION 4

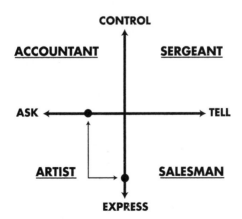

NOT ALL SERGEANTS ARE ALIKE

Now let's compare two people who are both SERGEANTS, but who differ in how they communicate. Compare SERGEANT A and SERGEANT B, shown in **ILLUSTRATION 5**.

ILLUSTRATION 5

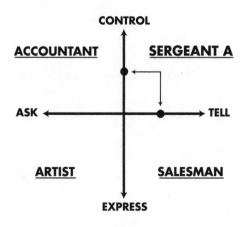

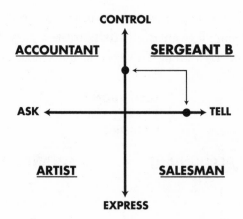

Notice that SERGEANT B *TELLS* more than SERGEANT A. Not only does this mean that the two SERGEANTS are different, but we can also make some predictions about their differences.

First, we can predict that SERGEANT B is more likely to take charge, be directive, or be forceful than SERGEANT A. Why? Because SERGEANT B has a stronger TELL trait than SERGEANT A. Thus, SERGEANT B is more likely to give orders or be firmer in the way he gives orders.

However, since SERGEANT B's TELL trait is stronger than SERGEANT A, we can also make another prediction. If both SERGEANTS have a tendency to be insensitive, we can predict that SERGEANT B is more likely to be more insensitive than SERGEANT A. Why? Because his TELL trait is stronger.

People who TELL often need to work on their listening habits. They are more likely to be more concerned about getting their point across than listening. And, when TELL is combined with controlling one's emotions, this often translates into being insensitive. Thus, since SERGEANT B's TELL trait is stronger, he will probably struggle more with being insensitive than SERGEANT A.

(*Reminder*...We are only assuming for the purposes of this illustration that SERGEANTS A and B struggle with being insensitive. We must remember that not all SERGEANTS have to battle insensitivity. To claim that all SERGEANTS are insensitive is to needlessly stereotype SERGEANTS.)

Take a minute and think through this comparison. You don't have to master the complete concept of how traits interact to reveal a type. But for now, just recognize that SERGEANTS can each be different because of the weakness or strength of their plot points. Recognizing the differences between people who are the same type not only helps us avoid stereotyping, but also increases our predictive accuracy when trying to estimate how someone will act in the future.

IDENTIFYING YOUR OWN TYPE

In Chapters 3 and 4 you plotted yourself on the CONTROL-EXPRESS and ASK-TELL gauges. Now plot yourself again on the gauges in **ILLUSTRATION 6** on the following page. Don't let the fact that the CONTROL-EXPRESS gauge has been turned to the vertical confuse you. Just plot yourself on the two gauges like you did in the last chapter. You may want to look at your original plot points on pages 35 and 49. Now draw a line out from each plot point until they intersect.

You have now identified your COMMUNICATION type, and you didn't have to answer any more questions. Please record your type in the space provided. Now let's examine the actions associated with each type.

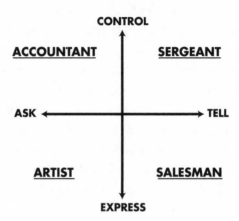

ILLUSTRATION 6

YOUR TYPE: _____

COMMUNICATION TYPES AND ACTIONS

TABLE 5, on the following page, lists the positive and negative actions that we are likely to see displayed by the four COMMUNICATION types. Also listed are "Other Tendencies," which are potential actions that aren't necessarily positive or negative.

What these lists reveal are the *possible* actions that we are likely to see when two traits interact with one another, providing a more complete picture of how someone communicates. Not every action listed for each type, however, will be evident in everyone who is a specific type.

ARTIST A, for example, might only display two-thirds of the actions listed for an ARTIST, while ARTIST B might display three-fourths of the listed actions. What we will find, though, is that an ARTIST will possess more of the actions listed in the ARTIST list than those actions in the SALESMAN list.

It is possible, however, that an ARTIST might learn to cultivate one of the actions outside of his type that he can use in specific situations. For example, he might learn to take charge (a SERGEANT action) when he teaches Sunday school to youngsters or when he must make simple presentations at work. He might have acquired this action through training or from a parent when he was a child. The majority of his actions, though, will be those of an ARTIST because of the interaction of his two traits—ASK and EXPRESS. (This concept of learned actions outside of one's type inventory is further addressed in Chapter 6.)

Types are also a guideline for predicting the possible actions that a person may display over *time*, rather than pinpointing how a person will specifically act or respond in every situation.

An ARTIST, for example, may not display all of his actual actions at one time, or even during a short period of time. He may experience an entire month at work without using his natural tendency to *avoid conflict*, a common ARTIST action. (Some people would call this a holiday!) But, because we have identified his type, we know that *avoiding conflict* is a *possible* action that he might display.

Take a few minutes and scan through **TABLE 5**. Familiarize yourself with the kinds of actions you will be able to identify. Remember, these are actions that people display when they *communicate*, not when they perform tasks.

TABLE 5
SERGEANT: CONTROL/TELL

POSITIVE ACTIONS	NEGATIVE ACTIONS	OTHER TENDENCIES
Takes charge	Overbearing	Strong-willed
Directive	Myopic	Self-sufficient
Self-confident	Egotistical	Unsympathetic
Influential	Machiavellian	Willing to use force
Assertive	Relentless	Stubborn
Determined	Hot-tempered	Forceful
Pragmatic	Won't accept direction	
Action-oriented	Impatient	
Persistent	Insensitive	

SALESMAN: EXPRESS/TELL

POSITIVE ACTIONS	NEGATIVE ACTIONS	OTHER TENDENCIES
Outgoing	Impulsive	Talkative
Optimistic	Overly ambitious	Dreamer
Passionate	Undisciplined	Emotional
Politically attuned	Manipulative	Plays favorites
Excitable	Easily discouraged	Reactive
Happy-go-lucky	Idealistic	Dramatic
Friendly	Egotistical	Open
Trusting	Gullible	Desire to please
"Joiner"	Unfocused	

ACCOUNTANT: CONTROL/ASK

POSITIVE ACTIONS	NEGATIVE ACTIONS	OTHER TENDENCIES
Easy-going	Uninvolved	Introspective
Thoughtful	Weak	Aloof
Analytical	Suspicious	Picky
Detail-oriented	Pessimistic	Stuffy
Poised	Unexcitable	Introverted
Calm and cool	Slow	Tranquil
Orderly	Critical	Debater
Efficient	Compulsive	Perfectionist
Objective	Resists interaction	Stubborn
Moralistic		Focuses on history
Dependable		Proper

ARTIST: EXPRESS/ASK

POSITIVE ACTIONS	NEGATIVE ACTIONS	OTHER TENDENCIES
Creative	Critical	Idiosyncratic
Sympathetic	Moody	Respectful
Agreeable	Argumentative	Tolerant
Avoids conflict	"Spineless"	Enduring
Supportive	Emotionally rash	Retiring
Sensitive	Low self-esteem	Focus on how they feel
Deep-feeling	Unsure	
Self-sacrificing		
Loyal		
Amiable		
Compassionate		
Self-effacing		

Remember, these are actions that people display when they communicate—their *talk*. So, a SALESMAN'S negative action, *overly ambitious*, only applies when he communicates, *not* when he takes action—his *walk*. How he performs tasks and makes decisions are a function of two other traits, which are covered in Chapter 8.

Also note that some types may share the same or similar actions. For example, both ARTISTS and ACCOUNTANTS can display the negative action of being *critical* when they communicate. This is because they both share the ASK trait which can contribute to failing to take the initiative when *communicating* one's perspective.

ASSIGNMENT #4

Goal: Scan the possible actions for your own type.

Time Required: 30 minutes.

Find your type, read over the list of actions, and check off the actions that you believe are a part of your personal inventory. As recommended in previous exercises, it is also advisable to find a trusted friend to assist you so that your list is complete. Sometimes we are unaware of a specific positive or negative action that we possess.

As just noted, you may find that *some* of the actions from the other types adjacent to yours might fit your personality. For example, if you are a SERGEANT, you may possess an action of a SALESMAN. This is because both types share the TELL trait. It is unlikely, however, that you will have many common actions with a ARTIST, who is ASK/TELL, because ARTISTS and SERGEANTS don't share any common traits. This is why ARTISTS and SERGEANTS are what can be called "opposite types."

If you find that you have a large number of actions from two adjacent types, such as ACCOUNTANT and ARTIST types which both share the ASK trait, you may be a *combination type* which is explained in the next section.

COMBINATION TYPES

A person is a *combination* type when one of his plot points is near the middle of a gauge. Thus, because he operates within a *range*, he shares actions from both sides of the gauge. This causes this person to share actions from two different types, thus a *combination* type.

There are two reasons why someone may be a combination type. The first reason is that one of his plot points is near the middle. Thus, because he has a *range* in which he operates, part of his range extends over to the other side of the gauge, as shown in **ILLUSTRATION 7**.

ILLUSTRATION 7

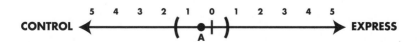

The second reason why someone may be a combination type is that he has a bigger range than most of us, and one of his plot points is closer to the middle, **ILLUSTRATION 8**. Notice that this person's plot range (**POINT A1** to **POINT A2**) is almost three full points.

ILLUSTRATION 8

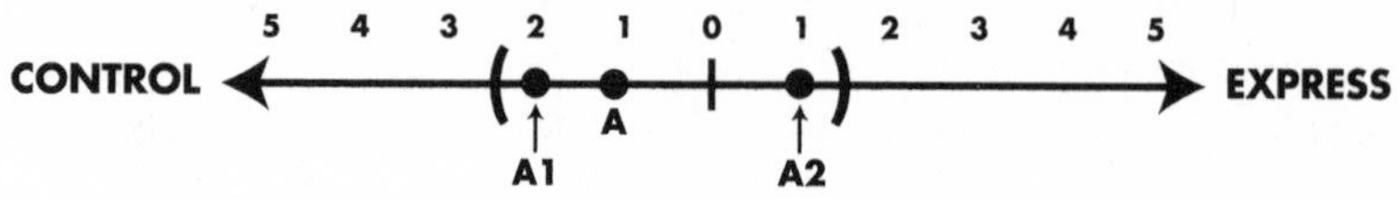

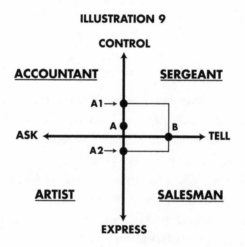

ILLUSTRATION 9 shows an example of someone who is a combination type who operates on both sides of the CONTROL-EXPRESS gauge. His plot point is **POINT A** but his range extends to **POINT A1** and **POINT A2**. Because he operates on both sides of the CONTROL-EXPRESS gauge, he is both a SERGEANT and a SALESMAN—a *combination* type.

ILLUSTRATION 9

CONTROL

ACCOUNTANT   **SERGEANT**

A1→

A

B

ASK   **TELL**

A2→

ARTIST   **SALESMAN**

EXPRESS

Although not very common, when you find someone who truly operates on both sides of a gauge, you must first identify both of his types. Then take the list of actions for both types and combine them together to evaluate the possible actions he might possess. This is more work, but it is better than always being confused by this person's gallery of actions, which may seem contradictory. It is also helpful to note the situations in which each type and its associated actions has a tendency to display itself.

Combination types are common in multi-role environments, such as small entrepreneurial companies in which a person must wear many hats and carry out varied kinds of responsibilities. Leaders who are combination types, should take the time to point out to their subordinates that they are a combination type and which type is likely to surface in which situation. For example, it is common for SERGEANT-SALESMEN to let their SERGEANT type dominate in situations that require directives, while the SALESMAN type will surface in selling or idea driven sessions. This requires a bit of maturity to do this, but can pay big dividends by retaining a stable management team.

An Enigma Wrapped in the Walls of a Castle Library

A number of years ago, I was asked to pay a visit to a prominent restauranteur, whom we will call Ned. His peers often referred to him as the "Walt Disney" of the restaurant industry. He possessed the uncommon combination of a knack for managerial details and artistic firepower, allowing him to develop one of the most successful restaurants in America. Unquestionably, he was one of the most interesting people I have ever met.

An art graduate of a West Texas university, one of his first jobs was running the family dry cleaning business. A huge jump from one end of the thought process to the other.

When I arrived at his office, I noticed that his office was also a lesson in contradictions, reflective of some combination types.

The corporate offices were in a Fortune 500 defense contractor's plain concrete building, complete with metal curtains shading the windows from sunlight and industrial listening devices. So you would expect a fairly conservative office interior.

Well, the lobby of his offices were fairly traditional. The door to the lobby was made from handsome leaded cut-glass panels, showing an artistic flair. Nothing in the lobby, though, prepared me for Ned's office.

He had dismantled a richly wooded library that resided in an European castle, sent it to the US by ship in containers, and reassembled it down the corridor from the lobby. Behind his desk, dimly lit, was a painting by one of my favorite American maritime master painters.

Attired in a conservative but richly tailored suit, I didn't hear a word of what Ned said to me during the first few minutes of my visit. I was overwhelmed.

Ned was an ARTIST-ACCOUNTANT, and, understandably, a genuine enigma to his senior management staff. If he were not a thoughtful and considerate CEO, he would have been a terror to try and please. On one side he was an expressive artist, and on the other side he was a controlled and detailed CEO with a bottom-line corporate mission.

I made a conscious decision, after our meeting, to understand how this type of person was wonderfully put together. About ten years later, when I started to develop the profiling system in this book, I got my wish.

HELPFUL TIPS ON TYPES

These are some helpful guidelines when reading a person's type.

Respect each person's natural traits and positive actions—Everyone has a contribution to make. We must respect the fact that we are all different. Imagine an organization in which everyone is a SERGEANT: the president is a SERGEANT; the receptionist is a SERGEANT; the personnel manager is a SERGEANT. It would be miserable to work in an environment where everyone tried to direct and control everyone else. Be thankful for diversity of types. Even if you feel uncomfortable with another person's style of communicating and interacting with others, learn to respect the positive aspects of his type.

If you are biased against a particular trait or type, it is often the result of one of three reasons:

- This person is your opposite type and you feel uncomfortable because you don't understand them and his/her unique needs.
- This person is the same as your trait or type and reminds you of your shortcomings. (You probably share some of the same negative actions.)
- This person's trait or type reminds you of someone whom you justifiably or unjustifiably don't like.

Persisting in your bias will only diminish your ability to profile with clarity and will limit the types of people with whom you can successfully interact. To counteract the above, focus on looking for the positive actions in people who have the types or traits toward which you have a bias. Better yet, practice the next tip.

Learn from your opposite type—Often, if you try to emulate the positive qualities of your *opposite* type, your negative qualities will begin to diminish. For example, SERGEANTS and SALESMEN, who are both TELL, can learn to be better listeners—a common negative action they both possess. They can improve their listening skills by learning from and associating with those who ASK—ARTISTS and ACCOUNTANTS. In fact, this type of learning is the basis of many "management development" programs.

Learning from and associating with those whose traits are the opposite of ours is something we should practice both professionally and socially. In successful marriages, when spouses, who are opposites, value and try to emulate their spouse's positive actions, their own negative actions often begin to diminish with the passage of time.

For example, let's imagine that Bill has a strong TELL trait, and he is not a good listener. His wife, Marge, is medium ASK and she has excellent listening skills. If Bill works at emulating Marge's listening skills, his inattentiveness will begin to diminish. This doesn't mean that Bill will adopt, to the same degree, Marge's exceptional listening skills. But he can move from being a poor listener to a moderate listener in most situations and an excellent listener in specific short-term situations.

By making a conscious effort to learn from those who have different traits, we can also reduce biases, and we can appreciate the benefit of another person's strengths which we don't possess.

Learn to modify how you communicate with each type—Successful interaction with others demands that we be respectful of the positive actions associated with each type and try to accommodate another's shortcomings. Here are some examples:

If you're a SALESMAN or an ARTIST, learn to reign in your emotions when interacting with SERGEANTS and ACCOUNTANTS, who may have difficulty expressing emotion.

If you're a SALESMAN or a SERGEANT, practice listening more when with ACCOUNTANTS and ARTISTS, who don't TELL.

If you're an ACCOUNTANT or ARTIST, practice voicing your opinion a little more when around SERGEANTS and SALESMEN. You are less likely to be discredited because of a lack of input or a low-key manner when delivering your point.

What we are talking about here isn't mimicking another person's style of interaction; rather, we are trying to meet people halfway to promote better interaction and understanding.

Some misguided motivational speakers suggest that if we are communicating with Bill, that we should "mirror" or copy Bill's communication style to become like Bill. The rationale is: *If you act like them, they will like you.* The end result, however, is usually a phony, surface-based relationship.

As noted in Chapter 1, the foundational attitude of this book is rooted in the idea of treating others like you would like to be treated. No one wants to be artificially mimicked. People want to be treated uniquely, based upon their unique combination of traits, actions, skills, knowledge, likes, and dislikes. Let this perspective reinforce your philosophy toward profiling: *I know who you are. Good for me, better for you.*

BRIEF RECAP

1. Actions reveal traits.
2. Traits combine to form types.
3. When traits interact, a list of potential positive and negative actions as well as "other tendencies" can be cataloged.
4. Types are a *guideline* for predicting *possible actions* over time, rather than pinpointing how a person will specifically act or respond in every situation.
5. Types are not stereotypes:
   - Not every ACCOUNTANT, for example, will display every action listed in the ACCOUNTANT list.
   - Similar types, such as two ACCOUNTANTS, will not necessarily display the same actions with the same degree of intensity because their plot points may vary on each gauge.
6. Familiarity with the list of *possible* actions will:
   - Increase predictive accuracy.
   - Help you better interact with others.
7. Combination types are people who can operate on both sides of a gauge because of their plot point and range. An example is an ARTIST-ACCOUNTANT, who is both EXPRESS and CONTROL.

ASSIGNMENT #5

Goal: Learn to identify the different COMMUNICATION types.

Time Required: Two hours over a one-week period.

At the end of Chapter 4 you practiced plotting people on both the CONTROL-EXPRESS and ASK-TELL gauges. During the next week, you will do the same thing. But you will also identify each person's COMMUNICATION type and review each person's actions associated with his/her type.

1. Take a week and plot twenty people from each of the five categories listed below. Don't rush. It takes time to absorb the concept of types. Reflection is needed when we compare ourselves to others.

   - Family
   - Close friends
   - Social acquaintances
   - Work—People you work with in your organization
   - Work—People you interface with outside your organization

2. Identify each person's COMMUNICATION type.

3. Check off the actions associated with each person's type that you observe. If one person doesn't seem to fit the list of actions, scan the other types and see which type seems to fit better. Perhaps you didn't accurately plot someone on the ASK-TELL or CONTROL-EXPRESS gauge. If you did misread someone, consider what you missed. Were you operating out of a bias? Did you fail to read someone based upon the extreme ends of each gauge? If someone's actions appear to be a solid mix of two types, this person may be a combination type, and you will need to combine the actions found in each of the two types.

After you have completed the assignments in this chapter, you will have learned how to use two of the points on your profiling compass and how to combine them together to identify a person's COMMUNICATION type. In effect, you have learned half of the Korem Profiling System.

ILLUSTRATION 10 on the following page graphically depicts these first two steps for developing a COMPREHENSIVE PROFILE: (Step 1) Identifying whether people are ASK-TELL and CONTROL-EXPRESS, and (Step 2) How to combine these traits to identify someone's COMMUNICATION type—the *talk* part of our persona.

In Chapters 7 and 8, you will learn how to identify the last two traits and combine them together to reveal a person's PERFORMANCE type—the *walk* part of our persona. Before tackling the last two questions that will enable you to profile, we will review some helpful tips that will improve the accuracy of your reads.

ILLUSTRATION 10

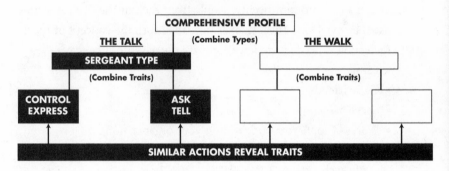

CHAPTER 6

Tips for Successful Reads

Before we review the last two gauges, some tips are reviewed in this chapter that will help you increase the accuracy of your reads. I have found that even seasoned profilers overlook some of the concepts in this chapter. Therefore, it is recommended that you periodically consult these ideas until they become instinctive.

Also, after you complete this chapter, it is recommended that you go back to the exercises in the previous chapters and see if you can't sharpen or even correct reads that you made of others. (Later chapters will provide additional guidance for improving the accuracy of your reads. Chapter 10 reviews the seven key reasons why people misread others and the antidote for each, and Chapter 14 provides additional suggestions for successful reads and details the five clue categories from which to make observations for your reads.)

1. READ OVERALL PERSONA WHILE LOOKING FOR "LEAKAGE"

As already suggested, there is no magic bullet that will enable you to profile someone. There isn't one specific action that you can look for and see a person's profile just tumble out. This is because we all have different ways of expressing the same trait.

For example, Keith may display his TELL trait by sharply pointing his hand at you when he speaks—sometimes simultaneously extending his first finger. For Keith, pointing his hand or finger is his way of being directive. Linda, however, may simply keep a strong, firm gaze on you while speaking to you and not use her hands at all. For Linda, the firm gaze is her way of being directive.

Because people have many different ways of expressing the same trait, it is advisable when first learning to profile that one focuses on:

- Observing a person's overall persona—the sum total of a person's actions, speech, posture, attire, and so on.
- Watch for any *leakage*—any breaks that appear in the consistency of a person's actions.

Each of these concepts is expanded below.

Overall Persona—When we observe a person's *overall persona*, we don't look for one specific action over another, rather we absorb the *combined* effect of a person's actions, speech, attire, etc. Then, when plotting someone on the ASK-TELL gauge, we ask: *Does this person's overall persona appear to be more like Mr. Rogers or General Norman Schwarzkopf?* The idea is to compare the overall persona of Mr. Rogers and General Norman Schwarzkopf with the overall persona of the person we are trying to read. Then, if stumped, you can take out the list of actions associated with ASK and TELL and ask yourself which set of actions seems to appear the most frequently.

When first learning to profile, about 50% of the people you read will be easy to plot. The person's persona will be easy to compare to the extremes. These people will typically have a plot point that is 3 or higher on a gauge, and thus their actions are more pronounced and easier to spot.

For about 25% of the people you are profiling, you will have to pay closer attention because a person's persona won't be immediately apparent. This often occurs when a person's plot point is around 1 or 2 on a gauge. Actions at this point aren't as pronounced when compared to a person whose plot point is 3 or higher. For these people, reviewing the list of specific actions associated with a gauge is very helpful.

The remaining 15–25% of those you profile will require some digging and practice. Some of these people will be illusive until you apply the concepts in this chapter and those in Chapter 10, which addresses the most common reasons for misreads.

In a workshop environment, it is interesting to watch beginners attempt to profile people from video clips they are shown. Most people predictably try to spot a certain look, phrase of speech, or facial expression that will reveal a trait. Then, when the specific action they are trying to spot doesn't appear, they misread that person's trait, and their success is usually limited. But, once the same group of beginners is instructed to take in a person's whole persona—and not focus on a predetermined action—and ask themselves, *Does this person's persona look more like Mr. Rogers or General Schwarzkopf?* their accuracy immediately increases. In fact, when people are instructed to take in the whole persona and compare it with the personas of Mr. Rogers and General Schwarzkopf, even though their accuracy goes up, they will tell you that one specific action did not tip them off, such as speech or nonverbal facial expressions. They just allow the sum of a person's actions to speak for themselves when compared to Mr. Rogers and General Schwarzkopf. Specific actions, such as speech, may sometimes tip them in the right direction, but when first profiling, taking in someone's overall persona is more efficient.

As a simple exercise, tape several of the better quality television news interview programs, such as *60 Minutes* or *20/20*. Now plot the people who are the subjects of each interview segment on the ASK-TELL and CONTROL-EXPRESS gauges. Compare each person's overall persona to that of Mr. Rogers and General Schwarzkopf (ASK-TELL) and Queen Elizabeth and Robin Williams (CONTROL-EXPRESS).

Also, make a note of what seemed to have tipped you off. You will often find that there is no definitive path that allows you to make an accurate read and plot someone on one of the gauges. The reason for this is that each person and situation is uniquely different. Sometimes a person's wild tie may tell you that he's EXPRESS, while another person's reserved office arrangement may suggest that she's CONTROL.

With experience one *will* eventually begin to pinpoint and even direct one's attention to look for specific actions. When first learning to profile, though, it is more helpful to take in the sum total of a person's actions, rather than trying to focus in on specific actions, such as: the specific content of a person's speech, the tone of his voice, or gestures. It's not that specific actions don't reveal traits. They can and do. But when first learning, it is my experience that people are less productive when they always look for a specific hand motion or a phrase of speech to determine someone's plot point. Making these kinds of assumptions when first developing one's skills will typically lead to ineffective stereotyping and unreliable profiling skills.

In addition to reading the overall persona, you must also look for *leakage* when you are profiling someone.

What is *leakage*?

Leakage—There are times when people deliberately or unknowingly conceal their actual traits. When trying to read these people based upon their observable overall persona, it's not uncommon to fail. To overcome this common stumbling block, you must also look for breaks in consistency or *leakage*.

Leakage is when there is a break in the consistency of a person's actions that *leaks out*. A person's actions seem to be consistent, and then there is that one action that doesn't fit. Someone appears reserved in a meeting (CONTROL), but when pressured, suddenly a clear EXPRESS trait erupts. Or a person who seems to be in the background during a dialogue (ASK) suddenly becomes forceful and directive (TELL).

The following is an example of a man who wasn't trying to fool anyone, but who often fooled those trying to profile him. By looking for leakage, however, his actual traits *leaked* out.

Leaking Eyes and Smiles

Bill was a salesman I interviewed who had been deceived by a "psychic surgeon." Bill related how the fraudulent healer from the Philippines seemingly reached into his body, without making an incision, removed damaged tissue, and repaired his hernia. All this and without the trace of a scar or even a slight scratch. The charlatan had fooled hundreds using sleight of hand to create the illusion that his hand could disappear into a "patient's" body. The tumor, which he "removed" from Bill, was actually a small animal organ that he concealed in his hand.

When I ask people to try and profile Bill by watching an unedited videotape of his interview, most profile him as CONTROL. They don't see Bill expressing any emotion as he recalls what he observed. Bill's facial expression doesn't change much, his voice is steady, and his speech content is void of anything dramatic. But leakage did occur during the taped interview—a break in his consistent actions.

Bill told me that the healer cured him of his hernia.

I politely asked: *Would your doctor say that you are healed?*

Bill's eyes sparkled, and smiling pleasantly for the first time, he said that he didn't know what his doctor would say. Specifically, expressive warmth could be seen in the area around his eyes that matched his warm smile. His eyes twinkled and the crows feet on the sides of his eyes lit up. It was Bill's way of expressing emotion when I politely asked him an important question.

Up until my question, Bill's face remained steady—almost placid. This is common when people know that what they are sharing is being recorded and will be seen on television. They try to appear calm and in control of the facts.

Most people when asked to profile Bill, will easily identify that he is about a medium TELL, by the directive tone of his voice. But, if one did not observe Bill for a couple of minutes, one might think that he was a SERGEANT (TELL and CONTROL). But, Bill, a salesman by profession, *leaked* a little bit of inconsistency through his eyes and smile that revealed that he was a SALESMAN type (TELL and EXPRESS).

There is no pat way that *leakage*—a break in the consistency of a person's actions—occurs. We are all unique and each have our own way of doing it. To spot a break, one must simply be observant. With experience, spotting breaks in consistency becomes second nature. While not all breaks in the consistency of a person's actions will indicate a specific trait, they should be noted. So if a person's persona seems to indicate that a person is ASK, and then a demonstrative TELL action surfaces, it is wise to test your first read and reexamine the ASK and TELL actions that you observe in that person.

2. TEST YOUR READS: CREATE POSITIVE AND NEGATIVE ASSUMPTIONS

After you make a read, it is wise to create positive and negative assumptions that will test your read.

For example, let's assume that you think someone is EXPRESS. Then it would be helpful to form a negative and positive assumption about your read, such as: *If my read is accurate, he will probably show some emotion when we talk about the possibility of a new position, but if he's CONTROL, he will probably be more stoic.* Here is another example if your first read is that someone is TELL: *If my read is accurate, he will probably be forceful in presenting his case for the new position, but if he's ASK, he will be less assertive and perhaps indirect in our discussions.*

Creating these kinds of positive and negative assumptions will force you to test alternative interpretations of the actions you observe, and will help you readjust your read if your first read is inaccurate.

3. PAST BEHAVIOR: BEST PREDICTOR OF FUTURE BEHAVIOR

Most of us are creatures of habit. We prefer to operate in the same way that we have operated in the past. People don't usually jump from extreme EXPRESS one day and then extreme CONTROL the next, unless they are confronted with a potentially life-changing experience. It just isn't comfortable. Remember, Rule #1 that promotes systematic accuracy: *People typically act in consistent, similar ways called traits.*

This common sense idea, which has been quantified through psychological testing, can be put to immediate use when reading people.

We can actually begin to develop hunches about a person's plot point by first taking a look at his *past* behavior. If past actions suggest that someone is EXPRESS, then we can start with this as a plot point.

To be sure that the data you have received about this person's past behavior is accurate, you then *test* your hunch by taking additional, real-time reads. Chapter 14 expands further on the idea of obtaining reads on past behavior. For right now, though, just remember that past behavior—actions—will typically help illuminate a person's plot point, unless that person has undergone a life-changing experience.

4. UNDER PRESSURE, ONE'S TRAITS ARE TYPICALLY REVEALED

This second idea is linked closely with the one just covered. As already noted, we typically prefer to operate as we have in the past. Yes, we may mature, become wiser, and so forth, but the *style* of how we communicate and perform will typically remain the same.

For most of us, when change does occur it manifests itself in whether we use the good or negative actions associated with our traits. Some of us learn to develop and strengthen our good actions, while others choose to turn from the good and let our negative actions dominate.

Under pressure, though, our actual traits and their associated actions are usually revealed. This occurs for the same reason noted in Tip 3—we prefer to use the traits and actions with which we are the most comfortable. When these two ideas are linked—the predictability of actions under pressure and past actions are the best predictor of future actions—a powerful idea emerges.

One of the most reliable reads we can make regarding a person's profile is to note how someone dealt with a *stressful* event in his *past.*

(*Life-changing* or *life-threatening* pressure/stress, past or present, doesn't qualify, because anyone can step out of character when their existence or daily life is in jeopardy. Death threats, for example, can elicit very strong EXPRESS actions even from someone who is strong CONTROL. Or, challenging a person's moral fiber can temporarily elicit strong TELL actions from someone who is ASK.)

Examples of positive and negative sources of stress that can elicit uncharacteristic actions include: divorce, unexpected promotion or recognition, public humiliation, loss of job, death of a spouse or friend, and so on.

Here are some practical places where one can obtain reads of how a person dealt with pressure in the past:

- During a downsizing, merger, or acquisition.
- How criticism was received (both justifiable and unjustifiable); how criticism was presented to another person.
- How someone adapted to stressful change; how someone initiated stressful change.
- How someone reacted when confronted; how someone reacted when he had to initiate confrontation.
- How someone worked under a deadline; how someone reacted to others when he was the initiator or presenter of a deadline.
- Response to a negative report; how he presented a negative report.

Each of these situations present opportunities to observe a person's actual traits in which stress is involved. It is important to note that a person might initiate the action that causes stress, or this person is on the receiving end of a stressful action initiated by another.

In a team environment, one can often develop a profile before ever meeting someone. How? By pooling information, gathered by team members, about how a person dealt with stress in the past. Chapter 13 takes a closer look at the idea of *team profiling* and how organizations can use this information to achieve objectives swiftly, efficiently, and sensitively.

Cautionary Note: It is unethical to artificially inflict stress upon a person simply to develop a profile. Only in limited situations in which the person *is aware that he is being observed* should this option be used, such as in some law enforcement or military environments. Current federal, state, and local laws as well as professional ethical codes of conduct should be very carefully reviewed before initiating this kind of action in order to obtain a profile. Finally, even if the action is legally, ethically, and morally justifiable, it should be the *last* option considered because of the possibility of unintentional or intentional abuse.

5. FIRST READS CAN BE PRODUCTIVE

When we first meet people, there is often a little bit of pressure and discomfort because it is the first time that we have interacted with them. In other words, there may be some *pressure* or awkwardness due to uncertainty. That's why the reads we make of people within the first few minutes of interaction often reveal their actual traits. This doesn't mean that the first actions we read are always the clearest, most accurate, or easiest to read. It is recommended, however, that you use your first impressions to create as many hunches as possible.

For example, suppose that Eric's first independent comment when you first meet is a question about your *feelings* on an issue. Because he asked about your *feelings*, rather than about your *perspective* (which is how a CONTROL person is more likely to ask the same question), your first hunch might then be that Eric is EXPRESS. Then, if you asked Eric a question about his *feelings* on the same issue, and if he provides a descriptive, personal response, you are closer to concluding that he is EXPRESS.

A very different read might be developed from this first observation if it appears that Eric asked you a question to control the interaction. Then your hunch might be that he is TELL—that he tried to *assert* himself and *direct* the conversation. In either case, the initial observation can produce hunches that can be quickly tested, providing a more reliable read of Eric's traits.

6. PEOPLE CAN LEARN ACTIONS OUTSIDE THEIR ACTUAL TRAIT OR TYPE

A famous journalist, noted for her strong TELL trait, once quipped about herself, "I got wide hips by learning to ask a question and not stepping on a person's answer. I learned to *not* intrude on a person's thoughts. When I was less experienced, I wanted to finish their statement for them."

Related to her traits, what this journalist was saying was: *I have learned an action that isn't naturally a part of who I am.* In this case, a reporter with a strong TELL trait, learned two ASK actions: to be *agreeable* and genuinely *inquisitive* when asking people about their opinions and thoughts.

Many of us can learn and master an action or two that is outside of our trait and type inventory of actions. It may not come naturally, but with practice we can do something that is uncomfortable for us. Some can acquire their actions through formalized training, while others do so through practice and sheer will.

One remarkable example is the story of a young entertainer who possessed a strong ASK trait *and* he stuttered. Yet, he had a strong desire to become an effective communicator. He knew that somehow he had to overcome his stuttering and his natural desire to resist being directive. What did he do? He took a job as a disc jockey for a low watt radio station! He reasoned that if he put himself under enough pressure, he could find a way to develop some directive actions and overcome his stuttering. He succeeded, and today he is an effective communicator for a national prison ministry speaking to and encouraging tens of thousands of inmates each year.

Acknowledging that people can learn an action or two that isn't in their type will help us when we are puzzled by an action that doesn't fit their profile. For this reason we must never rely upon just one read. We must take more than one read and test our reads to be certain that we are not observing a learned action.

Making more than one read reinforces Rule #3 for attaining systematic accuracy, which states: *Anything that is worth measuring is worth measuring at least twice.* While the *learned action* factor is not something that you will necessarily be confronted with on a daily basis, it is wise to remember it so that you aren't needlessly baffled or confused.

For the astute profiler, this raises the question: *How can one tell the difference between leakage of a trait and a learned action?* That is, how can one know the difference between a break in consistency that reveals a person's actual trait versus a learned action? The answer is experience. Taking more than one read, and testing your reads.

Will the Real ASK and TELL Please Step Forward

Mike Wallace, the noted journalist for TV's *60 Minutes*, conducted a fascinating interview in 1995 with Radovan Karadzic, then the Serbian leader in Bosnia. Both men are high TELL, yet both displayed the actions of an ASK person. By taking more than one read, however, the necessary *leakage* appeared that would enable you to profile each man with precision.

Mike Wallace, to the casual observer, would be plotted at about 3 ASK because of his ability to ask questions in an ASK style—extremely inquisitive and curious. However, at one point, Karadzic asked Wallace: "Who did more damage during W.W.II? Hitler or the Allies?"

In response, Wallace responded: "Damage to property. No doubt. The Allies. Of human life. No doubt. Hitler."

Wallace's language and tone in response to Karadzic's question were clearly TELL. When he said, *no doubt*, he sharply snapped his head forward and a strong TELL type of forceful gaze emanated from his eyes at Karadzic.

Karadzic, a psychiatrist before the Bosnian-Serb war, clearly showed his ability to portray someone who was ASK, which he probably cultivated as a psychiatrist. Before he posed his question to Wallace, he softly asked the following question with his head slightly tilted and without the least whisper of a directive trait: "May I ask you a question?"

Clearly, he had mastered the *agreeable* and *inquisitive* action of an ASK person, although the rest of the interview indicated a strong TELL person.

If you were satisfied with taking just one read of each man when their learned ASK actions were employed, your read of each man would have been inaccurate.

(Although anecdotal, I have observed that people who are TELL have an easier time trying to master an ASK action than an ASK person trying to master a TELL action. And for people who are TELL, they can only display ASK actions for short spans of time or in very specific contexts. Why? Because *people typically act in consistent, similar ways called traits*—Rule #1).

7. UNOBTRUSIVE READS ARE THE MOST EFFECTIVE

Typically, the more unobtrusive you are when reading others, the more accurate your reads.

If you walk up to someone and ask, "Do you control or express your emotions when you communicate?" you're not likely to receive a transparent answer. In fact, the person himself might not be able to articulate an answer because he has never thought about his profile.

Or, if you ask someone, "Did you express or control your emotions during the last merger?" it is questionable whether you will get an answer that is reliable. The person might respond with the answer that he thinks will best serve himself, or the answer that you want to hear, or he may not remember at all.

In most situations profiling accuracy can be enhanced by making unobtrusive reads, which are reads that we make in the background or indirectly. It's like when parents want to know how their child carries himself with his peers. Rather than directly asking the child, wise parents find opportunities to observe their child inconspicuously, like at a party or a school event.

Similarly, if we make unobtrusive reads when profiling people, our accuracy should improve. Here are some suggestions for when and how to make an unobtrusive read.

Background Information—One of the simplest unobtrusive reads is to find out how a person responded to a past situation. This can be done by making inquiries of others, or even dialoguing with that person about a past situation. A more detailed discussion of how to obtain and use background information is found in Chapter 14.

Observing Someone in the Background—A common practice in some sales organizations is to have a potential recruit travel for a week with a few of his future colleagues. Rather than solely relying upon an interview process, management can make unobtrusive reads by observing how the potential salesman responds when he is out on the street with those who carry out the same responsibilities.

During interviews, people can put on a "game-face," but in the field with potential peers, this usually gets stripped away. Applying this unobtrusive process is not only beneficial to management, it is also beneficial for the potential recruit so that he doesn't take on a job for which he isn't suited.

Nonthreatening, Open-Ended Questions or Requests— There are numerous courses taught on how to use questions or requests that allow people to be themselves more naturally when they respond. These strategies are often taught in behavioral interviewing workshops. The following is an example of how to adapt open-ended questions and requests to profiling.

Imagine that Don has just emerged from the battle of rush-hour traffic. Not only was he nearly hit by two rude drivers, one of whom drove a red truck, but he is also late for your presentation. This is also your first meeting with Don. He apologizes to you while simultaneously expressing quite a bit of emotion with what appears to be a strong EXPRESS trait. Then, two of his colleagues, Rick and Mary, enter your office.

A simple, nonthreatening and open-ended question that you could toss to Don might be: *Don, tell Rick and Mary what all you had to do just to get here this morning.*

The idea here is for Don to retell his morning traffic story to his colleagues so that you can see if he expresses himself with an EXPRESS trait—and with a similar or a little bit lower degree of intensity, since he is retelling his story. In this way you are able to test your read. If he uses the same trait with a similar degree of intensity, you will know that Don is probably EXPRESS.

Notice that your request is *indirect.* You ask Don to recall his experience for his colleagues. This enables you to observe Don more unobtrusively than if you simply asked him a direct question or made a direct request.

Also, notice the language that is used. It is *open-ended.* The request isn't: *Tell them about the guy in the red truck who pulled in front of you.* Rather, *Tell Rick and Mary <u>what all</u> you had to do just to get here this morning.*

The words *what all* are open-ended.

Don can relate whatever he would like about his morning drive, which frees him up to express himself more naturally. He can talk about the guy in the red pickup, or he might recall a similar incident the week before and how he reacted.

The idea is that the indirect question or request using open-ended language allows a person to more naturally and unobtrusively be himself. The dialogue does not force Don to respond with specific facts or subjective observations in a specific manner. He can express himself as he chooses, thus allowing his actual traits to emerge.

8. ENVIRONMENT AND TIME: DOES IT AFFECT ACTIONS?

As explained in Chapter 3, people operate within a *range*, and not at a specific plot on a gauge. This is useful to remember because some people move from one end of their range to the other, depending upon whether they are at the office or at home, or if they are talking to management or those down the corporate ladder.

For example, assume that Ted is an executive who is a SERGEANT type. He is also medium TELL—about a 2. At work because of the high-stress demands of his job, he often operates at about 3, but at home he is comfortable at about 1—where he doesn't feel compelled to use his TELL trait as often.

If you first meet Ted and his wife for dinner at their house, and later you unexpectedly do business with Ted, it would be wise to reassess your read of Ted based upon his professional environment. While he won't change from TELL to ASK—unless he is about a 1 on the TELL side—the *strength* of his SERGEANT actions will be affected and may catch you by surprise. At home, you may find that his SERGEANT actions, such as *assertive, takes charge,* and *influential,* are less pronounced than when you meet him at his office.

Because environment can affect which end of the range a person prefers to operate, it is common to take a job candidate to lunch or play a round of tennis—a completely different setting—so that one can observe a person's full range of actions.

Regarding the changing of a plot point on a gauge over a period of time, the plot point for most people remains consistently the same. For some people, however, a plot point can change over time, even moving from one side of the gauge to the other, such as moving from EXPRESS to CONTROL. While behavioral specialists have long debated the nuances of this issue, a common viewpoint is that plot points can change for various reasons such as sustained stress, which forces adaptation. An immediate response to a life-changing situation is another common reason. Some experts estimate that as many as twenty percent of US adults are currently going through some kind of plot-point change.

The plot points for most people, however, are usually fairly consistent over a period of time. I believe, however, that the number of people in the future whose plot point will change will increase in the US (and in many other countries) as the deteriorating social pressures of the past thirty years continue to persist, causing continued upheaval in individual lives. For this reason, those in managerial positions, for example, would be advised to semi-annually review the profiles of those in their department or division.

9. LEARN TO READ YOUR *OPPOSITE* TRAITS AND TYPES

Most people have difficulty reading people who are the opposite of their trait or type. This occurs because we don't live in the other person's shoes. How often do we hear spouses or those in opposite work groups, such as sales and auditing, voice the complaint: *They're just different. I don't understand them.*

When first learning to profile, we must respond to the fact that we typically have difficulty reading people who possess our opposite traits and types.

Logically, if reading our opposites is where we are likely to be weakest, *where should we expend more effort when learning to profile?* The obvious answer is focus on reading those who possess our opposite traits and types.

One way to do this is to find someone who is your opposite and ask him for help.

For example, if you are an ACCOUNTANT type, find a friend who you are iron-clad certain is a SALESMAN type—who doesn't share your ASK or CONTROL trait. Ask him to tell you about his thought process. How he reacts to situations. Ask him to describe how other colleagues and friends, who are also SALESMAN types, think and deal with people and situations. Ask for both positive and negative examples. Have him point out other people who are

SALESMAN types, and see if you can spot their specific SALESMAN traits and actions.

Or, if you find that you struggle with just one of the traits, find someone who you are absolutely certain is that trait and ask him to assist you as you read others.

One executive gave insightful advice to colleagues in his organization who were just developing their profiling skills. His suggestion was that if you are having a particularly difficult time reading someone, ask yourself: *Are they the opposite of my trait or type?* Often, he and those in his organization found that this was the case. Be careful, however, because there are other reasons for misreads, which are addressed in detail in Chapter 10.

APPLYING THE PROFILING TIPS

In order to illustrate how the ideas in this chapter can be practically applied, the following story is provided. It is based upon an actual case in which Jack, a sales consultant, was able to profile that Diane, the president of a prominent company, was a SERGEANT. Each tip that was applied is noted in brackets as well as the trait that was revealed or suspected.

Jack was first introduced to Diane at a benefit-sponsored tennis match. Jack couldn't initially tell if Diane was ASK or TELL, as Diane seemed pleasantly at ease. [Tip #8 Environment affects actions]

During the match, Jack and Diane agree to discuss a new equipment line that her company might be interested in purchasing.

A week before the meeting, Jack received a letter from Diane in which she wrote, "As you prepare for our meeting, be sure to focus on how your equipment can help us meet our bottom line productivity issues." [TELL . . . directive language]

Jack is also informed by a noncompetitive vendor that Diane is forceful when negotiating contracts. [TELL . . . . Tip #3 Past behavior predicts future behavior]

Upon entering Diane's office, she *firmly* meets Jack's eye, and, without fanfare, invites him to sit down. [TELL/CONTROL . . . Tip #5 First reads productive]

Still standing, Diane *warmly* asks, "Can I fix you a cup of coffee?" pointing to her personal coffee maker on the back corner of her credenza. [Tip #6 Learned action]

Jack politely refuses and they get down to business.

A few minutes later, they are interrupted by an intercom request from Diane's assistant. Diane must take a time-sensitive call.

"Look, I told you that we will not back off from opening the Central European market. Now follow through," she tells her caller. [TELL/CONTROL; Tip #4 Under pressure traits revealed and Tip #7 Unobtrusive reads—Jack indirectly observed Diane, confirming his initial reads]

Please review the ideas in this chapter periodically over the next few weeks, while you are developing your profiling skills. They will give you added insight and direction for making accurate reads. As suggested at the beginning of the chapter, review the exercises in the previous chapters and see if you can sharpen or even correct reads that you made of others by applying the ideas you have learned in this chapter.

You are now ready to learn the last two points on your profiling compass—the CONFIDENT-FEARFUL and PREDICTABLE-UNPREDICTABLE gauges—which are explained in the next chapter.

CHAPTER 7

The Last Two Questions: Confident-Fearful? Predictable-Unpredictable?

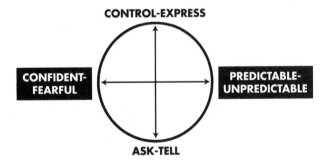

In this chapter, you will learn how to use the last two points on your profiling compass: how a person makes decisions and performs on the job. These two PERFORMANCE questions/gauges, which identify a person's *walk*, are:

1. Is this person confident or fearful when he makes decisions?
2. Are this person's actions typically predictable (conventional) or unpredictable (unconventional)?[1]

These two PERFORMANCE questions/gauges can be used in many practical situations, including:

- In a sales environment, knowing who needs to be presented with more, or fewer, options.

- Identifying who is and isn't resistant to accepting needed change.
- Secretaries and assistants reducing cancellation of appointments.
- Doctors identifying who needs more or less follow-up regimen.
- Investigators increasing their accuracy for detecting truthfulness.

Once you learn how to plot someone on these two gauges, you will also know the four key questions/gauges necessary to develop a *comprehensive profile*. Your profile compass will be complete. In the next chapter you will learn how to combine the PERFORMANCE gauges to identify a person's PERFORMANCE type, and Chapter 11 provides the already compiled sixteen COMPREHENSIVE PROFILES—your profiling map—which shows you what happens when PERFORMANCE and COMMUNICATION types are combined and how to interact with each combination.

QUESTION/GAUGE #3
CONFIDENT OR FEARFUL?

Is this person typically <u>confident</u> or <u>fearful</u> when making decisions?

Question/gauge #3, shown in **ILLUSTRATION 1**, is a "confidence" gauge. It will help you predict whether a person is typically motivated by fear or confidence when making decisions.

ILLUSTRATION 1

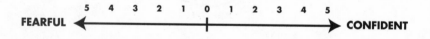

```
        5   4   3   2   1   0   1   2   3   4   5
FEARFUL ◄───────────────────┼───────────────────► CONFIDENT
```

On one end of this gauge are people who act confidently because they believe they can control or influence the events and circumstances in their lives. They believe they can influence their job and work environment, their family, or their social environment. Examples of people who could be plotted at the extreme end of this gauge are General Norman Schwarzkopf and Margaret Thatcher, the former British Prime Minister.

On the other end of this gauge are people who *do not* feel in control of their lives and are fearful. They generally act on the assumption that most events in their lives are outside of their control or are heavily influenced by external factors that dictate their personal success or failure. They take little responsibility or ownership for events which occur in their work, family, or social settings.

Of the four gauges, only the CONFIDENT-FEARFUL gauge has an inherently negative plot point. For each of the other three gauges, plot points are not positive or negative. Only one's specific negative actions are a negative. It is different, however, when a person is plotted about 3 or *higher* on the FEARFUL side of the gauge.

When a person is *extreme* FEARFUL, a plot point of 5, we won't find *any* positive examples of individuals who possess this trait. There are no positive actions associated with making decisions out of extreme fear. Think about it. What could possibly be good about making decisions based out of extreme fear? Another word that could be used for a person who operates at this end of the gauge is *paranoia*. Adolph Hitler possessed this trait.

Although Hitler had a strong TELL trait, and could whip mass rallies into a frenzy with his forceful and assertive TELL actions, he typically made *decisions* out of extreme paranoia. Some examples: He perceived all ethnic groups and minorities to be a threat and sought to exterminate them; he rarely trusted the wisdom of his generals and often dismissed them, and replaced their war plans with his own irrational strategies.

David Koresh, the Waco, Texas, cult leader, is another example of someone who operated at the extreme end of FEARFUL. What observable actions did he exhibit? He built a tightly controlled cult compound and fostered extreme paranoia of the world amongst his followers. The result? In 1993, when law enforcement closed in on the compound, he directed his followers to burn down the compound, killing over eighty members of his cult. In the 1970s, cult leader, Jim Jones, took similar action when he directed over nine hundred people to drink Kool-Aid laced with cyanide.

When someone is plotted higher than 3 on the FEARFUL, it is likely that some actions associated with paranoia will become evident. The further one moves to the end of the FEARFUL side of the gauge, the more likely that negative actions will become full-blown. People with a plot point of about 3 or *less* on the FEARFUL end of the gauge, however, wouldn't be classified as being driven by paranoia. Many of these people can be described as *cautious*, and they can display some positive actions such as *analytical* or *guarded*.

Alan Greenspan, for example, who has dictated the interest rate for the Federal Reserve bank for a number of years, would probably be plotted about 1 or 2 on the FEARFUL side. He cautiously and with a little fear and trepidation has carefully weighed his detailed decisions before making a move. Some air traffic controllers are another example of people who might operate with a certain amount of caution/fear when making decisions. Some dentists would also qualify, as they exhibit caution before drilling for oil in our teeth! **ILLUSTRATION 2** shows an example of a person who is low FEARFUL, or cautious, in comparison to the extreme ends of the CONFIDENT-FEARFUL gauge.

ILLUSTRATION 2

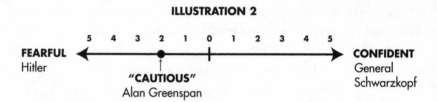

This isn't to suggest that all administrators in the Fed, air traffic controllers, or dentists will be plotted at 3 or less on the FEARFUL end of the gauge, but these are some examples that can help us visualize a moderate to low FEARFUL trait.

An amplifying thought regarding fear is appropriate here.

Everyone, even those who are extremely CONFIDENT, will experience fear in their lifetime in the midst of a life-changing or life-threatening situation. Common examples are: fear before impact in a car crash; fear before major surgery; fear of an uncertain future after the loss of one's spouse; and, fear of rejection while waiting for a letter of acceptance to a university.

What we are looking for when we plot people on the CONFIDENT-FEARFUL gauge is how people *typically make decisions on a day-to-day basis* in nonlife-threatening or life-changing experiences.

As noted in Chapter 1, when people go through life-changing or life-threatening experiences, they may or may not operate the same as they have in the past. Most of us have seen or heard of people who are at about 2 on the FEARFUL side of the gauge, but who act heroically to save someone's life. And we have also seen people who are usually extremely CONFIDENT, freeze up when confronted with life-changing pressure.

As a counterpoint, Hitler's paranoia and hatred of Jews was not founded in reality. Jews did not place him in a life-threatening or life-changing situation. Similarly, David Koresh amassed a mammoth arsenal against an imaginary foe. Both Hitler and Koresh operated at the extreme end of FEARFUL on a daily basis, which was confirmed by their actions. That there are people who operate out of extreme fear, raises the question: *Can these people change?* The answer is yes and this issue is addressed in Chapter 8.

CONFIDENT-FEARFUL ACTIONS

Actions that are often associated with being CONFIDENT or FEARFUL are detailed in **TABLE 6** below. Note that some of the actions associated with FEARFUL have an asterisk. These are actions which can be used both positively or negatively and are typically present only when a person is *moderate* to *low* (less than 3) FEARFUL. As was true for the COMMUNICATION traits, not everyone who is either CONFIDENT or FEARFUL will necessarily display all of the associated actions.

TABLE 6

CONFIDENT Actions: Poised, self-reliant, candid, conceited, independent, callous, durable/stable, arrogant, self-assured, and action-oriented

FEARFUL Actions: Analytical,* guarded,* cautious,* insecure, anxious, timid, unstable, envious, gullible, passive, self-pitying, and defensive

POSITIVE AND NEGATIVE EXTREMES OF THE CONFIDENT-FEARFUL GAUGE

ILLUSTRATION 3 shows positive and negative examples of the *extreme* ends of the CONFIDENT-FEARFUL gauge. As already stated, there are no positive examples of people who are extremely FEARFUL. Provided, however, are positive examples of people who are *moderate* to *low* (1–3) FEARFUL: people who might be described as *cautious, guarded,* or *analytical* when making decisions.

ILLUSTRATION 3

Positive Extreme FEARFUL

- **No Examples**

Positive *NonExtreme* FEARFUL

- **Alan Greenspan**
  (Cautious Fed who sets interest rates)

- **Prince Charles**
  (Royalty who rarely steps out and
  takes the initiative)

- **Some Air Traffic Controllers**

- **Some Dentists**

Positive Extreme CONFIDENT

- **General Norman Schwarzkopf**

- **Winston Churchill**

- **Margaret Thatcher**

- **Barbara Jordan**
  (Black Congresswoman from Texas
  and famous orator)

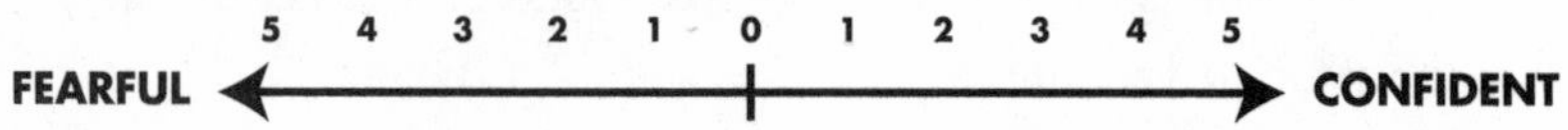

```
        5   4   3   2   1   0   1   2   3   4   5
FEARFUL ◀───────────────────┼──────────────────▶ CONFIDENT
```

Negative Extreme FEARFUL

- **Hitler**
  (Paranoiac dictator)

- **David Koresh**
  (Cult leader)

- **Charles Manson**
  (Cult leader)

- **Some people who have**
  extreme phobias

Negative Extreme CONFIDENT

- **Howard Stern**
  (Brash radio talk show host)

- **Leona Helmsley**
  (Owner of New York's Helmsley Hotel;
  convicted for tax evasion; said "Only
  little people pay taxes.")

- **Arrogant Athletes**
  (Choose your favorite)

PERSONALIZING YOUR CONFIDENT-FEARFUL GAUGE

After you have studied the positive and negative examples, personalize the
CONFIDENT-FEARFUL gauge in **ILLUSTRATION 4** with your selections for the positive and negative extremes. As you did with the first two gauges, if there is someone that you personally know that you would like to use as an example, be sure that

Chapter 7

The Last Two Questions: Confident-Fearful? Predictable-Unpredictable?

this person expresses his/her trait with the same degree of intensity as the examples provided. Now plot yourself on the gauge in comparison to the two extremes.

Remember, there is not an example of a person who is *positive* extreme FEARFUL. Also, select an example of a *non-extreme* person who uses his FEARFUL trait positively.

ILLUSTRATION 4

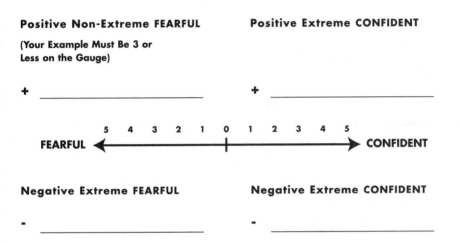

Positive Non-Extreme FEARFUL

(Your Example Must Be 3 or Less on the Gauge)

+ _____

Positive Extreme CONFIDENT

+ _____

5　4　3　2　1　0　1　2　3　4　5

FEARFUL ◄――――――――――――――► **CONFIDENT**

Negative Extreme FEARFUL

- _____

Negative Extreme CONFIDENT

- _____

HELPFUL CONFIDENT-FEARFUL QUESTIONS

If you have difficulty selecting which end of the gauge you tilt toward, ask yourself the following questions:

1. Do I prefer to initiate actions? (CONFIDENT)
2. Do I prefer to let others take the lead? (FEARFUL)
3. Do I prefer to act to take control of my circumstances? (CONFIDENT)
4. Do most things just happen to me as a result of events that are outside of my own control? (FEARFUL)
5. Do I make decisions confidently? (CONFIDENT)
6. Am I usually hesitant and somewhat fearful when making decisions and taking action? (FEARFUL)

If you are tempted to plot yourself in the center, remember: most people can be plotted on one of the two sides of the gauge. If necessary, ask a trusted friend for insight. Together, review the CONFIDENT and FEARFUL actions and note the specific *actions* you have displayed.

EXTREME AND NON-EXTREME EXAMPLES
OF CONFIDENT-FEARFUL

Most people aren't the extreme of CONFIDENT-FEARFUL, but fall between the center and one of the extremes. To help you visualize the difference between extreme and non-extreme examples, some positive and negative examples of each are provided in **TABLE 7.**

TABLE 7
EXTREME EXAMPLES

Positive CONFIDENT:	Hard-charging coach.
Negative CONFIDENT:	Arrogant tycoon.
Positive FEARFUL:	None.
Negative FEARFUL:	Manager who is unjustifiably paranoid of those around him.

NON-EXTREME EXAMPLES

Positive CONFIDENT:	Leader who exudes quiet confidence.
Negative CONFIDENT:	Slightly cocky athlete.
Positive FEARFUL:	Operator of a "fail-safe" system for a nuclear warhead or barge operator who navigates channels cautiously.
Negative FEARFUL:	Bureaucrat who tends to avoid confrontation when confrontation is necessary.

ASSIGNMENT #6

Goal: Learn to use the CONFIDENT-FEARFUL gauge.

Time Required: 30 minutes.

Using **ILLUSTRATION 5**, plot six people you know on the CONFIDENT-FEARFUL gauge. Think of people who can be plotted at 4 or higher on the FEARFUL side of the gauge and people who can be plotted at 3 or lower on the FEARFUL side. For those who are 3 or less, identify their positive actions from the list of CONFIDENT and FEARFUL actions provided in **TABLE 6** (page 93).

Chapter 7

**The Last Two Questions: Confident-
Fearful? Predictable-Unpredictable?**

ILLUSTRATION 5

Name	CONFIDENT-FEARFUL	Plot Point

#1 _____

#2 _____

#3 _____

#4 _____

#5 _____

#6 _____

QUESTION/GAUGE #4
PREDICTABLE OR UNPREDICTABLE?
Are a person's actions generally <u>predictable</u> or <u>unpredictable</u>?

Question/gauge #4, the "predictability" gauge, shown in **ILLUSTRATION 6**, helps us to determine if a person's actions are generally PREDICTABLE or UNPREDICTABLE—conventional or unconventional. This gauge helps us to make better predictions about how consistently people use their assets and skills.

ILLUSTRATION 6

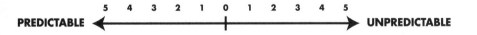

PREDICTABLE ← 5 4 3 2 1 0 1 2 3 4 5 → UNPREDICTABLE

On the PREDICTABLE side of this gauge we will usually see regularity and conformity in a person's actions. Queen Elizabeth II exemplifies this trait as she carries out traditions with uniformity. In movies, John Wayne, portrayed the dependable and reliable sheriff. People at this end of the gauge display positive and negative actions such as reliable, dependable, staid, stuffy, etc.

Alternately, the UNPREDICTABLE side of the gauge is characterized by actions that are infrequent, random, surprising, or unconventional. People on this end of the gauge can range from unconventionally creative to rebellious and reckless. This side of the gauge also gives us a measure of a person's tendency to act outside the norms of a given situation. The brilliant scientist, Albert Einstein, often displayed this trait, even forgetting to wear socks at awards ceremonies in which he was attired in a tuxedo. Comics, Robin Williams and Phyllis Diller, are other examples of those who operate "way out of the box"—outside the norm. Hitler, Manson, and Koresh, however, exemplify the extreme negative of this trait, displayed through their vacillating and explosive actions.

What follows in **TABLE 8** are positive and negative actions associated with the PREDICTABLE-UNPREDICTABLE gauge. Note that people who are UNPREDICTABLE find it a little bit easier to "get themselves into trouble" because of their freewheeling nature. These folks can also provide a spice of life, filling our lives with wonder and amazement.

TABLE 8

PREDICTABLE Actions:	Conventional, organized, staid, reliable, dependable, precise, stuffy, persistent, formal, punctual, consistent, logical, industrious, orderly, rigid, and self-disciplined
UNPREDICTABLE Actions:	Unconventional, aimless, reckless, negligent, inconsistent, spontaneous, frivolous, forgetful, nonconforming, rebellious, irreverent, intemperate, and freewheeling,

POSITIVE AND NEGATIVE EXTREMES OF THE PREDICTABLE-UNPREDICTABLE GAUGE

ILLUSTRATION 7 provides negative and positive examples of the extreme ends of the PREDICTABLE-UNPREDICTABLE gauge. You will note that there are no specific examples of notable people who are *negative extreme* PREDICTABLE. These people typically have the same notoriety as those who are negative extreme ASK: they never distinguish themselves. They are stuffy and staid and are not attractive people. Archie Bunker, the TV character from the show *All in the Family*, and the "entrenched bureaucrat" are examples of this person which most people can immediately visualize.

Chapter 7

The Last Two Questions: Confident-
Fearful? Predictable-Unpredictable?

As you review the examples provided, consider the positive and negative actions that each person uniquely possesses from those listed in **TABLE 7**. For example, while John Wayne's persona in the movies could best be described as one of *dependability*, Queen Elizabeth might best be characterized by *punctual* and *conventional*.

ILLUSTRATION 7

Positive Extreme	Positive Extreme

Positive Extreme

- **John Wayne**

- **Queen Elizabeth II**

- **Pope John Paul II**

- **President Dwight Eisenhower**

Positive Extreme

- **Einstein**
  (Often forgot to wear his socks)

- **Robin Williams**
  (Zany comic/actor)

- **Absentminded Professor**
  (Character in the classic Disney movie who invented Flubber)

- **Phyllis Diller**
  (Outrageous comedienne)

```
           5   4   3   2   1   0   1   2   3   4   5
PREDICTABLE ◄───────────────────┼──────────────────► UNPREDICTABLE
```

Negative Extreme

- **Entrenched Bureaucrat**

- **Archie Bunker**
  (Character in TV show *All in the Family*)

Negative Extreme

- **Hitler**
  (Moody and always vacillating)

- **Charles Manson**
  (Cult leader and murderer)

- **David Koresh**
  (Waco, Texas, cult leader)

- **Howard Stern**
  (Grossly irreverent radio talk show host)

- **Dennis Rodman**
  (Professional basketball player)

PERSONALIZING THE PREDICTABLE-UNPREDICTABLE GAUGE

After studying the extreme examples in **ILLUSTRATION 7**, personalize the extreme ends of the PREDICTABLE-UNPREDICTABLE gauge in **ILLUSTRATION 8** with your choice of examples.

ILLUSTRATION 8

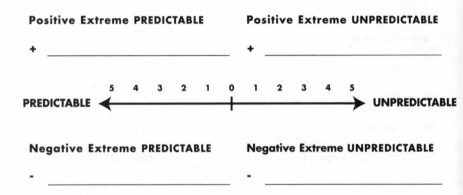

Positive Extreme PREDICTABLE   **Positive Extreme UNPREDICTABLE**

+ _____   + _____

```
        5   4   3   2   1   0   1   2   3   4   5
PREDICTABLE  ←———————————————|———————————————→  UNPREDICTABLE
```

Negative Extreme PREDICTABLE   **Negative Extreme UNPREDICTABLE**

- _____   - _____

Now plot yourself on the gauge. If you have some ambiguity regarding on which side of the gauge you should be plotted, review the following questions.

HELPFUL PREDICTABLE-UNPREDICTABLE QUESTIONS

1. Would most of my friends describe me as fairly conventional? (PREDICTABLE)
2. Would most of my friends describe me as fairly unconventional? (UNPREDICTABLE)
3. Am I usually consistent in how I handle people and situations? (PREDICTABLE)
4. Am I usually unconventional in how I handle people and situations? (UNPREDICTABLE)
5. Do I resist change, even when it is needed? (PREDICTABLE)
6. Do I welcome needed change? (UNPREDICTABLE)
7. Do I resist spontaneity? (PREDICTABLE)
8. Do I enjoy being spontaneous? (UNPREDICTABLE)

Chapter 7

**The Last Two Questions: Confident-
Fearful? Predictable-Unpredictable?**

EXTREME AND NON-EXTREME EXAMPLES OF PREDICTABLE-UNPREDICTABLE

TABLE 9 provides both extreme and non-extreme examples of the PREDICTABLE-UNPREDICTABLE traits.

TABLE 9

EXTREME EXAMPLES

Positive PREDICTABLE: Winston Churchill in his defense of England during the Battle of Britain.

Negative PREDICTABLE: Bureaucrat who adamantly resists positive change.

Positive UNPREDICTABLE: Unconventional inventor.

Negative UNPREDICTABLE: Reckless leaders and cult figures, such as Hitler and David Koresh.

NON-EXTREME EXAMPLES

Positive PREDICTABLE: Dependable support personnel in a company.

Negative PREDICTABLE: A sometimes stuffy and staid banker.

Positive UNPREDICTABLE: Ad executive who adapts well to changing trends and forecasts.

Negative UNPREDICTABLE: Absentminded employee whose mind constantly wanders.

ASSIGNMENT #7

Goal: Learn to use the PREDICTABLE-UNPREDICTABLE gauge.

Time Required: 30 minutes.

Plot six people that you know on the PREDICTABLE-UNPREDICTABLE gauge and write their names in the spaces provided in **ILLUSTRATION 9** on the following page. Then estimate their 1–5 plot point.

ILLUSTRATION 9

Name	PREDICTABLE-UNPREDICTABLE	Plot Point
#1		
#2		
#3		
#4		
#5		
#6		

USING PERFORMANCE GAUGES IN EVERYDAY SITUATIONS

Here are some practical applications of how you can use the two PER-FORMANCE gauges. These common sense suggestions are provided to help you understand how identifying PERFORMANCE traits can be put to imme-diate use. Use caution, however, as people and circumstances are and can be unique.

When a Person Is FEARFUL and . . .

1. You need to be directive, use a person who is lower FEARFUL.
2. You are providing choices, it is helpful to provide <u>fewer</u> choices.

When a Person Is CONFIDENT and . . .

1. You need to be directive, use a person who is higher CONFIDENT.
2. You are providing choices, you can provide <u>more</u> choices.

When a Person Is PREDICTABLE and . . .

You are suggesting change, be prepared for more resistance.

When a Person Is UNPREDICTABLE and . . .

You are suggesting change, he will likely be <u>more</u> receptive.

What follows are some specific situations in which various professionals have used the PERFORMANCE gauges.

Chapter 7

The Last Two Questions: Confident-Fearful? Predictable-Unpredictable?

The owner of an exclusive jewelry store adapted a couple of the above suggestions in his sales process. He found that it was more efficient to offer *more* choices to people who are CONFIDENT and *fewer* choices to those who are FEARFUL. He observed that customers who are FEARFUL often have a more difficult time making up their mind, shifting from one option to another. He also realized that he could present more choices to people who are CONFIDENT because they *are* confident and they tend to expeditiously eliminate options that do not meet their needs. (He also used this strategy to determine who might take *longer* to service if he chose to let his customers evaluate all possible options, thus enabling him to prioritize more efficiently his time.)

The jeweler also discovered a fine nuance.

Typically, if a buyer was 3 or higher on the PREDICTABLE gauge, he presented more choices because the buyer usually possessed a more predefined idea of what he wanted. This person's PREDICTABLE trait could sometimes even override a FEARFUL trait and cause decision-making to be slightly more predictable. (In the next chapter you will learn that this combination of traits is called a CONFORMIST type.)

Similarly, when a buyer was UNPREDICTABLE and CONFIDENT, he sometimes presented fewer choices because the buyer often wanted to see *everything* before making a decision.

Appointment secretaries in a physician's office came up with a clever plan to decrease cancellations. They focused their attention on identifying whether or not a new patient who phoned in was PREDICTABLE or UNPREDICTABLE. They found that those who were PREDICTABLE were more likely to keep appointments and appear on time. Those who were UNPREDICTABLE, however, tended to be more erratic when keeping appointments. So what did they do to reduce cancellations? They double-scheduled appointments for people who had a plot point of at least 3 UNPREDICTABLE.

The secretaries fleshed out this trait by listening for UNPREDICTABLE dialogue and by asking a new patient questions like: *Where do you record your appointments?* If the new patient airily replied, "Oh, I don't write it down, I'll just remember," then this person, who is more likely UNPREDICTABLE, might receive a double-booking.

If, however, the patient replied with a firm response, "Oh, I always put them in my appointment book," then this person, who is more likely PREDICTABLE, wouldn't be double-booked.

Some Swiss doctors developed a strategy for deciding which patients should and shouldn't receive a regimented follow-up for physical therapy, taking medications, and so on. Like the secretaries in the above example, the physicians noted whether or not a patient was PREDICTABLE or UNPREDICTABLE. Patients who were observed to be UNPREDICTABLE had this trait noted on their charts and were provided with a stricter and more carefully monitored regimen. Another example of: *I know who you are. Good for me, better for you.*

One group of auditors for an international organization faced a different kind of challenge. They needed to make recommendations for change in several different countries—countries that are typically resistant to change. How did they tackle their assignment so that their recommendations had a greater chance of acceptance? They looked for those in each organization who had an UNPREDICTABLE trait—those who were less resistant to change. Then, they sought opportunities in which these individuals could facilitate the needed recommendations, thus increasing the chances for a successful transition.

If you are an auditor, detective, or another type of investigator, the ability to read a person's PERFORMANCE traits can help diminish inaccurate reads of a person's truthfulness. For example, people who are CONFIDENT can appear more convincing—when compared to those who are FEARFUL—regardless of whether or not they are telling the truth. So if you perceive that someone is CONFIDENT, just be alert that he may fool you more easily.

People who are FEARFUL, however, sometimes send signals which make them appear that they are concealing the truth, when in fact they are simply less convincing because they are afraid. Their eyes may avoid contact. They may clear their throats. They may directly or indirectly plead with you to believe them. Additionally, a person who is FEARFUL, but who also possesses a strong TELL trait, can be convincing in some situations.

For example, Hitler, who was FEARFUL when making decisions, utilized his strong TELL trait to convince—or *talk*—Chamberlain into turning over the keys of Europe. This example illustrates the need to evaluate a person's *complete* trait inventory, especially in critical situations, before taking action.

Chapter 7

The Last Two Questions: Confident-Fearful? Predictable-Unpredictable?

Please use these suggestions cautiously, as they are only intended to point out common patterns. We must respect that people are unique and we can make mistakes, especially when first learning how to profile.

ASSIGNMENT #8

Goal: Practice plotting people on the CONFIDENT-FEARFUL and PRE-DICTABLE-UNPREDICTABLE gauges.

Time Required: One hour over a one-week period.

As you did with the first two gauges, plot six people from each of the groups listed on page 52. Then ask two insightful people whom you trust to help assess your accuracy. As with the previous major assignments, take a week to complete this assignment as time is needed for reflection.

BRIEF RECAP

1. You have learned how to use the four points of your profiling compass and answer the four questions which will enable you to identify someone's profile.
   - CONTROL-EXPRESS
   - ASK-TELL
   - CONFIDENT-FEARFUL
   - PREDICTABLE-UNPREDICTABLE
2. You have learned how to identify someone's COMMUNICATION type by combining the CONTROL-EXPRESS and ASK-TELL gauges.

The shaded area in **ILLUSTRATION 10** represents how many steps you have learned in order to develop someone's profile. There are just two steps left.

ILLUSTRATION 10

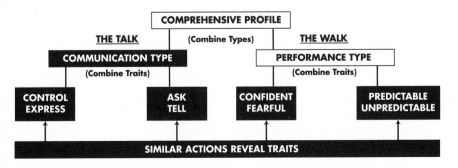

CHAPTER 8

Identifying Performance Types

In this chapter we will review the next building block of the Korem Profiling System: combining the CONFIDENT-FEARFUL and PREDICTABLE-UNPREDICTABLE gauges to reveal a person's PERFORMANCE type. Reading someone's PERFORMANCE type will enable you to evaluate more effectively how a person is likely to perform in a given situation, tackle responsibilities, and make decisions.

In addition to reviewing each of the PERFORMANCE types, special attention is given to one of the types, the RANDOM ACTOR, which is potentially the most dangerous and volatile of the PERFORMANCE types. Additional insight into the RANDOM ACTOR is provided in Chapter 13.

As we did with the COMMUNICATION types, the two PERFORMANCE traits are placed over each other to create four quadrants. Each quadrant is then indicated by an easy to visualize label.

ILLUSTRATION 1

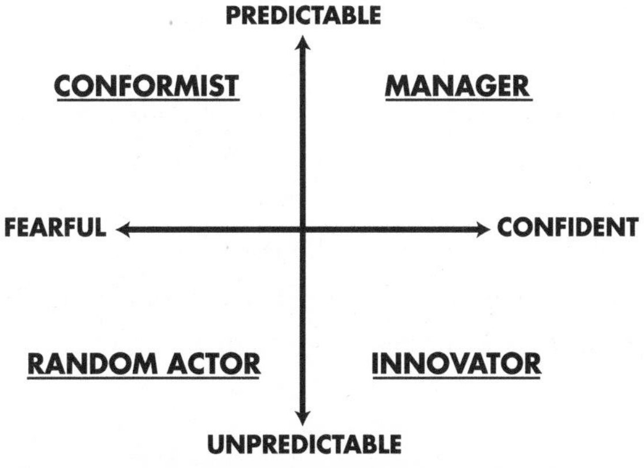

	PREDICTABLE	
CONFORMIST		MANAGER
FEARFUL		CONFIDENT
RANDOM ACTOR		INNOVATOR
	UNPREDICTABLE	

A brief summary of the traits associated with each type are:

MANAGER   CONFIDENT and PREDICTABLE
INNOVATOR   CONFIDENT and UNPREDICTABLE
CONFORMIST   FEARFUL and PREDICTABLE
RANDOM ACTOR   FEARFUL and UNPREDICTABLE

Plotting each type is accomplished in the same manner as the COMMU-NICATION types. **ILLUSTRATION 2** shows how two different MANAGER types are plotted. As we learned with the COMMUNICATION types, what determines the difference between MANAGERS is the specific plot points on each gauge. By recognizing that not all MANAGERS are alike, we avoid stereotyping.

ILLUSTRATION 2

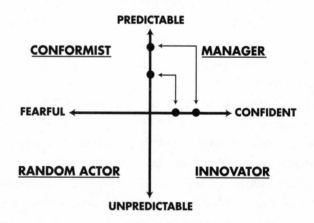

THE PERFORMANCE TYPES

A brief summary of each PERFORMANCE type is as follows:

MANAGER—It's logical to imagine a CONFIDENT/PREDICTABLE person as a manager. One can just as easily label this person as an *Organizer* or *Decision-maker*. MANAGERS prefer to make decisions in methodical and stan-dardized ways. They tend to execute their decisions or actions in self-directed ways which is why they are often easy to manage. MANAGERS are most comfortable in steady, calm, and predictable environments. They can be relied upon to "live within the system." For this reason they are often suited to lead others in an organizational environment.

INNOVATOR—An INNOVATOR (CONFIDENT/UNPREDICTABLE) is the idea-generator in a group or organization. This type will usually "try anything once." They are motivated by change and variety and are sufficiently self-confident to challenge situations and take risks. The higher their UNPRE-DICTABLE trait, the more likely they will be viewed as "absentminded" professor types. When their negative actions are dominant and their plot points are extreme, these people become anarchists, negligent of their duties and responsibilities, rebellious, and destructively antagonistic. Other suitable labels for this type are *Inventor* and *Creative Spark Plug.*

CONFORMIST—On the positive side, CONFORMISTS (FEARFUL/PREDICTABLE) are typically very compliant, dutiful, reliable, and obedient. *Supporter* or *Sustainer* are other labels that could be applied to this type of person. They are usually precise and at least as manageable as the MANAGER. The negative side of CONFORMISTS is that their sense of insecurity and fear when making decisions can instill in them an aversion to taking risks. While CONFORMISTS can fit into most environments, people will tend to view them as somewhat nervous or uninteresting the higher their FEARFUL trait because they are motivated by a fear of failure.

RANDOM ACTOR—Throughout the text, it has been pointed out that there aren't good or bad traits (except for extremely FEARFUL), just good or bad actions. The same is true for each of the COMMUNICATION and PER-FORMANCE types. The exception to this rule is the RANDOM ACTOR (FEAR-FUL/UNPREDICTABLE), who has few redeeming PERFORMANCE actions—especially when his traits are to the *extreme.* Logically, would you want to work with someone who makes decisions out of fear and who is simultane-ously unpredictable? Fortunately, at the present, RANDOM ACTOR are the least common of the four PERFORMANCE types.

Depending upon the individual and situation, RANDOM ACTORS are typically deception driven, manipulative, scheming, and volatile. When their traits are 3 or higher, they are capable of most types of manipulative and dan-gerous actions, operating out of a strong need for self-defense and self-protection. Those who are clinically psychotic are often extreme RANDOM ACTORS (plot points of 5), although this doesn't mean every RANDOM ACTOR is necessarily psychotic. About the only endearing quality of some RANDOM ACTORS is that they will be extremely loyal to whomever is able to control their fate and allay their fears. Other suitable labels for this type are *Manipulator*, and to the extreme, *Public Menace*. A more lengthy discussion of the RANDOM ACTOR will follow in this chapter and, as already noted, in Chapter 13.

IDENTIFYING YOUR PERFORMANCE TYPE

To identify your PERFORMANCE type, using your plot points from Chapter 7, plot yourself on the CONFIDENT-FEARFUL and PREDICTABLE-UNPREDICTABLE gauges in **ILLUSTRATION 3**. Now extend a line from each plot point until the two lines intersect, and write your type in the space provided.

ILLUSTRATION 3

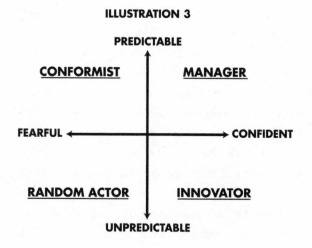

YOUR TYPE: _____

PERFORMANCE TYPES AND ASSOCIATED ACTIONS

TABLE 10 lists the possible positive and negative actions as well as "other tendencies" for each of the four PERFORMANCE types. Remember, the key word is "possible" since not every MANAGER, for example, is going to display every action. Take a few minutes to familiarize yourself with this handy reference list.

TABLE 10
MANAGER: CONFIDENT/PREDICTABLE

POSITIVE ACTIONS	NEGATIVE ACTIONS	OTHER TENDENCIES
Organized	Bureaucratic	"Square"
Persistent	No risk tolerance	Predictable
Thrifty	"Pesty"	Logic oriented
Goal-oriented	Unyielding	Can operate
Decisive	Entrenched	independently
Efficient	Compulsive	Adapts to a system
Practical/pragmatic	"Nitpicker"	Prefers to operate within
Precise	Staid	boundaries
Conventional	Will unnecessarily	Resists change, disruption
Dependable	defend status quo	of schedules
Logical		Relies upon experience
Assumes responsibility		v. creativity to solve
		problems
		Prefers challenge with
		predictable outcome
		Will initiate within
		boundaries

INNOVATOR: CONFIDENT/UNPREDICTABLE

POSITIVE ACTIONS	NEGATIVE ACTIONS	OTHER TENDENCIES
Risk-taker	Reckless	Nonconformist
Free-thinking	Anarchist	Unconventional
Creative	Frivolous	Idea driven
Self-assured	Egocentric	Negligent
Initiates action	Rebellious	Needs freedom
Isn't afraid of change	Aimless	Uninhibited
Decisive	Antisocial	Motivated by change
Likes/seeks challenges	Irresponsible	Spontaneous
Innovative	Disorganized	Operates without
Problem-solver		structure
		Relies upon creativity to
		solve problems v.
		experience

CONFORMIST: FEARFUL/PREDICTABLE

POSITIVE ACTIONS	NEGATIVE ACTIONS	OTHER TENDENCIES
Loyal	Unquestioning	Obedient
Manageable	Subservient	Compliant
Precise	Uninteresting	Analytical
Reliable	Uncreative	Repetitive actions
Cautious	Indecisive	Guarded
Supportive	Mindless	Rule-oriented
Dutiful	Insecure	Doesn't require
Compulsive	Fear of failure	challenge
	Unwilling to assume	Avoids risks, ownership
	blame	of problems
	Gullible	Follower
	Neurotic	

RANDOM ACTOR: FEARFUL/UNPREDICTABLE

NEGATIVE ACTIONS	OTHER TENDENCIES
Dangerous	Impulsive
Deceptive	Hard to read
Anxious	Rigid/unbending**
Insecure	Dependent
Distrusting	Seeks protection
Indecisive	through control
Moody	
Egocentric	
Lack of conscience	
Secretive	
Irresponsible	
Vacillating	
Unwilling to accept	
responsibility	
Self-absorbed	
Manipulative	
Hot-tempered	
Volatile	
Antisocial	
Blindly loyal*	

* More likely if person has ASK trait

** More likely if person has CONTROL trait

As we noted with the COMMUNICATION types, some of the PERFOR-MANCE types may share the same or similar actions. This is due to the fact that types that share a common trait might share some similar tendencies. For example, MANAGERS and CONFORMISTS both share the positive action of *precise*. This is because they are both PREDICTABLE. Those who are PRE-DICTABLE often prefer a semblance of order, which can translate into a desire for precision—things that predictably fit together.

In Chapter 9 you will be shown to different ways that both PERFOR-MANCE and COMMUNICATION types can be used in practical applications using SNAPSHOT and FINE-TUNED reads. For now, complete Assignment #9. We will then spend some time looking at the most difficult of the four PER-FORMANCE types to understand—the RANDOM ACTOR.

ASSIGNMENT #9

Goal: Identify the possible actions for your own type.

Time Required: 30 minutes.

Find your type and read over the list of actions. Then, check off the actions that you believe are a part of your personal inventory. Seek the coun-sel of a wise and trusted friend if needed as previously suggested.

OBSERVATIONS ABOUT THE RANDOM ACTOR

The RANDOM ACTOR type can be one of the most troublesome individ-uals one will encounter. For this reason, we will spend some extra time look-ing at who these people are, how to interact with or confront them, and the possibility that they can change. Further amplification of each RANDOM ACTOR profile, such as a SERGEANT/RANDOM ACTOR, is found in Chapter 11, and additional insight into RANDOM ACTORS is included in Chapter 13.

The Extreme Factor—Not everyone who is a RANDOM ACTOR will necessarily pose a threat. The lower a RANDOM ACTOR'S FEARFUL and UNPREDICTABLE traits, the less likely he will be severely volatile, manipula-tive, and so on. Of the two traits, the higher the FEARFUL trait, the more like-ly that negative actions will surface, as this drives paranoia, self-centered decision-making, and so forth. A practical benchmark for approaching this individual with caution is if the FEARFUL trait is higher than about 2 or 3.

Remember, people operate within a *range*. This means that a RANDOM ACTOR who is a 2 on the FEARFUL end of the gauge, can actually operate up to 3, and in some cases, even 4. That means that this person's negative actions are likely to be stronger, and thus more volatile.

When a RANDOM ACTOR'S FEARFUL trait is less than 2, or if his range rarely extends past 3, he is not as likely to pose an immediate threat and one might be able to engage in a productive relationship. In fact, a person who is plotted as 1 on the FEARFUL gauge might even display some of the actions of a person who is CONFIDENT because his *range* might extend to the CONFI-DENT side of the gauge. If this occurs, his CONFIDENT actions, though, will only be marginal.

RANDOM ACTORS with a Good Side?—Keep in mind, the RAN-DOM ACTOR PERFORMANCE type only identifies how a person is likely to *perform* in a given situation and make decisions, telling us something about a person's *walk*. A person's COMMUNICATION type, however, identifies how he prefers to *communicate*—the *talk*. Because RANDOM ACTORS also have a COMMUNICATION type as a component of their profile, they can display positive actions in the *talk* part of their lives. This means that while RANDOM ACTORS can be troublesome when called upon to *perform*, when they communicate, they can display any of the positive actions associated with each of the four COMMUNICATION types, such as:

- SERGEANT—Determined, takes charge, or self-confident
- SALESMAN—Passionate, outgoing, or friendly
- ACCOUNTANT—Easygoing, orderly, poised, or thoughtful
- ARTIST—Creative, gentle, or sensitive

This is one reason that people who are deceived by RANDOM ACTORS often say: *But he seemed like such a nice man.* They are disarmed by positive actions in the RANDOM ACTOR's COMMUNICATION type.

Because RANDOM ACTORS can draw upon positive actions from their COMMUNICATION type, it is best to operate with a RANDOM ACTOR on a communication level and avoid asking this person to "perform." Why? Because when the RANDOM ACTOR is called upon to perform—the *walk* part of his life—that's when RANDOM ACTORS fall apart. Then they can display actions, such as: manipulative, moody, dangerous, and insecure. When the COMPREHENSIVE PROFILES are covered in Chapter 11, which is the combination of a person's COMMUNICATION and PERFORMANCE types, we will review suggestions for interacting with each of the four different RANDOM ACTORS, such as the SALESMAN/RANDOM ACTOR.

Can RANDOM ACTORS Change?—As discussed in Chapter 6, people can change their traits when they experience a life-changing experience. RANDOM ACTORS are no exception. The key for a RANDOM ACTOR is to move from FEARFUL to CONFIDENT—or at least to low FEARFUL. This means that they must learn to *trust* without selfish motives, a character deficiency that is often tied to experiences and choices made during formative years as a child. It is common for RANDOM ACTORS to have been maligned when children due to abuse, neglect, absent parents, or, in some unique cases, a severe trauma that is not parent related. Trust is something that has been violated. RANDOM ACTORS can move from FEARFUL to CONFIDENT, however, when they experience trust (or choose to trust) for the first time.

Some make this change when they yield to a spiritual rebirth, learning to trust in God for that which they cannot control. This is how some convicted felons, who are RANDOM ACTORS, are legitimately transformed (not just a phony "jailhouse" conversion to convince a parole board).

For others, trust involves learning to trust other people. This means accepting the risk of being hurt or harmed. When someone marries, for example, one trusts one's spouse that he/she will remain faithful, even though there is always the risk that trust will be violated. But it is unselfish trust—love—that drives one forward and accepts the risk, be it great or small.

The following story illustrates one RANDOM ACTOR's tragic and twisted response when trust was violated.

Love Is a Trick

In 1981, I obtained what is believed to be the only filmed confession of a cult-like leader. James Hydrick, a twenty-two-year-old martial arts instructor with a criminal record, had developed what he described as a cult-like following in Salt Lake City. Hydrick used sleight-of-hand tricks to convince his "followers" that he possessed powers and that he could teach them to develop the same powers. After a lengthy undercover investigation, which included filming the modus operandi behind each trick, I confronted Hydrick (using a strategy described later in this chapter). After he was confronted, he agreed to explain on camera: (1) How he fooled millions of people on US television into believing he had powers; (2) How he built his group; and (3) His thought process and motivations for developing a cult-like group.

At one point during our taping, we did a word association sequence with Hydrick. My colleague, Hugh Aynesworth, assisted me. The most revealing moment was when he was given the word "love."

He replied: *To me, love is a trick.*

Severely abused as a child and placed in an institution for the mentally retarded when he was nine—and he wasn't retarded—Hydrick's reply illuminated his lack of trust for any adult in a position of authority.

Sadly, he never made the conscious character decision to learn to trust others. His half-sister did, and she had experienced similar abuse. Because she chose a different path through an act of character, she now leads a healthy and fulfilled life.

One day Hydrick called her, lamenting his childhood. He listed all the reasons why he couldn't assume responsibility for his actions, which had oft landed him in prison. She rebuked him. She pointed out that he did have a choice. He did not have to be a slave to his past. She endured the same kinds of abuse, and she chose to redeem her suffering by using her experiences for the benefit of others. He could do the same, she encouraged. Yes, even today, if he chose to trust, her brother could change.

The lesson to be learned from their exchange is that even those whose trust has been severely maligned, can learn to trust.

Trust is a choice, not a fate.

Long-term Relationships—In a business environment, it is unwise to engage in long-term relationships with RANDOM ACTORS who are in decision-making roles. This is especially true if their traits are extreme (3 or higher). Alternately, it is possible to engage in successful short-term relationships if the traits are not extreme—about 2 or less—and their range does not extend past 3. However, one should still proceed with caution.

If you are in a personal relationship with a RANDOM ACTOR, such as an immediate relative, and you must find a way to get along, attempts should be made to encourage this person toward trusting others. As already noted, RANDOM ACTORS can move from FEARFUL to CONFIDENT, or at least low FEARFUL. This usually involves, however, a life-changing experience during which they choose to trust someone else. The loss of a job, a spiritual rebirth, the death of a friend, loss of health, and so on can all set up a context in which the RANDOM ACTOR can choose to trust in someone else that can affect a long-term change from FEARFUL to CONFIDENT. When attempting to get along with this person, appeal to the positive actions you observe in his/her COMMUNICATION type. Consider and measure carefully, however, the risks of asking this person to make decisions or perform important tasks, as their negative RANDOM ACTOR actions type are likely to surface.

When a RANDOM ACTOR Is in Your Organization—A simple guideline for managing a RANDOM ACTOR in your organization is to *monitor* his activities closely and resist giving him significant responsibilities. Additionally, when possible, explore the potential for guiding this person along a path in which he can learn to trust others, or at least operate on the *lower* side of his FEARFUL range. Also, build a relationship based upon the positive actions that you observe in his COMMUNICATION type.

Confronting a RANDOM ACTOR—The following recommendation is only suggested for brief, one-time confrontations. This tactic is *not* suggested for long-term or repetitive confrontations.

When you must confront a RANDOM ACTOR, tactically do whatever is necessary to drive down his *immediate* fears. In many cases, this will make his actions in the *short-term* become *more* predictable. The effect of this strategy can work as follows in the mind of a RANDOM ACTOR.

When they are jolted by fear, initiated by a confrontation, their actions in some situations may become more unpredictable. Some people may bolt for the door, others may attack you, while others may lie in wait for you on another day. Additionally, if a RANDOM ACTOR is in a leadership role, one should not confront him in front of those he is leading. This will typically only drive up his fear—fear of exposure, rejection, etc.—pushing him to operate at the extreme end of his range.

The advantage of operating with RANDOM ACTORS in this manner is that they can be easier to guide, direct, or arrest (in the case of law enforcement).

This strategy is *not* likely to work in situations that require more than one confrontation. Why? Because Rule #1 that promotes systematic accuracy states: *People typically act in consistent, similar ways called traits.* This means that over a period of time, RANDOM ACTORS, like most everyone else, will revert to those traits that feel comfortable. So, if you confront a Random Actor over a long period of time, he will eventually revert back to his actual traits.

The above approach was used to obtain a confession from James Hydrick, previously noted, and encourage him to be arrested without incident.

Obtaining a Confession

James Hydrick had the same background profile as David Koresh, the Waco, Texas, cult leader. Both men were pedophiles, obsessed with weapons, threatened to kill others and themselves, and put forth contrived and manipulative religious dogma.

Before confronting Hydrick, I researched how he had dealt with confrontation in the past (remember: *Past behavior is the best predictor of future behavior*—Chapter 6). I discovered that when Hydrick was a boy in Aiken, South Carolina, a crime prevention officer with a fatherly bent, Frank Galardi, had several confrontations with Hydrick. Hydrick, whose father was a wayward bouncer at a nightclub, responded favorably to the officer's admonitions because he sensed that Frank truly cared about him.

Before confronting Hydrick, I enlisted the help of a Salt Lake City attorney, whom Hydrick had lived with for about a year after his release from the Los Angeles County Jail on a kidnapping and robbery charge. The attorney, John Bates, possessed the same firm, fatherly appeal as the juvenile officer.

I told John that I intended to confront Hydrick and explain that his tricks had been exposed. I explained that I also hoped that Hydrick might explain on camera what motivated his deviant need to make others believe that he had powers, prompting people to follow him in a cult-like environment. John agreed to help and the confrontation took place in John's office a week later.

With John present, I explained to Hydrick that I had film footage exposing his tricks and that I wanted him to explain on camera his motivations, methods, and so on. As I talked, John intermittently reassured Hydrick that this truly was the best thing for him to do. I didn't confront Hydrick in front of his followers, which would have driven up his fear and made him more unpredictable—the key tactical error made by law enforcement when they initially confronted Koresh. Rather, the con-frontation was facilitated with John's assistance, a person whom Hydrick knew genuinely cared about what happened to him.

Hydrick agreed to a videotaped interview and many people benefited from his transparent telling of his story. His "confession" helped to disband his group and numerous others in the US when the documentary, "Psychic Confession," aired in 1983. The documentary is still used today as a training film in law enforcement and psychology classes, illuminating how to approach a cult-like figure, who is typically a RANDOM ACTOR.

ASSIGNMENT #10

Goal: Learn to identify each of the PERFORMANCE types.

Time: Two to three hours over a one-week period.

1. Review the specific actions associated with your type. Check off those actions that you actually display and confirm with a couple of friends or relatives.

2. As you did with the COMMUNICATION types, identify the PERFOR-MANCE types of thirty people, six from each of the five categories listed on page 52. Be sure to select people whom you get along with as well as those you don't. Remember, the only inherently negative type is the RANDOM ACTOR. Also, review the specific COMMUNICATION type actions you observe in each person.

You have now learned all the steps necessary, except for one, to identify someone's COMPREHENSIVE PROFILE. The shaded area in **ILLUSTRATION 4** on the following page represents how many steps you have learned in order to develop someone's profile.

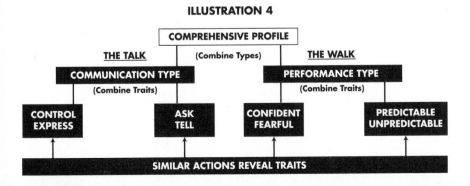

ILLUSTRATION 4

Before learning the last step, combining the PERFORMANCE gauges together to identify someone's PERFORMANCE type, we will examine two important subjects.

First, you will learn how to use the SNAPSHOT and FINE-TUNED reads, which will enable you to put PERFORMANCE and COMMUNICATION types into immediate and practical use. Then, we will review the seven most common reasons why people misread others. These two chapters contain vital information, so please be patient just a little bit longer.

CHAPTER 9

Snapshot and Fine-tuned Reads

As noted in Chapter 1, the Korem Profiling System provides access to three amounts of information using the same four gauges. In some situations you will need the full data sheet of information provided in a COMPREHEN-SIVE PROFILE (Chapter 11). There will be other instances, however, when a smaller amount of information will be adequate. That's when a SNAPSHOT or a FINE-TUNED read can be useful. Now that you know how to identify COM-MUNICATION and PERFORMANCE types, you can use both kinds of reads.

In this chapter you will learn how to assess and apply each type of read in a variety of environments, including:

- How sales personnel can remember the unique attributes of clients.
- Technicians on service calls smoothly servicing individual needs.
- How to write job advertisements to attract people with a specific type.
- New plant managers quickly interacting with a multitude of workers.
- Entrepreneurs establishing ground rules for partners in a new venture.
- Teachers and parents uniquely nurturing children with the same type.

The difference between a SNAPSHOT read and a FINE-TUNED read is that the SNAPSHOT read provides a brief, short-list general descriptor of some-one's type. It is primarily useful in first-time or noncritical interactions.

A FINE-TUNED read, however, identifies most of the *specific actions* in a person's COMMUNICATION or PERFORMANCE type. Tracking someone's specific actions using a FINE-TUNED read provides two distinct advantages over a SNAPSHOT read.

FINE-TUNED reads can help you:

• Interact with people based upon their unique strengths and weaknesses.

• Remember the unique characteristics about a person.

You have already learned two of the three steps necessary to develop each type of read, so your learning curve will be short.

We will begin with the simplest of the two reads, the SNAPSHOT read.

DEVELOPING A SNAPSHOT READ

A SNAPSHOT read is a brief summary statement of a person's type. It helps you quickly size up people, shortening the time necessary for effective interaction. SNAPSHOT reads are useful because they:

• Provide general information about a person.

• Are helpful when interaction is brief or short-term and detailed information isn't required.

• Are helpful when first interacting with someone.

• Require little time to assess.

When you use a SNAPSHOT read of someone's COMMUNICATION type, you are trying to determine how to communicate with that person.

When you use a SNAPSHOT read of someone's PERFORMANCE type, your focus is on how someone is likely to perform a task or make a decision.

You will use the following three steps to assess a SNAPSHOT read:

1. Plot a person on each gauge.

2. Identify the person's type.

3. Apply the brief summary statement to that person's type.

You already know steps #1 and #2. In order to complete step #3, you will use one of the eight summary statements provided.

THE EIGHT SUMMARY STATEMENTS

Each SNAPSHOT read in **TABLE 11** is a summary statement comprised of common positive and negative actions found in each type.

TABLE 11

Snapshot Reads for Communication Types

SERGEANT (CONTROL/TELL)—Prefer to *control* emotions and *tell* others what to do or what they think. They often like to *take charge* and can be *strong leaders*. Their downside is that they can also be *overbearing* and *insensitive* to others.

SALESMAN (EXPRESS/TELL)—Prefer to *express* their emotions and *tell* others what they think or what to do. They initially appear *outgoing* and *open* and are suited for sales and communication roles. Their downside is that they can get *discouraged* easily and can have *idealistic* expectations.

ACCOUNTANTS (CONTROL/ASK)—Prefer to *control* emotions and *ask* others what they think. They typically *wear well under pressure* and are suited as support, *sustainer* roles. Their downside is that they can be *weak* and *critical*.

ARTIST (EXPRESS/ASK)—Prefer to *express* their emotions and *ask* others what they think or what to do. They typically are *creative* and are *sensitive* to the needs of others. Their downside is that they can become *moody* and *lack self-confidence*.

Snapshot Reads For Performance Types

MANAGER (CONFIDENT/PREDICTABLE)—They are typically *confident* when making decisions and their actions are *predictable*. They are suited for managing others because they are usually *organized* and *efficient*. Their downside is that they can be *self-centered* and *bureaucratic*.

INNOVATOR (CONFIDENT/UNPREDICTABLE)—They are typically *confident* when making decisions and their actions tend to be *unpredictable*. Because they are *unconventional* and *willing* to take risks, they can be the creative spark plug in an organization. Their downside is that they might not be suitable for a structured environment, and they can be *rebellious*.

CONFORMIST (FEARFUL/PREDICTABLE)—They are typically *cautious* when making decisions and their actions are *predictable*. They are often easy to manage because they are *loyal* and *dutiful*. Their downside is that they can be *unquestioning* and become immobilized due to a *fear of failure*.

RANDOM ACTOR (FEARFUL/UNPREDICTABLE)—They are typically *fearful* when making decisions and their actions are *unpredictable*. These potentially volatile types of people tend to be *manipulative, self-absorbed*, and sometimes even *dangerous*.

As you can see, a SNAPSHOT read is a summary statement that is compiled by taking a couple of positive and negative actions from each type as well as identifying that person's traits. Obviously, not every person who is a SERGEANT will have all four actions—take charge, strong leaders, overbearing, and sensitive—noted in the SNAPSHOT read for a SERGEANT. Some SERGEANTS may only have three of the listed actions because each SERGEANT can have a unique set of actions. Condensing the SERGEANT's action list from **TABLE 5** (page 63) into a short summary, however, simply allows us to quickly remember the kind of arena in which most SERGEANTS prefer to operate. This, in turn, helps us to recall how to interact with someone who is a SERGEANT.

The SNAPSHOT read is not designed to be detailed or equally precise and reliable in all situations. You will use the FINE-TUNED read or a COMPREHENSIVE PROFILE when you need a more reliable and durable read that includes more details.

If someone that you read is a *combination type*, as described in Chapter 5, you will need to apply *two* descriptive statements to this person. If, for example, someone is an ARTIST/ACCOUNTANT combination type, then you would apply the summary statements for both an ARTIST and an ACCOUNTANT. SNAPSHOT reads of combination types should be used sparingly, however. FINE-TUNED reads or COMPREHENSIVE PROFILES are preferred as they provide a more complete base of information to understand these often difficult-to-understand individuals.

WRITING YOUR OWN SUMMARY STATEMENTS

While you can use the summary statements that are provided for each SNAPSHOT read, you can also personalize each SNAPSHOT read for your specific needs. For example, you might work in an idea-driven office environment, such as an advertising firm. Here, the potency of one's ideas and being *persistent* in conveying one's idea may be more important than being a leader. For this reason, it may be helpful to replace the "strong leader" descriptor with "influential" or "persistent."

To write your own summary statement for a specific type, follow the steps below. Start with the COMMUNICATION or PERFORMANCE type that is of the greatest importance for you to remember in your professional and private life. Assuming that you start with a specific COMMUNICATION type, ask yourself: *What are the most important actions that I personally need to remember about this type so that I can immediately recall how this person prefers to communicate?* Then complete the following three steps:

1. Review the possible actions for that type.
2. Select two positive and two negative actions that will help you immediately recall how this person prefers to communicate. (Later, you can add as many actions as you would like to memorize.)
3. Create a brief two-sentence summary statement using the actions you have selected. First, state the traits associated with that type, then follow with the positive and negative actions.

After you have used the Korem Profiling System for a while, customize your summaries for each type. This will help you recall how to interact more effectively with each type of person in the way that is the most meaningful for you. The key to constructing useful summaries is that you focus on actions that are typically the most important for you to recall when interacting with others.

Here is a sample of a customized SNAPSHOT read for SERGEANTS using alternative actions.

SERGEANT (CONTROL/TELL)—Prefer to *control* emotions and *tell* others what to do or what they think. They often are *influential* and *persistent*. Their downside is that they can be *aloof* and *unwilling to accept direction*.

You may also want to create different SNAPSHOT summaries for different kinds of professional and social situations. For example, certain actions may be more important to you when interviewing versus when managing those who work for you. In your private life, you may want to use one summary statement when socializing and another version around the house with your children.

With use, you will find that SNAPSHOT reads will also help you remember more of the actions associated with each type. You will meet someone, recall his SNAPSHOT read, and note that two actions are not present, but two other actions are. Making a mental note of this person's additional actions, provides a useful way for broadening your recollection of the actions associated with each type. Eventually, this will enable you to increase the length of each summary and reduce the need to memorize different variations of each summary.

USING SNAPSHOT READS

TABLE 12 provides a list of some noncritical and critical situations when a SNAPSHOT read can improve your interactions with others. Please note that because SNAPSHOT reads are based on limited observations, they will usually be less reliable and more vulnerable to change over time than a FINE-TUNED read or a COMPREHENSIVE PROFILE.

TABLE 12

■ **Noncritical or brief one-time only interactions**

- Sales with nonrepeat customers that require a short period of interaction, such as over-the-counter retail.
- Brief, noncritical interactions, such as: auditors conducting a low-key fact-finding interview; casual acquaintances in one's company; providing instructions to temporary personnel.
- Social gatherings.
- Many first-time exchanges.

■ **Critical interaction that is short, but is over a sustained period of time**

- Manager of a large plant interacting with many workers on the shop floor.
- Repeat sales in which the interaction is short, such as many types of industrial sales.
- Pressure situations for medical personnel, social workers, or law enforcement officers when one must quickly assess how to interact with someone.
- Technician who is dealing with people where the human face on the service is important.
- Screening applicants over the telephone.
- At the beginning of a hiring interview.
- A reporter conducting an interview during a fast-breaking story.

The following are suggested applications for using SNAPSHOT reads.

Hiring—You are running an ad in a local newspaper for an administrative assistant who will work with a SERGEANT type. You believe that an ACCOUNTANT type (ASK/CONTROL) is best suited for the job. To attract people who are ACCOUNTANT types to your ad, use words in your ad from the list of ACCOUNTANT actions that will appeal to this person—or similar words that fit the ad. Some examples: "Executive seeks *detailed* and *efficient* assistant . . ." or "Can you restore *order* to the office of an executive?" or "Amiable, friendly environment seeks *dependable* . . ." If you are uncertain about specific wording, find someone that possesses the type to whom you are trying to appeal and ask for their input.

Sales—You own a retail jewelry business. As noted in Chapter 7, you can typically provide more choices to people who are CONFIDENT (MANAGERS and INNOVATORS) than those who are FEARFUL (CONFORMISTS and RANDOM ACTORS). This is because people who are CONFIDENT tend to quickly eliminate undesirable options more quickly than those who are FEARFUL and often less decisive. Therefore, to improve your sales process, it might be wise to train sales personnel to quickly identify PERFORMANCE types and include the descriptors of *indecisive* for RANDOM ACTORS and CONFORMISTS and *decisive decision-maker* for MANAGERS and INNOVATORS. Or this information can be used to predict who one might have to expend greater energy servicing.

Managing—Your company has just acquired a new plant. SNAPSHOT reads can help you quickly size up the situation when you visit the facility for the first time. By reading the COMMUNICATION types of key employees, you can quickly decide where and how to seek critical information. For example, ACCOUNTANTS and ARTISTS will often be evaluative/critical of the situation. SALESMEN, however, are more likely to provide the positives of a new situation. And SERGEANTS will typically paint a picture that allows them to maintain as much control as possible.

Confrontational Settings—You are an investigator. You suspect fraud and must ask questions. When pressured, SERGEANTS and SALESMEN often tend to use their directive/forceful skills to defend themselves the stronger their TELL trait. ARTISTS and ACCOUNTANTS, however, often become less forceful, more silent, the higher their ASK trait. Recognizing these natural tendencies can help one avoid false conclusions about truthfulness simply because one person is more or less forceful/convincing than another.

ASSIGNMENT #11

Goal: Memorizing and customizing SNAPSHOT reads.
Time Required: One hour.

Using the format for a SNAPSHOT read described on page 125, write a customized synopsis for one COMMUNICATION type and one PERFORMANCE each. Make certain that one summary can be used in your professional career and the second summary in your private life.

DEVELOPING A FINE-TUNED READ

The FINE-TUNED read is more detailed than a SNAPSHOT read. FINE-TUNED reads use the *entire* action list for a specific type, identifying a more complete inventory of someone's specific actions. FINE-TUNED reads require observation over a period of time in order to identify the specific actions that a person possesses. FINE-TUNED reads are useful because they:

- Provide more detailed information about a person's strengths and weaknesses.
- Are vital when interaction must be precise.
- Are useful for long-term interaction.

The three steps for assessing a FINE-TUNED read are as follows:

1. Plot a person on the two gauges for the type that you want to assess. For example, if you want to assess a FINE-TUNED read for a COMMUNICATION type, plot that person on the ASK-TELL and CONTROL-EXPRESS gauges.
2. Identify the type.
3. Over a period of time, check off the specific actions that you observe in that person on the appropriate action list—**TABLE 5** (page 63) or **TABLE 10** (page 111). The time necessary to observe as many actions as possible will be driven by the number of situations in which you can observe people and how much information you can obtain about their past history.

Like the SNAPSHOT read, you have already learned the first two steps necessary to create a FINE-TUNED. Step #3 is simply observing a person's specific actions associated with his *type* and then checking off those actions on the action list for that type. This provides a way to track specific actions. On the following page is an example of a FINE-TUNED read of Jeremy, who is an ARTIST. The actions checked off are those that have been observed in Jeremy over a period of time.

Fine-Tuned Read of "Jeremy" Who Is an Artist

POSITIVE ACTIONS	NEGATIVE ACTIONS	OTHER TENDENCIES
✓Creative	Critical	Idiosyncratic
✓Sympathetic	✓Moody	✓Respectful
✓Agreeable	✓Argumentative	✓Tolerant
Avoids conflict	"Spineless"	Enduring
✓Supportive	Emotionally rash	Focus on how they feel
Sensitive	✓Low self-esteem	
Deep-feeling	✓Unsure	
Self-sacrificing		
✓Loyal		
✓Amiable		
✓Compassionate		
Self-effacing		

MANAGING FINE-TUNED READS

For important professional and personal relationships, it is recommended that you make a copy of the action list for each person's type and check off those actions that you observe. Keep this list filed and periodically review and update it. Over time, people's specific actions can change due to maturity, change of environments, and so on.

When you know that you will have a critical interaction, take out the action list and review it so that you can take into consideration all of the specific actions you have observed. This will help you to be more objective and sensitive to each person's unique personality inventory.

ASSIGNMENT #12

Goal: Identify your personal FINE-TUNED read.

Time Required: 30 minutes.

1. Check off the specific actions you possess in both your COMMUNI-CATION and PERFORMANCE types.

2. Ask a trusted friend or relative to review your list with you to be sure that it is complete. When identifying negative actions, candid honesty is the best policy. When people deny that they have a specific negative action, they may also choose to put on mental blinders so that they won't see the same action in others. In this way they don't see a reflection of themselves. A second common response is needlessly over

reacting when someone else displays this action. The reason: it reminds them of themselves. In either case, anything less than transparent honesty about one's actions will only impede one's profiling skills and inhibit effective interaction with others.

USING FINE-TUNED READS

Identifying specific actions can be useful because people with the same type can and usually do differ. For example, if you are hiring someone to run an enterprise, you may want someone who is a SERGEANT type who specifically *takes charge* rather than just *influences*. However, if you want someone to work in an environment that could be frustrating, you might want to know if a particular SERGEANT is also *persistent*, to have a better idea if they can fight through frustration.

TABLE 13 details situations in which you might use a FINE-TUNED read.

TABLE 13

■ **Critical one-time interaction that may or may not be short in duration**
- When you must pinpoint one or two specific actions.
- Teacher meeting with a troublesome parent.
- Crucial negotiations.
- High-powered sales environment.
- Counselors in a clinic.
- Investigators conducting interviews.

■ **Critical on-going interaction that may or may not be short in duration**
- When you must pinpoint one or two specific actions.
- Sales in which individualized personal rapport is crucial.
- Medical doctors on rounds or seeing a cancer patient during office visits.
- Manager making final hiring or promotion decisions.
- Managers working with teams.
- Any relationship with a family member or friend.

Here are some specific applications in which FINE-TUNED reads can be beneficial.

Promotions—You have three candidates in your organization who are all ACCOUNTANT types. You have a slot open for a new controller, and you anticipate stress in this department for a year or two due to a recent merger. Therefore, you want an ACCOUNTANT type who specifically *wears well under pressure.* By identifying which of the three candidates possesses this action, you will be able to make a better selection. This is not only beneficial for the organization, but it is also beneficial for the person you will promote, making sure that he is the best suited for the environment.

Sales—Virtually any on-going consultant or strategic selling relationship will require fine-tuned reads. Fine-tuned reads help one extend beyond shoot-from-the-hip interactions. Competitors are always looking for ways to capture your clients. Fine-tuned reads can help you keep business, giving you the tool necessary to directly respond to your client's unique personality.

One successful financial broker and consultant maintains a FINE-TUNED read for each of his clients in his contact database. Before each critical consultation, he reviews his client's unique actions and adjusts his written proposals and presentations accordingly. Through this one simple action, several difficult-to-please clients told him that his presentations were the best structured and the easiest to digest of any of his competitors.

Working with a Partner—In entrepreneurial environments, talented people often come together because they are driven by an exciting vision. But how often do you hear the story: *They started off with a flurry, but their differences eventually destroyed their venture.* Fine-tuned reads at the front end of a relationship can do the following:

- Pinpoint potential weaknesses in a relationship so that ground rules, buffers, and other relationship-saving devices can be explored and put into place before trouble erupts.
- Encourage a respect for the fact that partners often have—and should have—different types and actions that can complement each other to get a bigger job done.
- Help forecast the types and *specific* actions desired in senior personnel to complement the strengths and weaknesses of the partners.

Instructing and Disciplining Children—Fine-tuned reads can be of immeasurable help when instructing and disciplining kids. For example, let's assume that there are two siblings, Timmy and Sarah. Both are ACCOUNTANT types, but the weaknesses of each child is different. One of Timmy's weaknesses is that he tends to be slow. Sarah, however, tends to be pessimistic.

One way to help Timmy would be to give him responsibility accompanied by appropriate discipline if he didn't carry out his responsibility on time. He should also be encouraged to pursue a potential friendship with a schoolmate who is energetic.

Sarah, however, struggles with pessimism. She needs to develop a more positive bent on life. To help her move past her pessimism, her parents can encourage Sarah, an avid reader, to read books about people who have overcome great obstacles to achieve their goals. Also, Sarah may need more personal praise than Timmy, who will likely need more disciplining because of his laziness.

ADDITIONAL THOUGHTS ON FINE-TUNED READS

FINE-TUNED Reads Are Not Complete—Don't assume that a FINE-TUNED profile will provide all you need to know about a person. A FINE-TUNED read of a person's COMMUNICATION type, for example, is not a complete profile of the person. It is only a detailed description of his COMMUNICATION or PERFORMANCE type.

Actions Outside the Target Type—Let's assume that you have identified that Bob is a SERGEANT type. Then, as you develop his FINE-TUNED read, you notice that he also has a couple of SALESMAN actions, such as *outgoing* and *optimistic*. As discussed in Chapter 5, this is probably due to one of three factors.

First, Bob may share actions with the SALESMAN type because both share the TELL trait. Second, he may have learned a specific action, like a reporter with a TELL trait who learns to ask questions like an ASK person. Or third, he may have a plot point near the middle, and thus he is a *combination* type, described in detail in Chapter 5. If Bob is a SERGEANT/SALESMAN *combination* type, then you will have to review the actions for both the SERGEANT *and* the SALESMAN.

ASSIGNMENT #13

Goal: Learn to assess a FINE-TUNED read.

Time Required: One hour.

1. Identify the COMMUNICATION and PERFORMANCE types of ten people whom you have known for a period of time. Be sure that they are

evenly distributed amongst professional and personal acquaintances.

2. Check off the specific actions that you have observed in each. If you have difficulty, seek assistance from someone who knows the same people.

SUMMARY OF WHEN TO USE SNAPSHOT AND FINE-TUNED READS

Selecting when to use a SNAPSHOT or a FINE-TUNED read will be dictated by your interaction needs. **TABLE 14** provides an easy-to-use comparative summary of when to use each type of read.

TABLE 14

SNAPSHOT Read

- Need general information.
- Interaction is brief and short-term.
- When first interacting with someone.
- Have little time to assess.
- Noncritical, one-time only interactions.
- Critical, short interaction over a sustained period of time.

FINE-TUNED Read

- Need information about specific actions.
- When interaction must be precise.
- Critical long-term interactions.
- Critical one-time or on-going interaction that may or may not be short in duration.

A typical situation in which it is desirable to use both reads is when you are interviewing someone for a job. When beginning the interview, make a SNAPSHOT read to:

- Determine if the person has the COMMUNICATION type that you are seeking.
- Help you better communicate and pose questions during the interview.

As the interview progresses, you can then begin to develop a FINE-TUNED read, based upon what you observe, the résumé, references, previous work history, and so forth.

ASSIGNMENT #14

Goal: Practice using both SNAPSHOT and FINE-TUNED reads.

Time Required: Four hours over a two-week period.

1. Memorize the SNAPSHOT reads for both the COMMUNICATION and PERFORMANCE types.

2. Plot fifteen different people on the four gauges and determine their types. As you identify each person's type, recite from memory each person's SNAPSHOT read. *Reminder*: Be sure to include people form each of the five categories listed on page 52 whom you like as well as people whom you dislike.

3. Use the same group of fifteen people in #2 and assess a FINE-TUNED read of each person. If you haven't had sufficient contact with some individuals, replace them with another person from the same category.

CHAPTER 10

Seven Key Reasons for Misreads

There are several recurring reasons why even seasoned profiling professionals will misread others. This chapter will point out both the cause of these misreads and the antidotes.

Misreading people is something that plagues everyone. It's just a part of life. People can act uniquely on a given day simply because they choose to do so or because of a unique situation. The ideas in this chapter, however, will help you reduce your inaccuracy when you were the cause of the misread. And perhaps even more valuable, when you do misread someone, you will be able to pinpoint, in most situations, the exact reason for the misread. This will not only enable you to accurately redefine your read, but you will also gain insight that will decrease the chances that you will misread someone with the same trait in a similar situation in the future.

Before you begin this chapter, review the concepts in Chapter 6 as some of the concepts in this chapter build on those already presented. Finally, pencil in specific dates on your calendar, about two weeks apart, over the next four months when you will review this chapter and Chapter 6 until recall of the core concepts and antidotes becomes instinctive.

As you process these concepts and the antidotes in this chapter, think back to those people whom you have misread in *each* of your previous assignments. Don't just select one assignment. This will allow you to think through all of the traits and types and perhaps even discern a pattern of those you most commonly misread.

REASON #1
Confuse One Trait for Another

The most common misstep that even causes experts to misread someone is when one trait is mistaken for another. An example from history is when people are asked to identify whether or not Hitler was CONFIDENT or FEARFUL when making decisions. Many people will say *CONFIDENT*, because they recall his fiery oratory staged in front of his mass rallies. But we know that he was extreme FEARFUL when making decisions, exemplified by his extreme displays of paranoia. The reason that people misread Hitler is that he possessed a strong TELL trait. He could *talk* an extremely powerful game, but when called upon to perform when Russian troops captured Berlin, he operated out of fear and took his life.

Hitler's negative actions can also cause some confusion.

Some might assume, for example, that Hitler was *arrogant* and *conceited* when he made *decisions*, two negative CONFIDENT actions. Actually, when called upon to make important decisions, Hitler was *unstable, anxious*, and *defensive*—negative FEARFUL actions. What created the illusion of arrogance and conceit *when making decisions* was that he was *egotistical* (a negative TELL trait) in the *talk* part of his life. That is, when Hitler spoke, he was often egotistical. This is different from being arrogant or conceited when called upon to make a decision, which may or may not require him to communicate with others. In fact, it was this seeming contradiction that caused him to be an enigma to those around him. While appearing pompous and egotistical when he communicated, his decisions were made out of fear.

This may seem like splitting hairs, but if one doesn't carefully identify from which trait his negative actions originated, one might type Hitler as an INNOVATOR (which has a CONFIDENT trait) instead of a dangerous RANDOM ACTOR (which has a CONFIDENT trait).

Antidote—With some awareness this cause for misreads can be minimized by:

1. Recognizing which traits are the easiest to confuse for another.
2. Faithfully follow Rule #3 that promotes systematic accuracy: *Anything that is worth measuring is worth measuring at least twice.*
3. When profiling, always read each trait *separately*, and when necessary, review the list of actions for each trait. Don't look at someone and

think: *He looks like an ACCOUNTANT type.* Be disciplined to read each trait individually, because unique combinations of traits can fool you if not read separately. Don't take shortcuts, otherwise one day you will pay the price for a lack of discipline.

The most common traits which are mistaken for another and who is most likely to make each misread are as follows:

TELL for CONFIDENT—This is common when SALESMAN or SERGEANT types who are FEARFUL present a strong and/or powerful image when they communicate. The more pronounced the TELL trait, the greater the chance for misreading their TELL trait for CONFIDENT. Also, those who are ASK, FEARFUL, or low CONFIDENT are the most susceptible to making this misread because they are often not as instinctively familiar with the TELL and CONFIDENT trait. Thus, they are more prone to misinterpret TELL for CONFIDENT.

ASK for FEARFUL—It is common for people to misread ARTIST or ACCOUNTANT types (who are actually CONFIDENT) as being FEARFUL. What is misread is the ASK trait for FEARFUL. It is the ASK person's indirect or laid-back style of communicating is sometimes mistaken as being FEARFUL. This is especially true the stronger the ASK trait. People who are CONFIDENT or TELL are usually more susceptible to making this misread, because they are not as familiar with the nuances of a person who is ASK.

FEARFUL for UNPREDICTABLE—This misread often occurs when people who are FEARFUL act to protect themselves, such as reversing a previous commitment. This can create the illusion of unpredictability, even though someone is PREDICTABLE. People who are CONFIDENT are typically the most susceptible for making this misread, particularly the stronger their CONFIDENT trait.

PREDICTABLE for FEARFUL—People who are PREDICTABLE are often misread as being FEARFUL—even if they are CONFIDENT. It works like this: Some people just like things to be familiar, without deviation. They don't like changes in the appearance of reports, they like to eat at the same familiar haunts and not venture out, they don't change in their circle of colleagues and friends, and even prefer for their attire to be consistent. People who are UNPREDICTABLE or low PREDICTABLE are the most vulnerable to making this misread. They mistakenly interpret predictability as FEARFUL—that someone is *afraid* to try something new. The fact is they are not FEARFUL, rather they just prefer that things remain consistent and predictable.

In summary, to avoid confusing one trait for another, read each trait separately based upon observable actions, take more than one read, and be aware of which trait(s) you are more likely to confuse for another.

REASON #2
Difficulty Reading One's Opposite Trait/Type

The following reason for misreading people is closely associated with the one just covered.

As noted in Chapter 6, we usually have trouble reading people who possess our opposite trait or type. Why? Because they are different than we are and we are not as familiar with the nuances of our opposites. Some suggestions were provided in Chapter 6, but the antidote is worth repeating here.

Antidote—Recruit someone who is the opposite of *both* your COMMUNICATION and PERFORMANCE type to help you navigate and deepen the understanding of your reads. Be sure that whoever you select has keen insight. Additionally, you may need to find two people—one for each of your types if one person can't be found who matches both your COMMUNICATION and PERFORMANCE types.

Although this suggestion was presented in Chapter 6, my experience is that most people don't follow through and apply it without encouragement. If you want to develop refined profiling skills, this is something you cannot put off. A wise counselor/friend, who has your best interest at heart, can help you think through how others, like themselves, communicate, think, and so on with significant immediacy.

REASON #3
People Can Learn a Specific Action

As we've learned, people can learn an action that is outside of their actual type. If we plot someone on one of the gauges based upon observing that unique action, we will misread someone's trait and type.

For example, a teacher who is an ACCOUNTANT type, may have

cultivated the ability to *excitedly* communicate a subject, an action usually associated with someone who is a SALESMAN. This action may just be unique to this person, learned while a child from a parent or simply cultivated out of a desire to encourage students.

Antidote—Be certain your read isn't based upon just one read. Faithfully follow Rule #3 that promotes systematic accuracy—*Anything that is worth measuring is worth measuring at least twice.* If you do notice another action at some later point that seems to come from a different type or trait inventory, don't panic. Take more reads. Look at past behavior—the best predictor of future behavior. Eventually you will flesh it out. It may just take more time.

REASON #4
Life-changing Experience

This concept, which has been noted in earlier chapters, is unfortunately becoming more common in most countries, principally driven by deteriorating social conditions—divorce, addiction, abuse, etc. Other positive and negative factors such as marriage, birth of a child, death, illness, loss of job, demotion, or a move can also cause people to temporarily operate in a way that is inconsistent with their actual traits. In other cases, though, these kinds of events in a person's life can result in a permanent change of plot points, even moving a person from one side of a gauge to the other.

When hiring people, this can be a really troublesome problem when you think you have hired someone who is a good match for a job. A few months down the line, though, his plot point(s) changes and he is no longer suited for the position. The following antidote can help you minimize the chances for this happening—which benefits both you and the prospective employee.

Antidote—To increase the accuracy and possible stability of a specific person's traits, look at past behavior and breaks in consistency from the actions of his trait(s) or type(s).

When a person has gone through a life-changing experience that has temporarily shifted his plot point, checking out past behavior is one of the best ways to determine where a person is likely to land after they have absorbed and dealt with the full impact of the experience. When we go through a situation that stretches us—like a rubber band—we can return to plot points similar to our old plot points.

To check your read, inquire about past actions whenever possible. And specifically, how he dealt with non-life-changing pressure in the past. Precisely how you do this during an interview should be reviewed with legal counsel because of laws constraining the types of questions that can be asked during an interview that might be considered discriminatory, prejudicial, etc.

One possible tact that doesn't necessarily require an interview, however, would be to review a person's résumé and work history. See if his profile matches his previous job descriptions. Does a pattern emerge regarding the positions in which the person did and did not excel, which might reveal whether his profile was or wasn't suited for specific responsibilities?

Let's assume, for example, that you have a research position open in a marketing group that is best suited for a person who is ASK. Ellen applies for the position and during her first interview you believe that she is ASK. When you review her résumé, however, it is apparent that Ellen excelled in strategic sales environments, which typically requires that someone have a TELL trait. To be certain that you have not misread Ellen's ASK-TELL trait, you now test the option that she is presently going through a circumstance that has temporarily changed her ASK-TELL plot point—promoting her desire to use a TELL trait.

To test your read, you will focus on how Ellen handled a stressful situation in her previous position(s). For example, you might ask Ellen to describe how she personally handled the restructuring of her group, which was the catalyst for her decision to seek other employment. As she describes her reaction and response, listen carefully to how Ellen *communicates* what she did. Also, listen carefully for any clues to specific past actions that might further illuminate her ASK or TELL trait. (Chapter 13 provides additional guidance when handling this kind of situation.)

Perhaps she succeeded in her previous position with an ASK trait because of preparation skills and her ability to listen to and meet all of her client's technical needs. Or, you might discover that in those past situations she did use a TELL trait, exemplified by how she negotiated important contracts.

There is no sure-fire method that can be used in all situations to check out past behavior, but make the attempt to do so whenever possible. As more and more people are going through changes in their lives—when the ground is shifting under their feet, strategies that are within the law and professional ethical boundaries must be harnessed. (It is recommended that those charged with hiring responsibilities take a behavioral interviewing course that provides strategies that satisfy the demands of current state and federal laws.)

REASON #5
Culture or Choice Suppresses Actual Traits

Cultural Suppression—A corporate culture or even the culture of a country can suppress actions that can reveal a person's actual traits. If you don't take a second look—a second read—you can easily fall prey to a misread. Here are some examples.

In the military, enlisted men and women all wear the same uniform and salute in the same way. This can lead to assuming stereotypically that individuals in a unit are all PREDICTABLE, even though we know that all kinds of personality types join the armed forces.

In the 1970s, the corporate culture of one Fortune 500 company was known for its regimented style. Men and women typically wore blue or gray suits, and men's haircuts resembled military cuts, mirroring the image established by the company's founder. An outsider profiling this company's employees might mistakenly think that all were PREDICTABLE and CONTROL because of the "corporate uniform."

A more complicated example of cultural suppression of traits can be found in countries that have experienced repression. I witnessed this first-hand in Poland, shortly after the fall of Communism, where I have lectured regularly at universities since 1992. The repressive and flattening effects of Communism are still physically evident in the many gray-boxed apartment buildings in Warsaw. One can also observe a flattening effect in how people communicate. Unless one goes into someone's flat, where people really come alive, one would mistakenly think that Polish people are stereotypically PREDICTABLE and CONTROL.

Each of the above situations are examples in which culture suppresses actual traits, causing misreads.

Suppression by Choice—In this era of "interview training" and video-taped role-playing, many people are learning to project what they believe is the image that will get them the job. Often, interviewers will conclude that "trained" interviewees cannot be read as accurately as they might like. Some even give up on trying to read a person who has been through this type of training. However, even "coached" responses as well as "natural" responses can provide initial hunches that we can test several times before making our final read.

For example, a trained interviewee will typically try to avoid open-ended responses to open-ended questions. Instead, they will try to provide tight, succinct responses that they believe will put the best foot forward. Or they will try to *guide* the conversation to areas that they consider their strengths. This can be frustrating when trying to make accurate reads. The following, however, will help you profile even the most thoroughly coached candidates as well as those whose traits have been "flattened" by a culture.

Antidote—Regardless of whether a person's traits are suppressed by culture or choice, make unobtrusive reads that are noninvasive and look for breaks in consistency—leakage.

Let's first examine reading people when traits are culturally suppressed.

If you want to profile soldiers in basic training, you don't make reads based upon how they salute or stand at attention during a roll call. You make an unobtrusive, noninvasive read when they are relaxing in the barracks or enjoying a dinner at a local restaurant. You observe them when they can be themselves—preferably in a way in which you don't intrude.

In the corporate culture of the Fortune 500 company referenced, one way to make unobtrusive reads was to look for *leakage* in attire. Men who were UNPREDICTABLE or EXPRESS sometimes expressed their trait by wearing cuff links that had a unique flair. When in a critical meeting, they simply pulled the sleeve of their coat down, covering their "rebel" cuff links. When they went out to eat with colleagues at lunch, a tug of the sleeve, and voila...freedom of expression.

The women did it differently.

Some of those who were UNPREDICTABLE or EXPRESS relied upon earrings to express their trait. In a meeting, their hair covered their lack of uniformity, and at lunch...it only took a flick of the hand, pushing their hair behind an ear, and then, like the men, they enjoyed freedom of expression.

In Poland, you can often peer through the cultural facade by simply going to someone's home for dinner. Although living conditions are changing rapidly, many dwellings are still the old wretchedly constructed apartment buildings, a legacy of Communism. Additionally, people are still feeling their way when it comes to expressing themselves in public. But once you step into a flat, color abounds and the real traits of Poles come to life and are revealed—even to a foreigner who can't speak the language. (Additional suggestions for profiling in a cross-cultural environment are provided in Chapter 13.)

In most situations in which a culture disguises, conceals, or flattens out a person's actual traits, make unobtrusive, noninvasive reads in situations that allow people the freedom to be themselves while you look for *leakage*—breaks in consistency—that reveal actual traits. Unobtrusive reads are also an effective tool for reading coached interviewees, who try to convey a trait or traits that they don't possess.

In these instances, create hunches based upon the trait(s) that they might attempt to *avoid* or *conceal* as well as what they *present* as their strength. For example, let's assume that you are seeking someone who is an ACCOUNTANT type for a position. You require someone who can easily follow direction (ASK). During the interview, the candidate assures you that he can easily follow someone's directives. To be certain that he isn't just offering you a canned response, you might test your first read by asking him to describe how he followed someone's leadership in the past. As he relates his story, listen to the *communication style* in which he presents his story. Does he tend to control his emotions and use an ASK style for communicating, or does he come on forcefully (TELL) with a display of emotion (EXPRESS)?

By observing how trained interviewees communicate *and* their persistence in sticking to their "rehearsed, party line answers," you can often read their ASK-TELL tendencies. If they are unable to shift out of *telling* you their programmed answers and they do not seem able to easily ask questions about your inquiries (so that they can gain a broader understanding of the intent of your questions), you are probably dealing with someone with a TELL trait. If, however, they can easily shift and ask questions with an ASK flair, you probably have an ASK person.

When trying to identify CONTROL or EXPRESS traits during interviews with people who have prepared and practiced responses, it is typically more difficult for a person who is CONTROL to manufacture effortlessly and naturally EXPRESS actions, particularly the stronger his CONTROL trait.

Alternately, it is often easier for an EXPRESS person to temporarily harness his actions in order to present the appearance of CONTROL. Thus, if you ask someone to detail how he followed past directives, closely observe if the CONTROL or EXPRESS trait seems to dominate his communication style.

Identifying PERFORMANCE traits can be more difficult to identify during an interview because you are trying to identify how someone prefers to perform and make decisions in the context of verbal conversation. Identifying PERFORMANCE traits often requires more than one interview combined with a careful review of past work history, particularly when stress was involved in specific situations. Here are two examples.

Typically, someone who attempts to conceal his FEARFUL trait will do so by *verbalizing* that he is CONFIDENT. This doesn't mean that he will necessarily use a TELL trait, rather he will communicate with words that he is CONFIDENT. To test this kind of read, review specific situations in his past work history in which stress was involved and the kinds of responsibilities that he assumed. This will often provide a starting point for a read. Listen carefully for the PERFORMANCE style in which he handled past situations.

For example, did he seem to avoid a necessary confrontation? If he did confront someone, did he truly use a CONFIDENT trait or did he fearfully confront using a TELL trait? (As noted earlier in the chapter, TELL is often confused as being CONFIDENT. Remember, you must read each trait separately, separating a person's *walk* from his *talk*.) Did the confrontation reveal needless paranoia? Did the manner in which he handled past situations reveal CONFIDENT actions, such as being *independent, stable,* and *candid,* or were FEARFUL actions revealed, such as *guarded, cautious,* and *timid?* If he was in a support role (common for CONFORMISTS), was he in that role by choice and like it? If so, this might confirm that he is FEARFUL.

Identifying PREDICTABLE or UNPREDICTABLE traits is usually a bit easier. One tact is to review a person's past history and ask whether or not they enjoyed the *nature* of their prior positions. Often, a pattern will emerge. For example, those who enjoy responsibilities with predictability will usually be PREDICTABLE, while those who enjoy the challenge of changing environments or responsibilities will tend to be UNPREDICTABLE. Another tactic to test an uncertain read is to ask someone to provide *three* examples that illustrate why he enjoyed the nature of his previous responsibilities. Don't say,

"Please give me three examples...," rather, ask for an example. Listen to his response. Then ask for another example, listen, and repeat with a third request. Most interviewees who are trying to mask a trait will have a difficult time providing three detailed responses.

If you have any uncertainty when trying to identify a trait, don't hesitate to request an additional interview in a completely different setting. Or request that another colleague conduct a follow-up interview to test a read of a trait. The goal is to provide a good match that will benefit both your organization and the person you are hiring.

REASON #6
Emotional Reads

One of the times that we are the most vulnerable for misreading someone is when we are making reads based upon our emotions. Some examples:

- You had an exceptionally good or an exceptionally bad day.
- You've just been notified that your firm has just been selected to produce a documentary series.
- You've just been passed over for a career-advancing project.
- You've just come from your daughter's basketball game in which her team pulled off an upset.

Any of these positive and negative situations can present an opportunity for our emotions to interfere with making an accurate read. This doesn't mean that we should abandon our emotions or our intuition. We just need to be sure that when we are placed in an important or unexpected situation, that we check to see if our reads have been misdirected by our emotions.

As noted in Chapter 2, one of the worst kinds of situations is when people make an inaccurate emotional decision and then try to justify the decision—their read—with logic. This can allow pride to dominate as one defends a position, and real trouble can erupt. There is a better way.

Antidote—Recommit to read everyone based upon the extreme ends of your personalized gauges.

Remember how you first learned to use the CONTROL-EXPRESS gauge by comparing people to the extreme ends of the gauge: Spock and Queen Elizabeth (CONTROL) versus Robin Williams/Life-of-the-Party (EXPRESS)? In an important situation in which you may be emotionally charged and an accurate read is essential, mentally step back. Ask yourself if the overall persona of the person in front of you tilts toward Spock or Robin Williams—or whatever extreme examples you have chosen. Let the gauge be your guide. When you do, you will find that your intuition, which can be guided by your emotions, will sharpen—and, most importantly, you will know *why* it is sharper.

It is also a known fact that most people are attracted to others who are like themselves. While there is some common wisdom that says opposites attract, it is usually the case that opposites attract only within a finite range of differences. It is common for people to view those who are genuinely different from themselves (e.g., race, gender, religious or political persuasion, etc.) more skeptically or critically. Similarly, our feelings of attraction or affiliation can interfere with our ability to make reliable reads about people who are more like us. Therefore, regardless of whether someone is or is not like you, shares or does not share your perspectives, and so on, read their actions against the extreme ends of each gauge.

REASON #7
Combination Types

When a plot point is near the middle, it is common to misread people who are a *combination type* because they are operating at one side of their range on one day and at the other side of their range the next. For example, someone who is 1 EXPRESS and 3 ASK, might appear to be an ARTIST one day and ACCOUNTANT the next. While the concept of *range* was introduced in Chapter 3, it is helpful to remember the following antidote when you realize that you misread someone because of his range.

Antidote—Commit to vigilantly apply Rule #3 that promotes systematic accuracy: *Anything that is worth measuring is worth measuring at least twice.*

Always take more than one read and test your reads. Don't ever assume that your first or second read is accurate. Assume that there will always be people who will fool you. Not because they are trying to trip you up, but simply because of their plot point.

Therefore, be especially vigilant when you think someone has a 2 plot point or less—when there is a strong possibility that a person might be a combination type. People with extreme traits, around 4 or 5, usually won't fool you. Mentally, accept and prepare for the fact that you will need to take multiple reads for the 10–15% of those people you will meet who will be combination types. Accepting and applying this responsibility will not only increase your reads of these people, but you will also find that your reads overall will improve because of your heightened state of awareness.

So don't write off people who are combination types. Accept the challenge. Be vigilant. Take multiple reads, and watch your profiling skills begin to attain a professional quality.

ASSIGNMENT #15

Goal: To be able to recall the ideas presented in Chapters 6 and 10.

Time Required: One to two hours.

After you reading this chapter, read it again. Type a short list of the reasons for misreads and their antidotes. Carry it with you while you are developing your profiling skills. Also, type a condensed list of the tips presented in Chapter 6 and carry it with you as well. Refer regularly to these lists. You will find that this will increase your accuracy when making difficult reads.

CHAPTER 11

The Map: Sixteen Comprehensive Profiles

To this point, you have learned how to use the profiling compass—plotting people on the four gauges. You have also learned how to combine the gauges together to identify someone's COMMUNICATION and PERFORMANCE types, which enable you to develop SNAPSHOT and FINE-TUNED reads. You are now ready for the last step, combining the COMMUNICATION and PERFORMANCE types together to reveal a COMPREHENSIVE PROFILE, as shown below.

The COMPREHENSIVE PROFILE provides you with a *map* that shows you how a person's COMMUNICATION type interacts with his PERFORMANCE type.

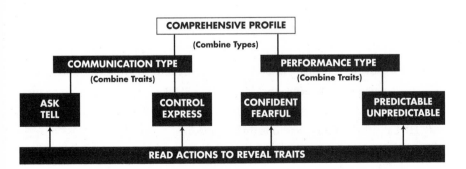

Each profile also details likely:

- Strengths
- Shortcomings
- Other tendencies
- Trait indicators (which traits are likely to drive specific actions)

Additionally, you will be provided with suggestions for:

- Interaction
- Presenting and selling ideas, products, and services
- Handling confrontations

THE BENEFIT OF COMPREHENSIVE PROFILES

COMPREHENSIVE PROFILES give you more predictive power and accuracy because they provide a richer layer of information than types by themselves. COMPREHENSIVE PROFILES are also valuable tools for understanding one's own tendencies and makeup. It is recommended that after you have identified your specific profile that you devote an hour or two to considering how others perceive you.

You will probably use COMPREHENSIVE PROFILES in most important situations, such as negotiations, hiring or promoting a key person, calling upon a new client, teachers interviewing parents, considering how to help one's spouse or children, and so on. COMPREHENSIVE PROFILES allow you to answer questions like: What kind of actions am I likely to see from a person who is a SERGEANT/MANAGER? What are the differences between a SERGEANT/MANAGER and a SERGEANT/RANDOM ACTOR? How do I need to interact with each?

For example, because a SERGEANT is CONTROL and TELL, we might assume that a SERGEANT can be depended upon in a crisis to give *direction*. But what if a person is a SERGEANT *and* a RANDOM ACTOR (FEARFUL and UNPREDICTABLE). Now we have a SERGEANT type who *can't* be depended upon to provide *consistent* direction under pressure because he is usually FEARFUL when making decisions. The COMPREHENSIVE PROFILE points out for us that there may be times when this person's FEARFUL trait will override his TELL trait when this person is under pressure.

This kind of information can be critical when making long-term decisions about relationships or even approaching first-time interactions.

Reviewing a person's COMPREHENSIVE PROFILE can also provide a safety check on your reads, helping you understand why first impressions may or may not match up with a person's actions over time. For example, perhaps you thought that someone was ASK, but he was really TELL. When you now read this person's profile, however, it becomes clear by the profile's descriptors that you missed a read because his COMPREHENSIVE PROFILE doesn't fit his actions.

Like the other components of the Korem Profiling System, mastering the use of the sixteen COMPREHENSIVE PROFILES requires study, practice, and periodic review, but the dividends will pay off for the rest of your life.

FOUR NEGATIVE PROFILES

As already stated, individual traits are not inherently good or bad, except for moderate to high FEARFUL. There are, however, good and bad actions associated with each trait. Regarding twelve of the sixteen different profiles presented in this chapter, the same rule applies: There are no inherently good or bad profiles. People can use their profiles both positively and negatively. The exception is the set of four profiles associated with the RANDOM ACTOR.

As detailed in Chapter 8, RANDOM ACTORS are potentially the most troublesome of the four PERFORMANCE types. So it follows that a COMPREHENSIVE PROFILE that has a RANDOM ACTOR PERFORMANCE type can also be troublesome.

The following suggestions summarize how to interact with RANDOM ACTORS, and should be used while reviewing the four RANDOM ACTOR COMPREHENSIVE PROFILES. (Additional observations on the RANDOM ACTOR is provided in Chapter 13.)

- The more extreme the FEARFUL and UNPREDICTABLE traits, the greater need for caution when interacting with this person.
- The positive actions of a RANDOM ACTOR will typically come from his COMMUNICATION type. Therefore, it is best to operate with this person on a communication level and not put him into a position in which he must "perform," thus triggering the actions from his PERFORMANCE type.
- Avoid long-term interactions.
- When one must interact, carefully monitor activities.
- When you must confront, work tactically to drive down fear so that actions

will become more predictable. (If and when this tactic works, it will only work in a short-term duration.)

- They can change and become more CONFIDENT when making decisions if they learn to trust, which often involves a life-changing experience.

THREE HELPFUL SUGGESTIONS

Evaluating the Profile of Someone Who Is a Combination Type—If a person is a *combination type*, such as a SERGEANT/ SALESMAN/MANAGER, you will need to review the profiles of both the SERGEANT/MANAGER and the SERGEANT/SALESMAN. (And, in some rare cases, in which someone is both a combination type in both his COMMUNI-CATION and PERFORMANCE types, you will need to review as many as four profiles.) This will require some significant work to flesh out which of the long list of possible tendencies will apply to this person. This means that you will have to be more astute when reading this person's actions and cataloging which profile is likely to surface in which type of situation. Yes, this can be time-consuming, but understanding the two (or up to four) arenas in which this person prefers to operate puts you much further ahead than if you didn't have any information at all. Additionally, when you do take the time to understand these people you will often experience great receptivity because you were willing to unselfishly invest time to understand and meet their complex needs.

Read Both Sell/Present and Confrontation Suggestions— Regardless of whether you are selling/presenting or confronting someone, read both the Sell/Present and Confrontation suggestions for each profile before taking action, as these two kinds of interaction needs can overlap. In some confrontations, for example, one might need to sell an idea in order to get a person to open up or to bring closure to a confrontation. And alternately, in some sell/present situations there is the possibility of a confrontation/rejection of one's ideas or products/services. By considering both suggestion categories, you will have a firmer foundation for operating with someone.

Reviewing Both COMPREHENSIVE PROFILES and FINE-TUNED Reads—Of the two, the COMPREHENSIVE PROFILE is a more powerful descriptor than the FINE-TUNED read. However, it is strongly recommended for critical situations that you review both a person's COMPREHENSIVE PRO-FILE and his FINE-TUNED read. You may find one or two specific actions that will better help you review a person's profile and develop strategies for inter-actions. For example, if a person is an ARTIST/INNOVATOR, observing a specific positive INNOVATOR action, such as *self-assured*, may indicate that this person will take action. This action might also suggest that he will needlessly "rock the boat," a typical shortcoming of his profile. Additionally, a specific action for a person's *type* might be the most important ingredient when working with that person—an action which is not necessarily spelled out in the COMPREHENSIVE PROFILE.

Lastly, as noted throughout the text, the word "typical" should not be interpreted as "always." These profiles are inventories of commonly seen actions for each combination of types. In addition to an individual's COM-PREHENSIVE PROFILE, you will need to take into consideration factors such as a person's unique combination of skills, intellect, or strategic positioning before interacting with that person.

SIXTEEN COMPREHENSIVE PROFILES

What follows are the sixteen different profile combinations. Since our natural instinct is to read someone's COMMUNICATION type first, the combination of types are presented with the COMMUNICATION type listed first.

SERGEANT Types
- SERGEANT/MANAGER
- SERGEANT/INNOVATOR
- SERGEANT/CONFORMIST
- SERGEANT/RANDOM ACTOR

ACCOUNTANT Types
- ACCOUNTANT/MANAGER
- ACCOUNTANT/INNOVATOR
- ACCOUNTANT/CONFORMIST
- ACCOUNTANT/RANDOM ACTOR

SALESMAN Types
- SALESMAN/MANAGER
- SALESMAN/INNOVATOR
- SALESMAN/CONFORMIST
- SALESMAN/RANDOM ACTOR

ARTIST Types
- ARTIST/MANAGER
- ARTIST/INNOVATOR
- ARTIST/CONFORMIST
- ARTIST/RANDOM ACTOR

For certain profiles that may be more difficult to understand or where additional information is needed for interaction, more descriptors and suggestions are provided, such as the RANDOM ACTOR profiles. However, the additional information should not be interpreted as implying that one profile is more important than another. Every individual, regardless of one's profile, is important. Also, don't try to memorize each profile, as each profile is formatted for easy reference. Retention will come naturally with use.

Using Common and Less Common Profiles to Focus Reads—One tool for deciding where to focus one's observations when making reads is to recognize which profiles are common and those that are less common. For example, let us assume that you have identified that Alice is an ACCOUNTANT. As you will see after you have reviewed the four ACCOUNTANT profiles in this chapter, there is a greater possibility that her PERFORMANCE type is a MANAGER or CONFORMIST than an INNOVATOR or RANDOM ACTOR. This is because ACCOUNTANT/INNOVATORS and ACCOUNTANT/RANDOM ACTORS aren't as common; ACCOUNTANTS are more likely to be PREDICTABLE than UNPREDICTABLE. With this knowledge, we can then focus our observations in the more likely direction that Alice is PREDICTABLE. Often, this will be the case, thus shortening our time for identifying Alice's profile because we looked at the most common patterns first.

Applying this strategy is not engaging in unwanted stereotyping, rather it is taking advantage of the fact that some profiles are more common than others. We still take more than one read and test our reads.

The following list of profiles is separated in two groups: those that are common and those that are less common.

Common Profiles	Less Common Profiles
• SERGEANT/MANAGER	• SERGEANT/RANDOM ACTOR
• SERGEANT/CONFORMIST	• SERGEANT/INNOVATOR
• SALESMAN/MANAGER	• SALESMAN/RANDOM ACTOR
• SALESMAN/INNOVATOR	• SALESMAN/CONFORMIST
• ACCOUNTANT/MANAGER	• ACCOUNTANT/INNOVATOR
• ACCOUNTANT/CONFORMIST	• ACCOUNTANT/RANDOM ACTOR
• ARTIST/INNOVATOR	• ARTIST/MANAGER
• ARTIST/CONFORMIST	• ARTIST/RANDOM ACTOR

Now let us examine the sixteen COMPREHENSIVE PROFILES, beginning with the four different SERGEANT profiles.

SERGEANT/MANAGER

The SERGEANT/MANAGER has the following combination of traits:

- CONTROL/TELL
- PREDICTABLE/CONFIDENT

This common profile will typically be seen as a "strong" personality. Many are often labeled "strong executive timber" in the corporate world the stronger their traits. SERGEANT/MANAGERS often hold the CEO's chair in a large organization. The profile combines a dominant, controlled social style with a self-initiating, consistent PERFORMANCE type which is CONFIDENT. People with this profile can make a bold first impression and then show that they can "do what they say" over longer periods of time. While this profile is naturally suited for leadership roles, it is also one that can turn callous and uncaring when negative actions aren't restrained.

Typical Strengths

- Combine emotional control and confidence.
- Perceived as being reliable to "deliver the goods" in almost any circumstances.
- Viewed as role models of how to maintain control.
- Viewed as "strong leaders."

Typical Shortcomings

- Can be rigid.
- Don't like change/unwilling to change.
- Over-dominate and over-control or stifle people who work with or for them.
- Often ineffective at developing/helping others.
- Can be poor listeners.
- Not effective when motivating diverse, complex teams that face creative problem-solving challenges.
- May have difficulty letting people work on their own. Often want to control and influence.

Other Tendencies

- Tend to hire "strong" people v. "growing" their successors or team.
- Prefer to let others *learn* on their own, but have difficulty letting others *work* on their own.
- Will make unilateral decisions when necessary to deliver final results.

Trait Indicators

- Shortcomings are most pronounced with high TELL, CONFIDENT, or CONTROL traits.
- Strengths more pronounced when TELL and CONFIDENT traits are stronger.
- Lower TELL trait is the most likely indicator that they can overcome any listening deficiency and address shortcomings.

Interaction Tips

- Be direct and concrete in language.
- Focus on bottom-line.
- When possible, help them adapt to ambiguity and the fact that they can't control all situations.
- Don't expect good "coaching" from them.

Sell/Present—Keep presentations short, crisp, and to the point. Use concrete language that displays a clear command of the facts and issues. Some emotional display is acceptable, but refrain from displays of emotions in place of facts. Don't try and "wing it" with fluff or you'll be shown the door.

Confrontation—When confronted, will typically turn to TELL trait to respond. Be prepared with facts and hard, concrete language. Develop strategic control before *and* after engagement. They typically won't back down. The higher TELL, CONFIDENT, and CONTROL, the more difficult to confront—the more preparation is needed. When possible, engage with a person whose TELL, CONFIDENT, and CONTROL traits are stronger.

SERGEANT/INNOVATOR

The SERGEANT/INNOVATOR has the following combination of traits:

- CONTROL/TELL
- UNPREDICTABLE/CONFIDENT

The SERGEANT/INNOVATOR has a profile much like that of the SERGEANT/MANAGER. The difference between the SERGEANT/MANAGER and the SERGEANT/INNOVATOR is the predictability trait. SERGEANT/MANAGERS prefer to be PREDICTABLE while the actions of the SERGEANT/INNOVATORS are more UNPREDICTABLE. This difference is the reason that this profile is one of the single biggest sources of entrepreneurs and others who lead in new and creative directions. SERGEANT/INNOVATORS have a COMMUNICATION type that allows them to "take charge" while their more open PERFORMANCE type will cause them to enjoy and thrive on change, risk-taking, and adventure.

Typical Strengths

- Comfortable with change and new and different ideas/appearances.
- Can be flexible in the amount of personal control they require in relationships.
- Can produce unique products and ideas.
- Tolerant of others' views and ideas. (This doesn't necessarily apply to tolerance of issues such as one's morals. Any of the profiles can be tolerant or intolerant regarding moral issues.)
- Prefer to solicit ideas during the development stages of a new effort.
- Appear controlled and not inclined to "lose their cool."

Typical Shortcomings

- May over-control the delivery of final product or work effort—due to their creative bent.
- SERGEANT characteristics may dominate when deadlines approach.
- Relationships with others (and projects) may not be as consistent as SERGEANT/MANAGERS, and thus can cause more instability in the work environment.

Other Tendencies

- May be seen by others as erratic or eccentric—stronger UNPREDICTABLE will magnify this quality/perception.
- Capable of developing a workable balance between career and outside interests.
- May appear inconsistent—may seek cooperation early in a relationship and then try to control later on.
- Will make unilateral decisions when necessary to deliver final results.

Trait Indicators

- Shortcomings are most pronounced when high UNPREDICTABLE gauge.
- Will appear most eccentric or hard to read when rated low on the CONFIDENCE dimension.

Interaction Tips

- Don't be misled by open problem-solving style; will still try to dominate later in relationship.
- Anticipate "high drive" work style resulting from desire to control implementation of lots of ideas.
- Present range of ideas before you present specific recommendations.
- Watch confidence indicators closely; they will reveal strength of desire to control.

Sell/Present—Stay two or three steps ahead of anticipated questions, which will show your creative ability to keep up with their UNPREDICTABLE trait. In this way you won't lose control of the situation, which they naturally seek. Also, infuse ideas that will trigger them to participate creatively, but in a predictable direction. Don't let creative dialogue get in the way of bringing closure to the sale or acceptance of suggestion/idea.

Confrontation—When confronted, they will turn to their TELL trait, but with less predictability than the SERGEANT/MANAGER. They will typically rely upon a mix of creative thinking balanced by controlling emotions. It may be helpful to confront with two people—one who is TELL and PREDICTABLE and another who is TELL and UNPREDICTABLE, thus providing a balance. The person with the PREDICTABLE trait can focus on fact issues and keep the dialogue on a more predictable course. The person who is UNPREDICTABLE can engage the creative issues. If only one person is possible, use a person who is TELL (preferably stronger than the person being confronted) and who is low UNPREDICTABLE so he/she can cover the fact issues while not being intimidated by their UNPREDICTABLE trait.

SERGEANT/CONFORMIST

The SERGEANT/CONFORMIST has the following combination of traits:

- CONTROL/TELL   • PREDICTABLE/FEARFUL

The SERGEANT/CONFORMIST has the dominant, CONTROL-oriented interpersonal style of the SERGEANT, coupled with the "dutiful and loyal" PERFORMANCE type of the CONFORMIST. This type is most easily characterized as the loyal, obedient middle manager, or lower level staff officer. Because of their fear-based motivations coupled with their social dominance and predictability, they will seldom risk new ideas or challenges, and they will seldom challenge others or the status quo. What makes SERGEANT/CONFORMISTS less troubling than SERGEANT/RANDOM ACTORS is their predictability. SERGEANT/CONFORMISTS dislike sudden or unpredictable change, and they fear the personal consequences of such change. They do not want to be surprised or to surprise those who may control their future or their fate.

Typical Strengths

- Faithful "right-hand" people who will deliver results once the task is defined or initiated.
- Motivated by loyalty, not personal fame or recognition.
- Will be described by others as persistent and tenacious.

Typical Shortcomings

- Do not make good leaders because they lack personal confidence to "take charge" in new or unfamiliar situations.
- Likely to be "blindly loyal."
- Others may question their "value" or contribution to an organization or project.

Other Tendencies

- Seldom risk new ideas/challenges.
- Rarely challenge system or superiors.
- May appear as dictators and autocrats to subordinates ("down the ladder") while appearing overly compliant to superiors or other "controllers" ("up the ladder").
- While socially strong, PERFORMANCE type will tend to be followers and not self-initiating.

Trait Indicators

- Higher FEAR trait is typically associated with more risk-aversion and tendency to avoid challenging any aspect of the system or the environment.
- Lower ratings on TELL and CONTROL will make them appear to be more consistent and easier to understand. The effect is a softer, less commanding SERGEANT.
- Higher TELL and CONTROL traits combined with FEARFUL is what makes them seem contradictory to others. (The effect is a strong directive in the *talk* but a weak showing in the *walk*.)

Interaction Tips

- Be sure to always deliver on promises and commitments.
- The higher the FEARFUL trait, the more likely they are to point a finger at you when you are not to blame for a problem. Therefore, evaluate entering situations where risk is a significant factor. This can especially be difficult, the higher the TELL trait.
- Expect rigid interpretations of rules; don't ask for compromises or exceptions.
- Allow time for SERGEANT/CONFORMISTS to gain approval of leaders.
- Don't misinterpret a defense of the "status quo" for being CONFIDENT.
- Don't be frustrated by their "mixed style" when they deal "up the chain of command" v. "down the chain of command." When they deal "down," they will tend to be more dominant, while they will appear to be less dominant when they deal "up" the chain of command.

- Like all CONFORMIST profiles, encourage them to recognize their natural tendencies toward loyalty and to consider carefully the integrity of those whom they serve—without paranoia—so that their trusting nature isn't abused.

Sell/Present—Remove ambiguity in both one's presentation and in the expected outcome. Do not expect SERGEANT/CONFORMISTS to take risks. If you do ask them to take a risk, expect *severe* reversals later if their security is in any way threatened. They are *not* problem-solvers and will lay the blame at your feet—or anyone else who is available. Best to find another person in the organization to sell to or act as a support if this person later gets "cold feet."

Confrontation—When confronted, they usually turn to their TELL trait to first drive down their immediate fears, and then they take the offensive using their SERGEANT actions. It can be helpful if the confronter is CONFIDENT and TELL. Remember, when backed in a corner, they will be driven by FEAR when making decisions. So, tactically work to reverse fear during the engagement as well as after the engagement when they have time to reflect and may choose to retaliate. Other profiles that have a CONFIDENT trait, such as a SERGEANT/MANAGER, might accept a blow and move on. They are more likely, however, to plot retaliation because of their fear of rejection and loss of stature with others.

SERGEANT/RANDOM ACTOR

The SERGEANT/RANDOM ACTOR has the following combination of traits:

- CONTROL/TELL
- UNPREDICTABLE/FEARFUL

The SERGEANT/RANDOM ACTORS, while not a common profile, may be one of the most difficult and troubling of all the profiles. The COMMUNICA-TION type of SERGEANT/RANDOM ACTORS will cause them to initially appear much like the other SERGEANT-based profiles, but their performance will vary widely across time and situations. This is because they are motivated by fear and their actions are UNPREDICTABLE. It's not uncommon to find someone with this profile in leadership roles in organizations that have a deceptive theme consistent in their culture. In history, Adolph Hitler possessed this profile. The combination of his SERGEANT traits, TELL and CONTROL, and his FEARFUL trait presented a rigid appearance; he used his TELL trait to try to control others and control his fears.

SERGEANT/RANDOM ACTORS will seek to maintain the strong, controlling image of the SERGEANT, but will frequently disappoint others with their unreliability and their unwillingness to take responsibility for their circumstances. Their fear-based motivation will cause them to feel and act "out of control" while their COMMUNICATION type will drive them to maintain the *appearance* of CONTROL. This combination of traits will produce a tension that can result in anger, impatience, depression, moodiness, or authoritarianism. Additionally, when they have a strong TELL trait, the illusion may be created of being high CONFIDENT. (Be sure to review general observations of RANDOM ACTORS in this chapter and Chapters 8 and 13.)

Typical Strengths

- Able to appear strong and dominant in *short-term* relationships like any of the SERGEANT-based profiles.
- Can be a strong "second in command" in situations requiring unswerving loyalty or in very controlled situations. (This may serve the purposes of their commanders, but produce a harrowing experience for those under them if their status is threatened.)

Typical Shortcomings

- No matter what their performance level, they will attempt to dominate and control others.
- Their unpredictability and fear-based motivations yield random actions that may have no relevance to the situation.
- They tend to act defensively, even when a threat isn't present.
- Lack the confidence of the INNOVATOR types to translate their unconventionality into creativity or to trust their judgment when acting outside standard operating procedure.
- Can be dangerous when placed in a position of unilateral and unmonitored power, especially the stronger their FEARFUL and TELL traits.

Other Tendencies

- COMMUNICATION type will appear as strong as other SERGEANT-type profiles, while performance indicators vary widely.
- This may be one of the most difficult profiles to read because of the strong contrast between the COMMUNICATION and PERFORMANCE types. Even though they TELL, they are FEARFUL when making decisions.

Trait Indicators

- Strength of RANDOM ACTOR traits will determine level of risk when dealing with them.
- Extreme ratings on the FEARFUL and UNPREDICTABLE gauges should be considered carefully for pathological implications.

- High ratings on the FEARFUL and UNPREDICTABLE gauges should prompt discussions about their ability to "outgrow" their RANDOM ACTOR PERFORMANCE type.
- People who choose to "grow" beyond their RANDOM ACTOR type by learning to trust, thus reducing their FEAR when making decisions, have the potential to become SERGEANT/INNOVATORS.

Interaction Tips

- Avoid implied threats or criticisms.
- Focus on building their self-confidence and providing structure to offset unpredictability.
- Avoid sudden changes in direction or plans.
- Do not give a lot of freedom when making decisions, especially where the threat of risk is involved, as this will increase the possibility that they will rely upon guile to defend or conceal their position.

Sell/Present—Avoid making presentations to these people when risk is involved and/or if they are high FEARFUL—especially if the interaction is long-term. Keep presentations direct and language clean/clear and unambiguous. When risk of failure is low or the FEARFUL trait is low, you can venture out to ideas as well, but otherwise, stick to the bottom-line.

Confrontation—First, be sure to review the guidelines for interacting with a RANDOM ACTOR detailed throughout the text. Because they possess a SERGEANT type, they will try to dominate. Therefore, be prepared to use a stronger TELL trait when closure is sought. The higher the level the confrontation, the stronger the TELL trait and the swifter the action required. Don't drag it out or they will try to dominate. Be swift. Appeal to some positive goal toward which the SERGEANT side of these people can direct their attention. When SERGEANT/RANDOM ACTORS threaten you, they will be overt, not subtle—like a rocket launcher fired at you with point blank precision.

SALESMAN/MANAGER

The SALESMAN/MANAGER has the following combination of traits:

- EXPRESS/TELL   • PREDICTABLE/CONFIDENT

SALESMEN/MANAGERS are a common profile characterized by predictability and self-confidence as well as a salesman/communicator COMMUNICATION type. They are perceived as "disciplined extroverts" who appear warm and open on first meeting, but demonstrate decisiveness, a willingness to take leadership roles, and a desire to deliver predictable performance.

Because of these qualities, they are often in sales and marketing or managerial positions. In many ways, this profile may represent an ideal leadership/ambassador style, especially for larger organizations where both charisma and consistency in performance are required to meet the needs of a wide ranging constituency of investors, customers, and employees. They may even provide superior leadership when compared to the SERGEANT/MANAGER or SERGEANT/INNOVATOR because of their initial focus on open, positive personal relationships. The SALESMAN/MANAGER will approach people and situations with an open, direct style followed by a focused concern with delivering performance commitments. They can be particularly effective in leading strong teams who are facing complex problems that require diverse input to achieve a solution.

Typical Strengths
- Inspire confidence in others.
- Reliable.
- Able to maintain both open relationships and consistent performance trends at the same time.
- Will take unilateral action when required, but don't always need to be in control.

Typical Shortcomings
- Not natural "learners"; not particularly adaptive.
- Will base decisions on experience rather than creativity; not inclined to look for new and different ways to approach questions or relationships.

Other Tendencies
- Take a pragmatic approach to new, opportunistic situations.
- Will surprise those who stereotypically view the SALESMAN type as all "hot air."

Trait Indicators
- Ability to rely on more than past experience and performance increases with low PREDICTABILITY trait.
- High TELL indicates less of a facilitator and more of a directive leader.

Interaction Tips
- Encourage them to consider alternative ideas and new solutions before settling on a given solution or answer.
- Provide clear, unambiguous directives.
- Be direct and open in all forms of conversation.
- Expect decisiveness, not extensive discussion.

- Sell new ideas based on their links to previous successes; build on experience.

Sell/Present—Sell the bottom-line with a firm TELL orientation. Reference past successes and how they predictably will lead to future successes. You may run into resistance if presenting a completely new concept, so try to link to similar products/services/strategies that were successful. If you use an ASK person for a presentation, be sure this person is articulate and well in command of the facts, because he won't be able to fall back on a TELL trait to keep things moving forward if there is difficulty.

Confrontation—First, adopt an open communication style. Use a stronger TELL trait than these people possess. If appropriate, appeal to the EXPRESS trait to encourage empathy. Be careful, though, because this could increase explosiveness when there is tension. If resistance is present, detail the predictable results that will ensue if cooperation is not forthcoming. Focus on concrete issues, potential loss of stature, and their experiences rather than abstract ideas and concepts.

SALESMAN/INNOVATOR

The SALESMAN/INNOVATOR has the following combination of traits:

- EXPRESS/TELL
- UNPREDICTABLE/CONFIDENT

This profile shares many similarities with the SALESMAN/MANAGER, and is able to avoid the key weakness of that profile: predictability. Look for these people to be the creative sparks in a sales/marketing/communication arena. Entrepreneurs often possess this profile as well. The combination of confidence and unpredictability results in a personal PERFORMANCE type that is likely to be more creative and innovative than the SALESMAN/MANAGER. However, the creativity may be achieved at the expense of focus and discipline that is required in a leadership profile, which is why they aren't typically suited for sustainer roles of a corporate mission. SALESMEN/INNOVATORS have an extroverted COMMUNICATION type coupled with a "free-wheeling" PERFORMANCE type. They are typically enjoyable and productive team-players, quickly engaging in interpersonal interactions and at the same time willing to explore new ideas and creative solutions to problems. Depending on the level of TELL (social dominance), they will either be a good facilitator of team activities or they may have a tendency to try to direct the team once the creative elements of the team's task are complete.

Typical Strengths

- Combine charisma with creativity and willingness to take risks.
- Can be good facilitators of problem-solving teams.
- Most effective in a less regimented or bureaucratic environment.
- Likely to be strong leaders in smaller, more entrepreneurial environments.

Typical Shortcomings

- Should not be called on to lead in situations where long-term, consistent, patterned results are the desired result, such as an unchanging sales environment.
- Can appear "out of control" or "off the wall" when profile is extreme.
- May be inclined to "job-hop" if not focused.
- Can be impulsive; usually not worried about the effects of impulsivity.

Other Tendencies

- May be described by others as always having a new idea or plan.

Trait Indicators

- The higher the TELL trait the more likely they will have the ability to lead; the lower the TELL trait the easier for them to be strong team players.
- "Out of control" style will be most noticeable when EXPRESS and UNPREDICTABILITY are high.

Interaction Tips

- Avoid assigning them long-term roles requiring routine performance.
- Focus on their tendency toward need for change and personal recognition.
- Give them leadership roles in problem-solving settings, not in solution implementation roles.

Sell/Present—Sell the benefit of ideas, innovations, and so on, rather than the bottom-line. Presenter can use low ASK trait as long as verbal skill and/or *ideas* are good, though TELL is preferable. The lower their TELL, CONFIDENT, or UNPREDICTABLE traits, the more likely they will seek advice from their team. Alternately, the *higher* these traits, the more likely they will feel comfortable taking action on their own. The latter may cause problems with their group, so it may be beneficial to include other members of their team in presentations, decision making, and so on.

Confrontation—It is advisable to confront with a stronger TELL trait. Also, either EXPRESS or CONTROL trait can be used. Focus on creative options that, if acted upon, will increase their personal stature. Alternately, when there is resistance, focus on how this can depreciate their stature, ideas, or creative input.

SALESMAN/CONFORMIST

The SALESMAN/CONFORMIST has the following combination of traits:

- EXPRESS/TELL
- PREDICTABLE/FEARFUL

This profile is less common than the SALESMAN/SERGEANT or SALESMAN/INNOVATOR profiles because it combines the qualities of extroversion (SALESMAN) with obedience or a sense of duty (CONFORMIST). The dominant COMMUNICATION type will almost always be noticed first, causing the more submissive side of the profile to be overlooked. The higher their TELL trait, the more likely they will lead with their COMMUNICATION type. This profile is often suitable for routine sales positions, such as the classic order-taker, or other industries that require extensive people contact, such as, customer relations. Do not count on them for high-powered creativity or initiative. When the SALESMAN type is combined with a low FEARFUL trait, they may be able to operate in environments that require a little bit of risk-taking, such as a low-key and salaried insurance sales position. Other suitable roles are communication responsibilities which require a willingness to be directed, such as some low-key media broadcast positions where one's strength is reading copy from a teleprompter rather than on-the-street reporting. SALESMEN/CONFORMISTS with a low FEARFUL trait are able to handle these kinds of low stress-provoking situations because they fall back on their TELL trait during interactions, even though they aren't CONFIDENT.

Typical Strengths

- Display loyalty typical of CONFORMIST type.
- Open, expressive, and endearing COMMUNICATION type.
- Well-suited for "rote" people-contact types of jobs (e.g., telephone sales, order-takers, customer service, etc.).

Typical Shortcomings

- Avoid risks in both social and performance arenas.
- Minimal leadership ability, other than TELL trait.
- Lack creativity.
- Not strong problem-solvers.
- Lack strong personal initiative.

Other Tendencies

- Not as reactive as other sales-based profiles.
- Not a good second-in-command because they will be seen as only passing on the orders and directions of whoever is really in charge.
- Can be the "life of the party," but will have difficulty contributing to group problem-solving efforts.

Trait Indicators

- High TELL trait can create impression of lacking in substance because of a lack of follow-through.
- High EXPRESS combined with strong CONFORMIST traits will give appearance of being sympathetic, but ineffective in helping others solve problems.

Interaction Tips

- Don't expect big results quickly. They tend to be socially open, but plodders.
- Give them explicit instructions about how they are to interact with others.
- Don't rely on their social skills to lead a group in problem-solving.
- Avoid quick changes that will be unsettling to their performance type.
- Like all CONFORMIST profiles, encourage them to recognize their natural tendency toward loyalty and to consider carefully the integrity of those whom they serve—without paranoia—so that their trusting nature isn't abused.

Sell/Present—Avoid structuring presentations that force them to make decisions out of confidence. Rather, appeal to the fact that your idea seems to fit in with the norm—what is acceptable in their organization. Use TELL trait with restraint, except when establishing friendly rapport. Then pull back TELL trait a bit so that it doesn't provoke their FEARFUL trait when they must make a decision. And, like other CONFORMIST profiles, find someone in their organization to undergird and strengthen any decision that is made.

Confrontation—To establish rapport, use EXPRESS trait to connect with their sociable SALESMAN style. Appeal to the status quo in which they feel comfortable operating. When confrontation is complex, work at obtaining concessions in small bites, so they don't overload due to their FEARFUL trait. The lower their TELL and EXPRESS trait the less likely for explosiveness. If retaliation does occur, it will probably be spontaneous, energized by their SALESMAN type. So, if tensions increase, appeal to their positive CONFORMIST actions, to reduce potential explosiveness.

SALESMAN/RANDOM ACTOR

The SALESMAN/RANDOM ACTOR has the following combination of traits:

- EXPRESS/TELL
- UNPREDICTABLE/FEARFUL

This profile is a picture of extroverted, dominant people who charismatically react to most situations out of their lack of self-confidence or fear of failure. It is not uncommon for cult leaders to possess this profile. David Koresh, the Waco, Texas, cult leader for example, or manic marketeers, who are given to bouts of severe depression. Their PERFORMANCE type causes them to appear unfocused and easily influenced by anyone or anything who might impact their fears. And when there is a focus, it is typically founded in an effort to derail their fears. In the workplace, this person often has the reputation for being a charmer and "hot air" with no substance when called upon to perform. Intellectual savvy coupled with manipulative control, however, can allow some to amass a following for a while, even though they inherently lack leadership. It works like this: Their SALESMAN COMMUNICATION type first captures the group, and then they reciprocally "capture" him because of their misguided needs/desires.

SALESMEN/RANDOM ACTORS typically move from one opportunity to another based solely on their need for variety and change, while trying to avoid any source of conflict or pain that will increase their fears. They always look for the "greener pastures on the other side of the fence" in their professional and private lives, or, in the case of Koresh, create a paranoiac greener pasture—a compound—while inviting/directing others to join him in his misguided fear. (Be sure to review general observations of RANDOM ACTORS in this chapter and Chapters 8 and 13.)

Typical Strengths

- More easily led or motivated by most leadership styles the lower their TELL and FEARFUL traits.
- Open, candid COMMUNICATION type.
- Always willing to risk emotions or tradition (but not willing to risk relationships).

Typical Shortcomings

- Will seek approval from or appease whoever is in control, especially when medium to low TELL.
- More willing to lead others in misguided efforts the higher the TELL trait.
- If they lead and attract others, it is through a combination of a strong TELL and EXPRESS trait, that sells fear and paranoia; thus, the group bands together for "protection."
- Lack both discipline and self-control.
- One of the most impulsive of all profiles because of the combination of UNPREDICTABLE, FEARFUL, and EXPRESS.

Other Tendencies
- Can't keep secrets.
- Avoid confrontation or conflict; when extreme, build compounds (literally and figuratively).

Trait Indicators
- Low UNPREDICTABLE may indicate some ability to control impulsivity.
- High TELL may indicate strong tendency to be "all talk and no do."

Interaction Tips
- Get everything in writing!
- Don't tell them anything you consider confidential or a secret.
- To maintain consistent performance, maintain firm control of their rewards and penalties for failure to perform.
- Never expect them to present the whole truth, such as the negative side of the story.

Sell/Present—Presenter should appeal to whatever positive actions are found in their COMMUNICATION type. Resist asking them to perform or act on something that is important, because they won't with any reliability. The higher the FEARFUL trait, the more likely for lack of performance. The higher the UNPREDICTABLE trait, the more random their performance. Best advice: Find another place to do business.

Confrontation—First, be sure to review the guidelines for interacting with a RANDOM ACTOR detailed throughout the text. Don't confront these people in front of their followers or peers. Their perpetual need and unpredictable methods for selling themselves or their agendas to others will negate rationale discussion. Find a strong TELL and CONTROL person whom this person has trusted in the past to support your efforts. Bring closure swiftly. Before engaging, develop strategy for protecting yourself, as they will probably be inclined to retaliate the higher their FEARFUL and TELL trait. When they attack you, it will be direct and loud, not subtle—"in your face."

ACCOUNTANT/MANAGER

The ACCOUNTANT/MANAGER has the following combination of traits:
- CONTROL/ASK   • PREDICTABLE/CONFIDENT

This common profile is an interesting combination that initially looks similar to the SERGEANT/CONFORMIST profile. Like the SERGEANT/CONFORMIST, ACCOUNTANT/MANAGERS prefer predictability and will not seek change for change's sake. Similarly, they will appear cautious and unwilling to take risks or challenge the system. It's common for finance, audit, and engineering groups to have someone with this profile running a division. The ACCOUNTANT/MANAGER will typically analyze a problem carefully before advocating or implementing a solution. Thus, the combination of predictability and asking/analysis will give an initial impression similar to the predictability-fear combination of the CONFORMISTS. However, the important distinction between these two profiles is their willingness to act independently in their areas of expertise, driven by their CONFIDENT trait, once they have analyzed a given problem. The ACCOUNTANT/MANAGER possesses a level of confidence that allows independent action when seeking predictable and stable results or performance. The CONFORMIST-based profiles lack this element of personal initiative.

Typical Strengths
- Analytical.
- Detail-oriented.
- Deliberate/Prudent.
- Perform confidently and consistently after completing necessary analysis.
- Typically good listeners.
- Understand how to develop others.

Typical Shortcomings
- May be unable to be directive or dominant.
- Can get bogged down in details rather than face the challenge of leading.
- May initially appear overly cautious, averting "risk" situations.
- May avoid direct confrontation.
- Can be pessimistic and rigid.

Other Tendencies
- Not inclined to challenge the system or assume risk-taking roles.
- Prefer "calculated risks."
- Will control work/performance, but not social situations or relationships.
- Some may view these people as nondirective, and not inclined to be autocratic, especially when compared with the SERGEANT/CONFORMIST, who possesses a TELL trait.
- Weak COMMUNICATION type that possess few strong positive actions may cause others to underestimate their ability to deliver results.

Trait Indicators
- High ASK will cause this profile to appear more like the CONFORMIST profiles; this same effect is enhanced when CONFIDENT is low.

- High CONTROL and high PREDICTABLE may indicate avoidance of all risks, overriding their level of confidence.
- Strong MANAGER traits should be interpreted as indicator of ability to deliver on commitments.
- Ability to develop others will be highest when CONTROL and PREDICTABILITY ratings are low and CONFIDENCE rating is high.

Interaction Tips

- Allow time for analysis and detailed discussion of issues.
- Avoid putting ACCOUNTANT/MANAGERS in roles that require strong interpersonal control or exchange.
- Be ready to back up recommendations with significant detail.
- Keep things neat and in order.
- Don't underestimate their ability to deliver.

Sell/Present—Presentations should be concise with unambiguous language. Use low EXPRESS or CONTROL when communicating. It's okay to use TELL trait because of this profile's CONFIDENT trait, but don't stray too far with ideas. Keep agenda neat and orderly. Don't be discouraged by the request for details. Expect it, and prepare. Finally, don't be fooled and think that a lack of verbal participation means a lack of interest. Listen carefully to input because it may only come selectively. When you ask a question, don't interrupt. Allow for their nondominant ACCOUNTANT style of communicating, but don't be fooled when final decision is CONFIDENT-based.

Confrontation—Have your details down and your approach well organized. These people do not like confrontations because of their ASK trait, which may necessitate a more open-ended questions approach. The stronger the CONFIDENT trait—and associated positive actions—and the greater the presence of positive PERFORMANCE type actions, the greater the likelihood they will accept personal responsibility. Confront with a person who is stronger CONFIDENT and who can move between TELL and ASK styles of communicating: ASK, when moving dialogue along, and TELL when bringing closure (if strength is needed at closure).

ACCOUNTANT/INNOVATOR

The ACCOUNTANT/INNOVATOR has the following combination of traits:

- CONTROL/ASK
- UNPREDICTABLE/CONFIDENCE

The ACCOUNTANT/INNOVATORS have a somewhat paradoxical and uncommon profile. While not usually dominant, they're comfortable taking risks and trying new and different ideas. This profile is best represented by the inventor genius or the "technical guru or wizard" often found in key research or staff roles. They often create technical or professional innovations but lack the social style typically required of a leader, executive, or manager. ACCOUNTANT/INNOVATORS are unlikely to move beyond the "director of" level in most organizations, although their contributions are often crucial to solving problems that require an innovative flair.

Typical Strengths

- Comfortable being in the background, playing support roles.
- Creative.
- Easily motivated by creative challenge.
- Curious.
- Able to separate emotional issues from tasks; not likely to "lose their cool."

Typical Shortcomings

- Impact of their contributions may be overlooked because COMMUNICATION type is not assertive.
- If they don't have technical credibility, can experience significant loss of value/standing in an organization because of their ASK trait.
- May appear intensely motivated by creative challenges, but unconcerned about delivering results.

Other Tendencies

- Survival in organizations is dependent upon ongoing intellectual contribution.
- Like other INNOVATORS, may be viewed as eccentric, erratic, or the "absentminded professor type" the stronger their UNPREDICTABLE trait.
- May appear less "results-oriented" than other profiles that have TELL or PREDICTABLE traits.
- Inclined to play the "devil's advocate."

Trait Indicators

- High UNPREDICTABLE may indicate inability to implement practical ideas, especially if combined with high ASK tendencies.
- High CONTROL and ASK will cause some to appear aloof.

Interaction Tips

- Give ACCOUNTANT/INNOVATORS autonomy and freedom to work on their own.
- Reward with professional recognition and acclaim, more than money or positions of power.

- Team ACCOUNTANT/INNOVATORS, who are ASK, with SERGEANT/INNO-VATORS, who are TELL, to achieve creative results in a timely manner.
- Prepare for "eccentric" social style (especially when high UNPRE-DICTABLE) and avoid impatience when listening to ACCOUNTANT/INNO-VATORS.

Sell/Present—Although these people are ASK, a SALESMAN (TELL/EXPRESS) type can do well as long as the focus is on ideas and personal rewards for acting on good ideas. When inquiring and seeking input, use nondirective, questioning style and open-ended questions. After asking a question, wait. When an important question is answered, wait some more. They are likely to offer additional information, as they are probably still processing the question and have more to say due to their INNOVATOR type. As with other ACCOUNTANTS, a lack of verbal rapport doesn't necessarily mean a lack of interest.

Confrontation—They are likely to defend personal turf and ideas indirectly and even ramble under pressure. Look for playing the "devil's advocate" as a deflection device. Using a moderate TELL trait, keep them focused on the issues at hand, and give them an opportunity to think through the issue(s) presented. Remember, they are UNPREDICTABLE, and are unlikely to be direct in their "taking action" process due to their desire to think through all the issues. SALESMAN or SERGEANT types, as a counterpoint, are more likely to TELL you immediately what they think in response to a confrontation. ACCOUNTANT/INNOVATORS are also less likely to become hostile the weaker their UNPREDICTABLE and CONFIDENT traits. Conversely, the higher these traits, aggression is more likely to be indirect and scheming. If the latter is the case, anticipate and prepare for the unexpected.

ACCOUNTANT/CONFORMIST

The ACCOUNTANT/CONFORMIST has the following combination of traits:

- CONTROL/ASK
- PREDICTABLE/FEARFUL

ACCOUNTANT/CONFORMISTS perform their tasks and make decisions in ways that completely avoid any risk or potential negative reactions from other people. They are indecisive, while simultaneously keeping their emotions passively "locked up" inside. ACCOUNTANT/CONFORMISTS will ask questions in social relationships, but they seldom share anything about themselves or make declarative statements of any kind. The higher their FEARFUL trait, the more they will fit the classic "frightened subordinate," who does whatever he is told and rarely expresses any emotion or feelings—suitable support people, as long as they aren't required to provide significant input or assume responsibility.

Typical Strengths

- Will perform most any detail job without "grumbling."
- Will rarely challenge an order or directive.
- Do not tire of repetitive, mundane tasks.
- Listen well, and appear interested in others.

Typical Shortcomings

- Seldom assert themselves, even when surrounded by people who have no influence over their situation or future.
- Avoid leadership roles.
- Likely to be viewed as one of the most neurotic of all profiles the higher the FEARFUL and CONTROL traits.
- Seldom expose self or emotions, even in close relationships.

Other Tendencies

- Are often unable to develop close friendships because of the combination of their ASK and FEARFUL traits. This is due to their inclination to be socially reserved because they lack a TELL trait. (Some SERGEANT/CONFORMISTS can develop these relationships because their TELL trait enables them to more easily overcome their FEARFUL trait and engage in dialogue. They *lead* relationships with their TELL trait.)
- Can be viewed by others as "led around by the ring in his nose."

Trait Indicators

- More likely to demonstrate some type of independence if CONTROL or FEARFUL are low.
- Follower orientation most pronounced when CONFORMIST traits are strong.

Interaction Tips

- Refrain from asking them to speak in public or make "presentations."
- Look for ways to reduce fear if you want them to speak up on an issue.
- Avoid issues that could force them to reveal emotions; deal in non emotional arenas.
- Avoid references to your own power, position, or confidence.
- For long-term relationships, gently place them in moderately challenging situations, combined with your encouragement, to help them move toward CONFIDENT.

- Like ARTIST/CONFORMIST, don't ask them to give others negative or critical feedback.
- Like all CONFORMIST profiles, encourage these people to recognize their natural tendency toward loyalty and to consider carefully the integrity of those whom they serve—without paranoia—so that their trusting nature isn't abused.

Sell/Present—If what you are presenting is important, a presentation for these people is likely to be frustrating. This is because they operate out of fear and you won't get much feedback when their FEARFUL trait is coupled with their ASK trait. Only sell essentials that don't spark fear, or find someone else in whom they trust and whom you can depend upon to assist in the decision-making process. Adopt a very laid back, nonurgent approach. Make sure the presentation naturally evokes an "I am comfortable" response. Otherwise, don't expect them to volunteer to make decisions.

Confrontations—If a response isn't needed quickly, ideally use an ASK person for the confrontation who is PREDICTABLE and can operate at the low end of CONFIDENT. This will put them at ease. Don't be as direct with one's confrontation as one would with other related profiles, such as an ACCOUNTANT/MANAGER or a SALESMAN/CONFORMIST. They have little to fall back on, such as a SALESMAN/CONFORMIST who can retreat to his TELL trait. When a response is needed quickly, however, use a person who can build trust and who possesses medium to strong TELL, CONFIDENT, and PREDICTABLE traits. Work quickly to bring closure before they freeze up and resist taking action.

ACCOUNTANT/RANDOM ACTOR

The ACCOUNTANT/RANDOM ACTOR has the following combination traits:

- CONTROL/ASK
- UNPREDICTABLE/FEARFUL

This uncommon profile possesses some paradoxical combinations that must be carefully understood. Usually, people who are FEARFUL and are inclined to CONTROL their emotional reactions will periodically "slip" and display aggressive reactions against their social environment. However, in the case of the ACCOUNTANT/RANDOM ACTOR, the lack of social dominance (the ASK trait) makes it difficult for these people to "act out" their emotional reactions. This combination can result in a potentially volatile profile the higher the FEARFUL trait. This will cause them to suffer significant psychological tension, acting out their reactions only when the tension becomes so great they can no longer tolerate the situation. Or, they will release their anger through cleverly plotted schemes or through passive aggression by what they don't say. In an organization, this type person may be found in corporate support roles, such as finance and human resource functions. It's possible for this person to rise up through the ranks as he relies upon his ACCOUNTANT type and/or unquestioning loyalty. But if there is extreme pressure, this person usually disintegrates. In the criminal arena, it is not uncommon to find that "mousy" child molesters will have the ACCOUNTANT/RANDOM ACTOR profile because their ASK style of communicating is appealing to young, trusting children. Additionally, Ted Kaczynski, dubbed the "Unabomber" for his series of letter bombs sent to numerous people during the 1980s and 1990s, possessed this profile. He resisted face-to-face confrontations, and instead made meticulously crafted, hand-carved, wood-encased bombs that he sent *through the mail.* (Be sure to review general observations of RANDOM ACTORS in this chapter and Chapters 8 and 13.)

Typical Strengths
- Appear reserved and under control in most situations.
- Able to listen to others and accept input.
- Will have a higher tolerance for emotional or psychological "pain."

Typical Shortcomings
- The higher their FEARFUL trait, will seek to avoid face-to-face confrontations over important issues in order to maintain emotional control.
- May employ "passive-aggressive" behaviors to deal with psychological tension.
- When ability to tolerate tension is surpassed, may be unpredictably volatile and reactive.
- Likely to express anger through scheming plans.

Other Tendencies
- Because of ACCOUNTANT COMMUNICATION type, may initially be misread as stable and consistent. Remember, it is from the COMMUNICATION type—the "talk" part of his life—that a RANDOM ACTOR will display positive actions. Ask this person to take action, however, and the actions of the RANDOM ACTOR take over.

Trait Indicators
- Strong RANDOM ACTOR traits are key indicators of volatility and reactiveness.
- Strong ACCOUNTANT traits indicate ability to delay RANDOM ACTOR responses because of their inability to vocalize and express themselves.

They won't yell, like SERGEANT/RANDOM ACTORS; they must first carefully think through how to carry out their plans, which may delay their taking action.

Interaction Tips

- Watch for signs of "buried" emotions and "pent-up" feelings.
- In a less directive context, help them to talk about issues and then focus on resolving fears and concerns.
- Watch for passive-aggressive responses as clues to concerns or potential "trigger" issues that will later cause them to "erupt."

Sell/Present—Because of their COMMUNICATION type, don't ask ACCOUNTANT/RANDOM ACTORS to buy into situations that require their personal interaction with others—only behind-the-scenes environments that are carefully controlled. It is easy to be initially fooled into thinking that they are compliant because of their ACCOUNTANT type, but the higher the FEARFUL trait, the greater the chance that swift and unannounced reversals will be carried out *indirectly*, to avoid a face-to-face confrontation. When possible, bring closure quickly, because the longer the time for reflection, the greater the chance they will renege on a commitment.

Confrontation—First, be sure to review the guidelines for interacting with a RANDOM ACTOR detailed throughout the text. Be prepared strategically. Make your case and bring closure quickly. Don't give them advance notice. And don't be misled by their low-key, ACCOUNTANT style of communicating. Look for preemptive scheming plans to resist you rather than relying upon the force of their personalities, like a SERGEANT/RANDOM ACTOR or SALESMAN/RANDOM ACTOR. Appeal to the positive actions you observe in their ACCOUNTANT type. Don't expect much emotional leakage to help you determine what is going on in their minds, but rather develop insight from past history—the best predictor of future behavior. You will probably only get one opportunity to confront them, as they will tend to withdraw the higher their ASK and FEARFUL traits. Regarding the confronter, it may be useful for this person to possess a TELL trait, provided that he can modulate his TELL trait and even employ an ASK style for communicating. Then, at the moment of opportunity, this person can naturally employ the strength of his TELL trait to demand closure or the truth. Finally, if they attack you, they will do it indirectly—a letter bomb sent through the mail, a magistrate embarrassingly serving you with papers at work, an attack on your credibility by placing cleverly layered lies in places that you don't think is important, and so on.

ARTIST/MANAGER

The ARTIST/MANAGER has the following combination of traits:

- EXPRESS/ASK
- PREDICTABLE/CONFIDENT

This profile can be a bit of a paradox, and can fool people. From a performance perspective, ARTIST/MANAGERS are CONFIDENT and PREDICTABLE. They predictably perform and act based on their self-confidence in their ability to accomplish a task and make decisions. Their COMMUNICATION type, however, is an ARTIST, which often results in a tendency to ignore their leadership potential (MANAGER PERFORMANCE type) because of their ARTIST actions when they communicate. The ARTIST/MANAGER's tendency to be emotionally expressive, however, is counterbalanced by the MANAGER's tendency towards predictability and avoiding sudden change. An example of this profile is the amiable advertising executive who combines an artistic COMMUNICATION type with performance actions necessary to lead a group of creative people and bring a project in on-time and within budget. The head of a research medical staff is another common place to find this profile.

Typical Strengths

- Dependable.
- Creative.
- Can bridge the gap between creative and hard-nosed business demands.
- Comfortable and open in initial meetings.
- Usually a warm, optimistic initial outlook.

Typical Shortcomings

- May use poor judgment when trying to avoid conflict or confrontation with others due to their ASK-EXPRESS combination.
- May be insensitive to the fact that the combination of their expressive/creative flair and their MANAGER type will confuse people.
- May tend to be self-centered and/or compulsive when they have a creative agenda, which they may conceal due to their ASK trait.

Other Tendencies

- Typically better facilitators of teams than strong leaders of large, diverse organizations; an exception is noted under "Trait Indicators."
- Present a good balance between the predictability of a MANAGER and the ARTIST's appreciation and sensitivity for change.
- May surprise subordinates with contrast between amiable COMMUNICATION type and more task-oriented PERFORMANCE types.

Trait Indicators

- Low MANAGER traits will quickly detract from performance effectiveness due to the impression created by their ARTIST COMMUNICATION actions.
- Strong ASK trait coupled with high MANAGER traits can create strong team leader profile that can accomplish much through others in environments that do not require a strong directive (TELL) leadership style. This is particularly helpful in creative/innovative environments where team players must have the freedom to experiment and create, such as software systems development, advertising and design, education, and so on.

Interaction Tips

- Be open and expressive in initial meetings.
- Allow extra time in meetings/work plans for ARTIST/MANAGERS to "warm up" to people.
- Once a task or project is started, realize that the MANAGER characteristics will make ARTIST/MANAGER a more demanding taskmaster.
- To promote team welfare, encourage them to explain to others why their profile might be confusing—and beneficial.

Sell/Present—One should adopt a laid-back approach that presents predictable results. Expressing emotions is helpful, but not crucial. Also, either ASK or TELL presenters can be effective, provided that ASK presenters are CONFIDENT, and TELL presenters provide time for them to process questions. One can shift between bottom-line and "idea" issues, but don't be surprised if they show creative and bottom-line tendencies simultaneously. The balance between creative and bottom-line elements in your presentation should be evaluated based upon the respective strengths of their ARTIST and MANAGER types.

Confrontation—For volatile situations, avoid using much EXPRESS as this may trigger their desire to display negative EXPRESS actions, unless their showing sympathy or compassion toward someone or something is an essential factor. Either an ASK or a TELL person can be employed for the confrontation, provided that the TELL person doesn't override the ARTIST's need to process thoughts before responding. Approach them in a way that drives them toward sensitivity (their COMMUNICATION type) and away from being self-centered (their PERFORMANCE type).

ARTIST/INNOVATOR

The ARTIST/INNOVATOR has the following combination of traits:

- EXPRESS/ASK
- UNPREDICTABLE/CONFIDENT

The ARTIST/INNOVATOR type is one of the most likely sources of great creative genius and they are usually easy to read. Here the ARTIST COMMUNICATION type combines with self-confidence and unconventionality to produce the open, free-thinking style required to challenge the status quo, while simultaneously remaining attuned to the emotional impact of their actions. This type of person can be characterized as being completely in touch with his personal needs and desires as well as with the needs of the people and the situations around him. Look for these people in research and development, small creative shops, creative start-up companies, medical environments that require exploratory risk-taking, etc. One significant difference between ARTIST/INNOVATORS and ARTIST/MANAGERS is that INNOVATORS who are not low UNPREDICTABLE, should not be called upon to lead others over a sustained period of time—no matter how impressive their intellectual prowess.

Typical Strengths

- Creative.
- Self-confident and willing to trust own ability/judgment.
- Will personally deliver results.
- Good listener.

Typical Shortcomings

- Lack desire for control; will not manage or dominate in situations when they should.
- May be viewed as "unorthodox" or unwilling to "play by the rules."
- May cause conflict because they are not afraid to "rock the boat."
- May not be a strong leader.

Other Tendencies

- Willing to try almost anything once.
- Open to people and ideas.
- Unconventional.
- Can be the pure "artist"; work only for art's sake.
- Little concern for detail, order, or consistency.
- Can appear idealistic or naive.
- Like the ACCOUNTANT/INNOVATOR, likely to play the "devil's advocate."

Trait Indicators

- High EXPRESS coupled with high UNPREDICTABLE trait can produce extreme "agitator" profile. They will tend to challenge the current system or proposal.
- High ASK may be best assurance that they are able to link ideas and reactions (abstract) to real world (concrete) situations, as they are more inclined to "take in" information and process it before they communicate.
- The higher the UNPREDICTABLE trait, the less likely that they are suitable for even short-term leadership roles.

Interaction Tips

- Expect lots of challenges and criticisms.
- If detail or precision is required, it must be provided by someone other than the ARTIST/INNOVATOR.
- Provide realistic balance to their idealism.
- Don't require them to provide strong control-oriented leadership, even when they have the leading-edge ideas on a team.

Sell/Present—Don't be afraid to show emotion during presentations and appeal to the new creative venues that will be created. Bottom-line issues are secondary. A TELL person can do the job here as long as he is stimulating ideas and not stifling their ability to respond (due to their ASK trait). Remember, it may take these ASK people, who are INNOVATORS, longer to respond as they weigh all the creative options. So ask for a response, and wait—and, wait some more, even after they offer their first response. Bring closure by focusing on vibrant ideas with which they will be associated.

Confrontation—Use a low CONTROL person who can reach out to their EXPRESS trait as necessary to allow them to open up. Appeal to the opportunities for understanding, feelings that will be settled or restored, new creative venues, etc. that will remain open or be created by coming forward or resolving the conflict. The higher the UNPREDICTABLE trait, the greater the likelihood of a rebellious and/or frivolous attitude, such as a taunting devil's advocate response. Keep the attention focused on the nonpersonal to avoid triggering their EXPRESS trait, which may tend to cause them to tilt toward the illogical/irrational; the exception is when an appeal to positive ARTIST actions is needed, such as sympathetic/compassionate.

ARTIST/CONFORMIST

The ARTIST/CONFORMIST has the following combination traits:

- EXPRESS/ASK
- PREDICTABLE/FEARFUL

People with this profile have the COMMUNICATION type of an ARTIST—open, expressive, and sensitive, but fail to show creativity in their performance. Because this profile's PERFORMANCE type is characteristically compliant and obedient (FEARFUL and PREDICTABLE), these people do not translate their sensitivity into new, creative, or unique performance. This seeming contradiction between their COMMUNICATION and PERFORMANCE types can result in tension that can create neurotic actions the stronger their FEARFUL and EXPRESS traits; they want to be sensitive and step forward, but they are stymied by their fear.

This rather uncommon and unexpected profile demonstrates the need to avoid preconceived stereotyping. While we tend to expect ARTISTS to take some risks in personal relationships because of their willingness to express emotion, we find that for these ARTISTS that their "talk" doesn't match their "walk." In this case, ARTIST/CONFORMISTS extinguish their potential because they demand predictability in their performance and demand a safe, risk-free environment for managing their lack of confidence. This is very different from ARTIST/INNOVATORS, for example, who are willing to accept risk and try new ventures, taking advantage of their creative capacity.

Typical Strengths

- Open COMMUNICATION type coupled with willingness to loyally follow; a very yielding COMMUNICATION type.
- May have potential for combining a precise work ethic with a creative bent.
- Not likely to overreact like other ARTIST types, because they are restrained by their CONFORMIST type.

Typical Shortcomings

- Won't try new ideas and adventures, despite open COMMUNICATION type.
- Avoid risks that might endanger relationships with others, even in the face of opportunity.
- Under emotional stress, inclined to be impulsive when they communicate and then "take back" what they have said or done.
- While appearing open and easy to understand, they make decisions in ways that appear mundane or boring, earning the label of "underachiever."

Other Tendencies

- Can be hard to read because of contradictions in COMMUNICATION and PERFORMANCE types.
- Can serve as good "eyes and ears" for SERGEANT types who want to be more "in touch" with others; may be seduced into informant role.
- Avoid conflict.

Trait Indicators

- High ASK makes this profile most useful "eyes and ears."
- High EXPRESS may produce implosive reactions.
- High FEAR will cause profile to appear untrustworthy to peers and those not in control.

Interaction Tips

- Don't force into quick decisions or reaction situations—impulsivity will reduce quality of decisions/reactions.
- Like ACCOUNTANT/CONFORMIST, don't ask them to give others negative or critical feedback.
- After an agreement is reached, allow time for it to "settle in" before assuming it is a "done deal."
- Like all CONFORMIST profiles, encourage to recognize their natural tendency toward loyalty and to carefully consider the integrity of those whom they serve—without paranoia—so that their trusting nature isn't abused.

Sell/Present—Like other CONFORMIST profiles, resist approaching with important decisions the higher their FEARFUL trait. ARTIST/CONFORMISTS require a lot of time to process requests, and the strategic use of a person with a low or moderate TELL trait may be helpful to get them to "move." (However, the longer the process, the greater the likelihood that their FEARFUL trait will kick in as they mull over the options. Additionally, TELL presenters will typically be ineffective in reaching them over a long, sustained period of time.) Avoid too much EXPRESS, which may trigger more irrationality in their FEARFUL decision-making process. Best advice: Find backup support, such as one of their colleagues, to bolster their lack of decision-making initiative.

Confront—You are confronting people who have both fear and sensitivity and will retreat into themselves. For this reason, these people usually aren't dangerous or highly volatile. The exception would be if they were low PREDICTABLE and faced with a life-changing crisis, which could move them over to FEARFUL—the RANDOM ACTOR. Use an ASK/EXPRESS person to dialogue and a low TELL person to force the decision or bring closure, but only if the ASK person isn't successful. Finally, in most cases, ARTIST/CONFORMISTS won't attempt crippling or life-threatening retaliation.

ARTIST/RANDOM ACTOR

The ARTIST/RANDOM ACTOR has the following combination of traits:
- EXPRESS/ASK
- UNPREDICTABLE/FEARFUL

ARTIST/RANDOM ACTORS are an uncommon profile who usually fool most people who meet them. They operate out of the same fear-based, UNPREDICTABLE PERFORMANCE type as the other RANDOM ACTOR profiles, but like the ACCOUNTANT/RANDOM ACTOR, they fool people because of their ASK trait, appearing less Machiavellian or threatening than a RANDOM ACTOR with a TELL trait. When they communicate, they are likely to evoke empathy and seemingly portray interest in others, like a doctor with a good bedside manner. But, this is only when they communicate—the *talk* part of their life. When called upon to perform—their *walk*— their EXPRESS trait can cause their predatory nature to express itself by preying upon feelings and a sense of beguiling warmth. They will operate to protect themselves while placing little emphasis on conventionality or "appropriate" behaviors. A common place that we find ARTIST/RANDOM ACTORS is in the role of cult follower, where they can be led down destructive paths due to blind loyalty, or, the child molester who uses his ARTIST type to gain intimacy. Their ARTIST type also makes them extremely susceptible to depression and expressions of a fatalistic bent. (Be sure to review general observations of RANDOM ACTORS in this chapter and Chapters 8 and 13.)

Typical Strengths
- Open and sensitive to others.
- Capable of being creative.

Typical Shortcomings
- Susceptible to depression and neuroses.
- Can become fatalistic.
- Open to risks of self-harm and even suicide the more extreme their PERFORMANCE traits.
- Potential for severe mood swings.
- Easily intimidated by those "in control."
- More likely to be blindly loyal than SERGEANT/ or SALESMEN/RANDOM ACTORS.

Other Tendencies

- May struggle unsuccessfully to hide emotions from others.

Trait Indicators

- Low FEARFUL ratings are best indicator of profile's ability to express creativity like ARTIST/INNOVATOR.
- High FEARFUL trait can change creative genius into "insanity" or instability.

Interaction Tips

- Be prepared for spontaneous and open displays of emotion, both positive and negative.
- Because this RANDOM ACTOR profile has an EXPRESS trait, focus on minimizing fear-producing events or discussions, which might *emotionally* trigger self-inflicted harm.
- Do not put them in "sensitive" or politically complex relationships.

Sell/Present—Like all RANDOM ACTOR profiles, avoid making presentations that require important decision-making. Like the ARTIST/CONFORMIST, find another person in the organization to either make your case or help undergird their fears. When making presentation, presenter with an EXPRESS trait is ideal who should focus on ideas rather than bottom-line issues, using a slow, deliberate ASK style, while preemptively preparing for any potential fear-provoking, need-to-take-action points.

Confrontation—First, be sure to review the guidelines for interacting with a RANDOM ACTOR detailed throughout the text. Like the other RANDOM ACTOR profiles, try and operate with these people based upon the positive actions in their COMMUNICATION type. Reduce fear with soothing reassurances that keep their EXPRESS and FEARFUL traits in check. Only as a last resort should a person with a moderate to high TELL trait be employed. Appeal to their desire to be amiable and respectful. That is, appeal to the positive actions you observe in their COMMUNICATION type and vocalize with a reassuring tone. When they seek to harm you, they will often try to get in close, playing off your "feelings" and intimacy. So, be careful what you give away about yourself personally.

CHAPTER 12

Using the Comprehensive Profiles

In this chapter we will examine four different cases in which utilizing the COMPREHENSIVE PROFILES was integral in solving problems. Each case is based upon an actual situation in which I either acted as a consultant or observed closely. Two assignments are provided at the end to help you put the profiles to work in your professional and personal life.

Case #1—*An outside consultant is working with a creative work group in the audit industry. Every time the consultant makes a proposal that the staff wants to initiate, the group's manager, Thomas, throws up illogical roadblocks that nearly derail the project. What course of action should the consultant take to save the project?*

The first step the consultant took was to profile the manager. He based his read upon correspondence that he received from Thomas, phone conversations, and a face-to-face meeting with the entire staff. He determined that Thomas was a SERGEANT/CONFORMIST. Here are some excerpts from Thomas's COMPREHENSIVE PROFILE.

- Because of their fear-based motivations coupled with their social dominance and predictability, they will seldom risk new ideas or challenges and they will seldom challenge others or the status quo.
- SERGEANT/CONFORMISTS dislike sudden or unpredictable change, and they fear the personal consequences of such change. They do not want to be surprised or to surprise those who may control their future or their fate.

- The higher the FEARFUL trait, the more likely they are to point a finger at you when you are not to blame for a problem, so evaluate entering situations where risk is a significant factor. This can especially be difficult, the higher the TELL trait.
- Expect rigid interpretations of rules; don't ask for compromises or exceptions.
- Do not be frustrated by their "mixed style" when they deal "up the chain of command" versus "down the chain of command." When they deal "down," they will tend to be more dominant, while they will appear to be less dominant when they deal "up" the chain of command.

First, it is pretty obvious that whoever hired Thomas to be the manager of this group didn't do a very good job. Rarely, if ever, do you want a SERGEANT/CONFORMIST to manage a creative group because he has a natural aversion to risks, which is an integral part of a creative process. Still, the consultant has to get the job done. But he knows that all blame will be placed on his desk by Thomas if anything doesn't perform as expected—even if it isn't his fault.

To overcome this fear-driven profile, the consultant developed very close working alliances with two team members, Mark and Joy, who were medium CONFIDENT and not risk-adverse. Mark was low TELL and wasn't afraid of verbally articulating a position, while Joy was ASK and demonstrated her confidence in the project through her actions rather than through dialogue. Together, the consultant relied upon these two people to keep the project moving forward.

When Thomas threw down unnecessary objections, the consultant provided responses through the two team members. He provided Mark with oral responses when a verbal response was necessary, and he provided strategic direction to Joy when a written response was needed, such as a revision to a proposal or to a strategic point. In this way, team members kept Thomas's FEARFUL trait "propped up" and he was rarely called upon to make decisions—his weakness.

By relieving Thomas of the majority of the decision-making process when modified actions had to be taken, Thomas's FEARFUL trait was minimized, the project was completed, and the consultant's reputation remained intact and untarnished.

The consultant also took action to protect his integrity if any phase did not perform due to factors out of his control. He wanted to avoid the usual "Well, you promised…" type of comments from Thomas. One strategic step he took was faxing frequent written updates to Thomas. This provided a vehicle through which anyone—Thomas's superiors, team members, or prospective future clients—could easily track the progress of the project. Each update also included observations about changes in delivery and completion dates, changes in strategy, etc. that were not directly communicated by Mark or Joy. He did not let these changes accumulate. In this way, the bumps and obstacles that all creative projects face were presented in *small doses*, which can prevent fear-overload by CONFORMIST profiles. This tactic can also minimize a severe reaction from a manager's superiors if the manager is forced to present several unexpected changes at one time. This is very important for a SERGEANT/CONFORMIST. In this way his superiors are less likely to exert overloading pressure, which the manager might be tempted to redirect at the consultant.

Keeping Thomas regularly informed of changes also aided the communication process. As a SERGEANT/CONFORMIST, Thomas's natural tendency is to be firm with subordinates (using his TELL trait), while he is more likely to retreat (because he is FEARFUL) if confronted by superiors, which can result in the derailing of a project, needless posturing, and so forth. By presenting changes in small doses, Thomas was never confronted with pressure from senior management which might have caused him to halt the project.

Case #2—*Frank and his staff are pursuing a lucrative contract with XYZ Inc., a Fortune 1000 company. However, Frank encounters an unusual challenge. The CFO of XYZ requests an exploratory meeting with his staff before moving forward. He tells Frank, though, that under no conditions may any of Frank's staff make contact with anyone at XYZ before this meeting. Then, the day of the meeting, the CFO slams the boardroom door shut and screams at his subordinates, while Frank and his staff are standing outside the door within earshot of the CFO's loud barks. What action did Frank take, based upon the CFO's actions, that increased his company's chances of securing a future contract?*

Sometimes it is just as beneficial to know when not to press forward as when one should move forward aggressively to secure a contract. When the decision is made not to move forward at an inopportune time, one can direct the same resources toward a more productive opportunity or wait until the time is right to resume sales and marketing efforts. This case is one such example.

Frank profiled the CFO as a SERGEANT/RANDOM ACTOR. He based this upon the reads of technical support people in his organization and observations of outside vendors who had done business with the CFO. Frank tested these reads during his first interactions with the CFO on the phone and during a prior meeting. Unfortunately, everyone was on target: the CFO was extremely volatile and manipulative.

Here are some of the highlights of the SERGEANT/RANDOM ACTOR's profile.

- SERGEANT/RANDOM ACTORS will seek to maintain the strong, controlling image of the SERGEANT, but will frequently disappoint others with their unreliability and their unwillingness to take responsibility for their circumstances. Their fear-based motivation will cause them to feel and act "out of control" while their COMMUNICATION type will drive them to maintain the *appearance* of CONTROL. This combination of traits will produce a tension that can result in anger, impatience, depression, moodiness, or authoritarianism.
- No matter what their performance level, they will attempt to dominate and control others.
- Their unpredictability and fear-based motivations yield random actions that may have no relevance to the situation.
- They tend to act defensively, even when a threat isn't present.
- This may be one of the most difficult profiles to read because of the strong contrast between the COMMUNICATION and PERFORMANCE types. Even though they TELL, they are FEARFUL when making decisions.

Even to the uninformed, a quick glance at these tendencies says: *Do not enter into long-term relationships with RANDOM ACTORS unless you are willing to deal with the consequences.*

Given the CFO's profile, Frank has two reasons for not doing business with XYZ. First, the key player is volatile, paranoiac, and unstable. Second, when SERGEANT/RANDOM ACTORS exit their senior level positions, housecleaning often follows. This can include the cancellation of contracts, termination of relationships, etc. Taking this into consideration, Frank still wanted to eventually do business with XYZ, so he took three courses of action.

First, during the meeting that eventually started after the CFO slammed the boardroom door shut, Frank politely disengaged his staff from negotiations using nonthreatening, open-ended language. Frank didn't want to needlessly create an enemy. Second, he instructed his staff to quietly develop strategic relationships with technical staffers at XYZ so that if and when the CFO exited, they would be positioned to move forward again—but with helpful alliances in place. Third, he directed his staff to focus their time and resources on other accounts.

Did Frank get the account? No. But, he made a wise decision for maximizing his resources and positioning his company for a better day in the future with XYZ.

Case #3—*Kathleen is an independent negotiator who brings documentary producers and cable networks together. For two months she has been trying to purchase the rights to an historically significant documentary series produced by a British production company. Wendell, her contact, has been very difficult to pin down. It is the first time he has negotiated a contract for his company. One day the deal is on, the next day it is off. Her only contact with Wendell has been through correspondence and telephone conferences. She thinks he is a RANDOM ACTOR, and she is willing to do whatever is necessary to secure this important documentary. What course of action did she take in order to secure the contract?*

Kathleen profiled Wendell as an ARTIST/RANDOM ACTOR whose UNPREDICTABLE and FEARFUL traits were about 2 or 3. Some of the highlights of this profile are:

- Capable of being creative.
- Susceptible to depression and neuroses.
- Can become fatalistic.
- Potential for severe mood swings.
- Easily intimidated by those "in control."
- When making presentation, presenter with an EXPRESS trait is ideal. He should focus on ideas rather than bottom-line issues, using a slow, deliberate ASK style, while preemptively preparing for any potential fear-provoking, need-to-take-action points.

Unlike Frank's situation in the previous case, Kathleen pursued her contract with Wendell because she was *not* entering into a long-term relationship. Her relationship with Wendell was only short-term. Once the deal was signed, there would be no more obligations or action points with Wendell. Additionally, she believed that working with Wendell was an acceptable risk because his UNPREDICTABLE and FEARFUL traits were only about a 2. As noted in Chapter 8, it is possible to engage in short-term relationships with RANDOM ACTORS as long as their PERFORMANCE traits are not extreme.

Tactically, it was crucial that Kathleen do whatever was necessary to drive down Wendell's fears/apprehensions. It was Wendell's first major contract. His future reputation was on the line, and he would almost singularly be motivated by the opinions of his superiors. Driving down Wendell's fears in this pressure situation was also more likely to make his actions more PREDICTABLE, but only in the short-term, as described in Chapter 8.

So what did Kathleen do?

She flew to England for a face-to-face meeting with Wendell. She was determined to identify the positive traits in Wendell's ARTIST type and operate with him on that level. As they *communicated*, she wanted Wendell to see with his own eyes that she could be trusted and that her first desire was to see Wendell sparkle in the eyes of his superiors. Was her costly trip guaranteed to work? No. But she was confident that her US client was the best vehicle for Wendell's documentary series. She also felt that if Wendell would trust her, both would end up winners.

The result?

Wendell signed, and his company's documentary series aired with much acclaim in the US. Wendell also increased in stature within his company. And yes, Kathleen was able to discuss future projects with Wendell because his *trust* in her was established—the key in successfully operating with a RANDOM ACTOR. She made sure, however, that none of the transactions required a long-term commitment on Wendell's part.

I know who you are. Good for me, better for you.

Profiling with this attitude does work.

Case #4—*All teenagers become odd in different ways when they go through "the change." In our family we call it "lala land." Kids can't help it, just* *like you and I couldn't help it when our hormones ravaged us. Pimples, new hair, rearranging of body parts . . . it's all a part of the mutation/transformation.*

Robert and Sharon have two teenage boys. They are convinced that the reason God created puberty was so that they would have an easier time letting go of their sons when they became men. They love their boys, who are both competitive with very different profiles, but nurturing and disciplining is a challenge. Here are some ways that they used profiling to keep the lines of communication wide open.

Their oldest son, Steve (16), is an ARTIST-ACCOUNTANT/INNOVATOR. Phil (14) is a SALESMAN-SERGEANT/MANAGER. Both boys, who are combination types, are extremely competitive, driven by their high CONFIDENT traits, which were nurtured by their parents and a handful of very caring teachers.

The difference in the two boys was humorously apparent by the time they were three and five. Phil, the MANAGER, could completely dress himself, shirt tucked in. Everything coordinated. Steve, the INNOVATOR, who was two years older, was lucky just to get out of bed. From the time Phil was three, he actually dressed and critiqued his older brother, morning after morning, until Steve was seven.

By the time the boys started their lawn-mowing business, Phil, now 10, was the organizer, and Steve, 12, had the warm, winning smile that endeared his neighbors to give them a chance.

When discipline was necessary, their parents took a slightly different approach with each son. For both sons they first reviewed the facts of the infraction, the punishment, and their expectation for change. When confronted with a huge error by Steve (the INNOVATOR), his dad would have Steve write a paper to be sure the expectation for change was concrete and unambiguous in Steve's idea-driven mind.

When disciplining Phil (the MANAGER), they followed the same initial process: review the facts of the infraction, the punishment, and their expectation for change. But when a specific situation needed to be emphasized, he was usually given a specific *task* that was a direct counterpoint of how he ineffectively handled/managed himself. For example, if Phil failed to take out the bathroom garbage pails for the second time in a week, his punishment went as follows: First, he empties the garbage from each bathroom into a large container in the garage. Second, he then returns each container to its respective bathroom. Third, he recollects the containers from each bathroom. Fourth, he replaces the emptied garbage that is in the large container in the garage back into each bathroom container. Finally, Phil must return each container back to its original bathroom with its original garbage. For emphasis, the whole process is then repeated about a half-dozen times.

In Robert and Sharon's house, both boys had to obey the same rules. They used two very different approaches, however, to help each boy learn his lesson in a way that matched his profile. They applied the same kind of thinking in all other important situations, such as times of encouragement, teaching, making "suggestions," and so on. The boys almost always sensed that Mom and Dad understood and took a unique interest in their successes and failures, their missteps and their maturing steps forward. Yes, this requires time, but it is parenting with a legacy of blessings.

ASSIGNMENT #16

Goal: Learn how to use the COMPREHENSIVE PROFILES to solve a professional problem.

Time: Approximately two hours.

Think of a problem that you encountered in your professional life which ended in an unsuccessful resolution but which might have been tackled successfully if you had known how to profile. Now do the following:

1. At the top of a legal pad, write a summary statement of your hoped-for outcome at that time. Be specific.
2. Write a summary statement of the *actual* outcome underneath your initial anticipated outcome.
3. Identify the profile of each person who was involved.
4. Review each person's profile and record their specific actions which had a direct bearing on the outcome.
5. With a blue or black pen, catalog on a separate legal-sized sheet of paper the facts on a vertical time line of what occurred. The simplest way to do this is to write down the sequence of events—one event on each line. In the left-hand margin, provide the time of each event, when appropriate.
6. After compiling the time line, record the tendencies/actions of each

profile that, if addressed differently, might have changed the outcome.

7. Review your personal profile and make notes about how your specific tendencies may have affected the outcome.

8. Referencing the sequence of events you prepared in Step #5, create another time line on another sheet of paper as follows: For each specific event that you *wouldn't* have changed how you interacted, write these in blue or black ink—one event for each line. After carefully reviewing the mix of profiles that were involved in the situation, both yours and the profiles of others, record how you would modify *specific* interactions, actions, and directives if faced with the same situation. Write these modifications on your time line in *red pen*. Be sure to be specific and not ambiguous. In some cases you may be looking for a completely successful outcome, while in other cases you will only be able to minimize damage.

9. Now review the entire modified time line, taking note of your suggestions (which are in red). Evaluate and then reevaluate your modifications. When possible, ask another person who possesses wisdom and insight to review your suggestions.

10. Finally, write out specific lessons and insights you have gained by applying profiling to this situation and how you will tackle future situations which are similar. Don't just talk this last step out. Write out your thoughts. You will find that even as you put your ideas down on paper that you will probably gain an additional insight or two.

ASSIGNMENT #17

Goal: Learn how to use the COMPREHENSIVE PROFILES to solve a personal problem.

Time: Approximately two hours.

For this assignment, think of a minor personal problem that you had with another person which had an unsuccessful resolution but which you might have been able to resolve successfully if you had known how to profile. Start with a less-than-volcanic problem to avoid unwanted intrusion of your personal emotions at this point. Only after you have practiced this exercise on a couple of less explosive situations should you consider examining a volatile and/or life-changing event.

Follow the ten steps provided in ASSIGNMENT #16. Addressing a personal situation can sometimes be more difficult than examining a professional problem. Therefore, be sure you set aside sufficient reflective time so that you won't be interrupted. Seek impartial and wise input when necessary. Once you have thought through and learned from one situation, try another. Resist tackling difficult situations until you have gained some experience.

If you are reviewing a situation together with a spouse, be patient. Let grace be the operative word. We all have strengths *and* deficiencies. Don't clobber your mate with newfound understanding and knowledge which you have gained from your profiling skills. One of the best pieces of advice I have ever received was from my colleague Dr. James Reese, who wrote the foreword for this book. He said: *If you really care, would you ever want to see your best friend fail and lose in life? Of course not. Well, it's the same with your spouse, especially in an argument. Don't hound the person you love until you win and he or she fails. That's a pretty shallow and hollow victory. Be on your spouse's side so that he/she wins and doesn't fail.*

Again, the philosophy introduced in Chapter 1 *must* be made to prevail: *I know who you are. Good for me, better for you.*

ASSIGNMENT #18

Goal: Learn how to use the COMPREHENSIVE PROFILES to interact with precision and/or succeed in a future situation.

Time: Approximately two hours.

Don't leave this chapter until you have made progress with at least one prior situation. Now think ahead to professional and personal situations that you know that you will probably encounter in the future. Then apply the following steps to a specific future situation.

1. Identify a future situation, such as how you will:
   - Refine a presentation for a previously puzzling client.
   - Encourage a student who needs to tackle a new challenge.
   - Help your team better interact, respecting each other's strengths.
   - Attempt to diffuse the anger of a colleague who must be confronted.
   - Conduct an interview so that fears are not unnecessarily provoked.
   - Engage a volatile/threatening individual.

- Consult a client so that he is more likely to enact your recommendations.
- Provide a patient with appropriate counsel.
- Show your spouse that you respect his or her unique style for communicating and performing.
- Communicate your vision for a project to a group with a unique profile.

2. Write a summary statement of your anticipated outcome.

3. Identify the profile of each person that will probably be involved.

4. Review each person's profile and record the tendencies/actions which might have a direct bearing on the outcome.

5. Review your personal profile and make notes about how your specific tendencies/actions may affect the outcome.

6. Write out a time line, referencing how you will interact, direct, listen, etc. with each individual.

7. Finally, write out a specific goal(s) of what insight you hope to attain by using profiling in this situation. Be specific and write down your expectations, as you did in ASSIGNMENT #17. Taking the time to articulate your thoughts on paper will help you refine and add to your expectations.

CHAPTER 13

Additional Observations and Suggestions

This chapter provides additional suggestions and guidance in the following areas:

- Three Questions to Shorten Your Reads
- Profiling Groups
- Strategy for Impromptu Profiling
- Strategy for Profiling Before Interaction
- Team Profiling
- A Hiring Strategy
- Cross-culture Profiling
- Random Actors: Additional Observations

Complete texts could be written that address many of these areas, but the following suggestions should keep you focused in the right direction as you develop your profiling skills. Also, before reading this chapter, it is recommended that you review the concepts covered in Chapter 6 as some of the concepts are further developed in this chapter.

THREE QUESTIONS TO SHORTEN YOUR READS

When there is a way to shorten the time necessary to develop a profile, we should use it. For example, let's say that your colleagues are absolutely certain that, based upon past interactions, George is a SALESMAN, but no one is certain about his PERFORMANCE type. Where do you focus your reads to quickly identify George's PERFORMANCE type?

This is where the following three questions will come in handy in most professional environments. They will quickly remind you where to look to identify a specific trait or type. These questions are:

1. How does a person handle *situations*? (PERFORMANCE traits)
2. How does a person handle *people*? (COMMUNICATION traits)
3. Does a person like the *nature* of his job? (All four traits)

The questions can be directed at the person you are profiling, associates and colleagues of the person you are profiling, or you can review present or past actions.

The first question, inquiring about how people handle *situations*, will point you toward PERFORMANCE traits, because it will answer how people handle problems, challenges, and so forth. This, in turn, will reveal how they will perform and make decisions. So, if you ask how George handles a restructuring process, you might find out that he welcomes change and adapts easily, suggesting that perhaps he is UNPREDICTABLE. If, however, he is very uncomfortable in that kind of *situation*, then he is more likely PREDICTABLE.

The second question, inquiring how someone handles *people*, can help you identify someone's COMMUNICATION traits. This is because the question focuses on personal interactions. If, for example, you are told that George is *emotional* and *sensitive* when he interacts with others, he is most likely EXPRESS, but if he is *private* and *introverted*, he is probably CONTROL.

Naturally, there will be some overlap regarding the traits these two questions can identify. An example might be when George uses his TELL trait in response to a situation. Or, when George uses his PREDICTABLE trait when interacting with someone.

Most of the time, however, these questions will point you in a direction that will enable you to quickly make the read you need.

The third question, whether a person likes the *nature* of his job, can also provide quick reads of someone's traits.

If Lee likes the nature of his work, it can indicate that his traits are a good match for the job. So, if Lee enjoys his engineering career, one could start with the hunch that he is PREDICTABLE and CONTROL and possibly ASK, common traits found in engineering groups. And, if Debra enjoys being the director of marketing, TELL and CONFIDENT are possible starting points.

When using this question, it is important to distinguish between the overall *nature* of the job from other factors, such as whether or not someone likes a specific project, a specific boss, or their work environment. These factors can be impacted by downsizing, poor market conditions, and so on, which may color someone's opinion about their current position. What we are looking for is if someone likes the *nature* of his work, apart from internal or external   factors which may affect one's attitude.

When people don't like the nature of their job description, then this might indicate a bad match of traits with the needs of the job. For example, if Jennifer is involved in sales, but doesn't enjoy selling herself or her product, even though she likes her product, then this might indicate that she is ASK and/or possibly CONTROL, as sales personnel often rely upon TELL and/or EXPRESS traits.

Therefore, when possible, make immediate reads and inquiries about how people feel about the nature of their job as this will often provide quick insight into their profile.

PROFILING GROUPS

Here's a puzzle...

My wife Sandy is the purveyor of one of Dallas's better known catering establishments. At one posh Christmas company party for about one hundred guests, she and her staff watched something odd.

One of the treats of the buffet-style feast was a giant, richly garnished silver punch bowl filled with jumbo shrimp on ice. With great amusement, Sandy and her staff watched as *every* guest did exactly the same thing on each of their plates. After consuming a shrimp, they lined up the tails—about six to ten a plate—in a precise arc around the edge of their plate. None of the one hundred-plus employees deviated, and there was no "shrimp-tail conspiracy" amongst the company employees to line up the tails.

Now the question is: *What was the profile of the company?*

The company was a software company primarily comprised of software engineers and technicians. The profile of the typical staff member was an ACCOUNTANT/MANAGER or CONFORMIST—people who were fastidiously detailed and precise. Placing the tails in a neat arc on their plates was simply an expression of being precise. The chain reaction was most likely initiated when one colleague unconsciously observed another colleague line up the tails on his plate. He then copied his colleague's actions because he possessed the same fastidious profile. The rest of the staff followed suit in the relaxed setting because being precise was something that felt natural and comfortable.

Even though individuals in an organization have individual profiles, when collectively compiled together, a work group often takes on a *group profile*, and it will display many uniform actions. This is because the majority of the members of a group have a similar mix of traits. The company that Sandy observed is just one humorous example.

Other common examples of work groups that often adopt a group type or profile are:

- **Research and Development**—INNOVATOR type
- **Sales and Marketing**—SALESMAN type
- **Administrative Staff at a Hospital**—ACCOUNTANT type

This doesn't mean that everyone in the group will possess the same type(s) as the group because individuals will have their own unique profile. The unique demands of the work group, however, typically draw people with traits which easily adapt to the demands of a specific work group.

In an audit group, for example, one usually finds ACCOUNTANTS or SERGEANTS for the COMMUNICATION type (those who are CONTROL) and either MANAGERS or CONFORMISTS for the PERFORMANCE type, reflecting predictability. If the group is large enough, though, one will often find one or two INNOVATORS, and these people usually work on innovating/creating new systems.

Identifying a group's profile can be a valuable tool when predicting how a group as a whole prefers to interact and operate. Identifying a group's profile can also be useful when evaluating how a specific person in a group may or may not operate in a given situation.

Typically, the stronger the influence of the group and the greater the desire of an individual to get along or conform, the more likely that his preference for operating may be steered by the profile of the group. This is usually reflected by the group either overriding individual preferences, or driving people to operate at the end of their range for a trait(s) that is closer to that of the group. So, if Mike is an INNOVATOR, but his group operates as a

MANAGER, look for the possibility that Mike may use his UNPREDICTABLE trait at the lower end of his range—toward PREDICTABLE.

Another common reaction occurs when someone who does not feel loyal to the group and/or does not have a long-term interest in interacting with the group will react *against* the group. This person will often move toward the extreme end of his range that is the farthest from the group's trait(s).

When considering how group profiles and individuals interact, it is important to bear in mind that we are considering typical daily preferences for communicating or performing. We are not addressing those situations in which people must make important moral or ethical decisions. As already noted, even those who are FEARFUL can choose, as an act of character, to operate with, against, or without a group.

Up or Down the Ladder—Another factor that should be considered when evaluating a group's profile and its affect on an individual is where someone is on the organizational chart. Typically, the further down the organizational chain of command an individual's position, the more likely that the group profile will affect the individual's profile. Alternately, the higher up the chain of command, the less likely the group's profile and tendencies will alter an individual's preferences for operating.

For example, Thomas, the SERGEANT-CONFORMIST in the last chapter, was the head of his group. The group's profile didn't affect his decision-making. He simply made the group more neurotic, because of his fear-based decision-making style. As a positive counterpoint to Thomas, there are leaders who are CONFIDENT and inspire those in their charge to operate at the end of their range that tilts toward optimum confidence. In this case the group may take on a more CONFIDENT flavor due to leadership from the top.

STRATEGY FOR IMPROMPTU PROFILING

The following are priorities to keep in mind when you must profile someone on-the-spot, without prior preparation or knowledge of past history.

Determine Which Type or Trait(s) Are the Most Important and Focus Your Reads—When you must profile people immediately without advance preparation, ask yourself which trait(s) or type is the most important for you to identify—the trait that will be of the greatest benefit to you. Then focus your reads on that trait(s) or type.

If you are in a social environment, the ASK-TELL trait may be the most important, enabling you to communicate sensitively with someone.

If you are negotiating a contract, you may want to identify the ASK-TELL trait first, enabling you to identify someone's communication tendencies. Your second choice may be the CONFIDENT-FEARFUL trait, so that you can identify likely tendencies when someone makes decisions and takes action. (By choosing to read these two traits first, you can also avoid confusing the TELL trait for CONFIDENT, as discussed in Chapter 10, enabling you to separate someone's *walk* from his *talk*.)

Or imagine that you are a personnel manager who, without advance warning, is given the assignment to conduct interviews on the same day for two different positions. One opening is for a receptionist and the other is for a draftsperson. This means that each interview should be started from a different perspective.

When interviewing candidates for the receptionist position, you should start by reading their ASK-TELL and CONTROL-EXPRESS traits, as most of their responsibilities will rely upon their COMMUNICATION type. As suggested earlier in this chapter, direct your reads toward how the candidate handles *people*. Alternately, when interviewing candidates for the drafting position, you should start with reading predictability and how they handle *situations*, as their PERFORMANCE type will be more important for their position.

Determine Which Clue Sources Should Receive First Attention—This chapter has already provided some tips for where to look when you are trying to identify a specific trait. Chapter 14 further expands on this concept, categorizing clue sources into categories that will quickly point you to a specific trait. The clues are broken down into categories such as speech, attire, background data, and so forth. Once you are familiar with the full range of options open to you, in impromptu settings, focus your reads on the clue source(s) which will point toward a specific trait.

Identify Positions of Key Players, Responsibilities, and What Is Important to Each—When meeting with a group of individuals, identifying the positions of key players and their responsibilities can aid initial reads, providing a starting point to create and test your reads. For example, the manager/leader of a group is more likely to be CONFIDENT and PREDICTABLE, while someone in research and development is more likely to be CONFIDENT and UNPREDICTABLE. Also, by identifying positions and responsibilities of leaders and subordinates, as well as what is important to each person, one can begin to create hunches about which person's traits are likely to influence others in the group, and when and how a person is likely to exert his influence.

Because there are a lot of places where you can focus your reads, simply ask yourself, "What is it that I need to know?" and focus your reads in that direction.

STRATEGY FOR PROFILING BEFORE INTERACTION

The following are suggestions for developing a profile *before* interacting with someone. Diligently applied, this strategy will give you an edge unlike any other skill, because you will regularly reduce the time necessary for successful interactions. All that is required is an orientation toward disciplined preparation.

Profile of Organization and Past History—Here, several key questions should be answered. Does an organization have an identifiable group profile? Does the organization's profile impact the profile of specific work groups, such as marketing or systems? Can the profile of the CEO and key decision-makers be identified from past interactions, input from outside vendors, or past reactions to mergers and acquisitions? How has the organization made decisions in the past? Did an individual's decision-making in the past reflect an individual or group persona?

Identify Positions of Key Players, Responsibilities, and What Is Important to Each—The idea here is the same as explained for impromptu profiling. Identify key positions, responsibilities, etc. which can provide starting points for reads.

Identify Opportunities for Making Unobtrusive Reads— Opportunities for making unobtrusive reads will depend upon whom you are reading, the environment in which he operates, and your imagination. Some common examples are:

- Observing someone on the job without calling attention to yourself.
- Observing how someone interacts with others.
- Insight from a colleague who dealt with this person in the past.
- Input from the assistant of the person you are profiling.

- Review of past correspondence, especially if written under pressure.
- Observations from outside vendors or competitors.

Each work environment will dictate when and where unobtrusive reads can be made. Care must be taken not to violate any ethical codes of conduct, nor to make observations in a way that inappropriately fuels suspicions/resentments. One's attitude should be the same that has been promoted throughout the text: *I know who you are. Good for me, better for you.* If your method for obtaining a read violates this philosophy, don't use it.

What Traits Were Revealed When This Person Was Confronted with Stress in the Past?—Because past behavior, particularly under pressure, is the best predictor of future behavior, make inquiries about past situations in which stress was a factor.

Some common examples are:

- Organizational downsizing or restructuring.
- Reactions to shifting markets.
- Reaction to performance evaluations.
- How a patient handled a past diagnosis.
- How a parent reacted to their child's difficulties in a prior class.

TEAM PROFILING

Team profiling is one of the most potent ideas presented in this text.

Team profiling is when a group of individuals pool their resources and reads in order to profile people in other organizations/groups *before* interacting with those individuals. The goal of team profiling is to *systematically* achieve *identified objectives* with greater efficiency.

The fundamental components of team profiling are:

1. Identify applications in which team profiling will help you achieve specific objectives.
2. Prioritize applications, objectives, and develop plans of action.

Thoughtfully appropriated and mastered, team profiling is one of the most valuable assets for teams of individuals who work together. Team profiling can also provide an organization with a distinct internal and external advantage over organizations which do not use this strategy.

The idea is common sense: several minds and perspectives are often better than one. When several people, with equal profiling skills, compare their reads of the same person, the group's accuracy is likely to be more accurate than if one person is relying solely upon his own reads. Also, a group of team members can brainstorm and break down each process to create and identify opportunities for evaluating past actions, obtaining unobtrusive reads, and enlisting the help of internal and external players.

Team profiling creates significant strategic advantages over one person profiling by himself, which are:

1. Increase the frequency of being able to profile people before interacting with them.

2. Achieve targeted communication and productivity objectives.

When team profiling is used to profile those within an organization, efficiency in communication and productivity will immediately result. When used to profile those outside an organization, an exceptional competitive edge can be captured, particularly in consultant and sales environments.

The two most important factors that will cause team profiling to become a reality are:

1. Management requires that each team member develop profiling proficiency.

2. Specific applications are targeted in which profiling, when applied, will meet specific objectives.

The team profiling bottom line is: Team profiling must be made a *priority* and applied so that it can produce *measurable* results.

We'll now review the two components of team profiling.

1. Identify Application Needs and Specific Objectives— Identify when your group can best benefit from profiling others. This means detailing your various work processes and then identifying a wish list of how profiling can specifically and quantitatively improve each process. Some sample descriptions of how profiling can be used to improve performance quantitatively in specific applications are as follows:

Sales—Customize presentations and closes to increase sales.

Consultants—Improve interaction and accommodate different profiles so that needed recommendations will be acted upon.

Educators—Improve communication with parents during conferences so that students with learning disabilities can get help at home more quickly, which will translate into better grades, retention, and comprehension.

Audit—Efficiently gather data during interviews so that reports will provide a more accurate measure of corporate performance.

Human Resource—Direct team management strategies to shorten the time necessary to restructure a division.

When identifying applications, be specific. If you are an educator, the following description of an application won't work: *improve communication.* The description isn't specific. It's vague and unfocused. There is nothing by which one can measure improvement. It's more productive to state specifically: *Improve communication with parents during conferences so that students with learning disabilities can get help at home more quickly, which will translate into better grades, retention, comprehension, etc.* Another sample description might be: *Improve communication in staff meetings so that committees can reduce the time necessary to evaluate proposals.* By being specific, you can also better identify specific opportunities for making unobtrusive reads, examining past actions, etc.

In the case of a teacher meeting with parents, enlisting the help of a colleague who had the same student the year before might be the first step used to identify a parent's profile. Step two might be tailoring how recommendations should be communicated so that a parent would be more likely to take action. For example, for parents who are high UNPREDICTABLE, it might be appropriate to make more follow-up calls, than for parents who are more PREDICTABLE and regimented (similar to the approach taken by the Swiss doctors in Chapter 7).

There will be applications in which one won't be able to measure quantitatively the success of applying team profiling, such as improving the quality of organizational communication, goodwill, and so forth. These may be viable long-term goals. Experience, however, has demonstrated that initially focusing on a couple of specific and measurable objectives will increase the motivation of team members to sharpen and apply their profiling skills.

2. Prioritize Applications, Objectives, and Develop Plans of Action—Once you have developed a list of applications in which profiling will increase productivity, promote effective communication, and so on, prioritize which applications are the most important and work on those first. Then detail specific objectives for each application, such as: shorten interviewing process, increase number of closes, improve team communication during project meetings, promote trust, and so forth. Finally, develop an action plan to achieve the desired objective for each application utilizing the combined ideas for impromptu profiling and profiling people before interaction.

Here is an example of how one high-tech sales team might identify an application and specific objectives, and suggestions for obtaining reads.

Application:	Increase the effectiveness of sales presentations.
1st Objective:	Increase sales by 5% during the next quarter.
2nd Objective:	Reduce the time necessary to establish customer rapport.

Opportunities to evaluate past actions:

- Ask other divisions for their reads of past transactions.
- Obtain input from noncompeting outside vendors.

Opportunities to make unobtrusive reads:

- Pre-sale technical consultant meetings with a potential client.
- Observe a client meeting with his staff when questions about service, financing, etc. are raised.

Here is another example of how an audit group might apply team profiling. In this situation measurable results can be evaluated for both of the objectives, although the first objective will be harder to quantify.

Application:	Improve data gathering.
1st Objective:	Reduce unnecessary fear during interviews. There is the possibility of a merger and data-gathering interviews should not needlessly provoke fear.
2nd Objective:	Improve the quality of information obtained during interviews.

Opportunities to evaluate past actions:

- Previous oral presentations.
- Past "announcements" (when objectives of an audit are outlined).
- Previous times of stress, such as acquisitions and mergers.

Opportunities to make unobtrusive reads:

- During announcements.
- During preliminary audit status drafts, reports, etc.

- Verbal discussions over audit matters.

- Closing conferences.

As noted at the head of the chapter, team profiling is one concept for which an entire text could be written. However, most teams with determined leadership should be able to take this framework and successfully build on it so that team profiling can become an integral part of its success.

The Ethical and Moral Standard—I was asked by a consultant: *What if one division gets wind that another division is profiling them? Couldn't this promote distrust?*

My response was that everyone in a corporate culture should be encouraged to develop profiling while promoting the philosophy that advances goodwill: *I know who you are. Good for me, better for you.* If profiling is solely used to obtain a personal edge, it will promote distrust. If profiling is used to improve productivity *and* the quality of organizational life, then trust will be promoted.

The president of a major plastics manufacturing company, who possessed a natural intuitive gift to profile, asked me to teach profiling to his entire senior staff. When I asked what the goal of the training was, his exemplary response was: *I know that it will make them better team players and more effective leaders.* It is with this kind of sound ethical philosophy that senior management must thoughtfully promote the use of team profiling skills.

A HIRING STRATEGY

The following is a simple strategy for using profiling when hiring personnel. It can reduce the screening and interviewing process by as much as one-third. This strategy is principally recommended for small businesses that advertise in a local newspaper, but some of the ideas can be adapted for use in larger organizations. Additionally, it is recommended that this strategy be used along with a reliable self-assessment test.

The steps for applying this strategy are as follows:

1. Develop the Profile—Make a list of the COMMUNICATION and PERFORMANCE type *actions* you would like to see in the person who will fill the position. Be certain that your expectations are reasonable. Most of the COMMUNICATION actions, for example, should originate from one of the types. If your list of actions is scattered across two or three types, you may have to rethink your expectations, or you have to be willing to search until you find someone who is a *combination type*. Once you have identified the specific actions and both the COMMUNICATION and PERFORMANCE type, identify and review the COMPREHENSIVE PROFILE. Ask yourself: Do the positive and negative attributes described in the profile match my expectations? Remember, you are developing a profile for both the benefit of your organization and the person you are hiring.

2. Make a Trait and Action List—After you have developed the ideal profile and specific actions for the position, list them as shown in the example provided, separated by communication and performance actions, along with other important qualifications, such as *computer literate*. Note that you must also record the strength of each trait, on a scale of 1–5, as this will help you gauge the strength of specific actions. For example, CONTROL is noted as *about 2 or 3*, in order that this person, who will be doing a lot of phone work, will have the flexibility to relate to a broad range of people while addressing detailed issues. (The symbols next to each attribute are explained in Step 3.)

Naturally, it is unlikely that you will find someone who will match every item on your list. Additionally, some people will have a unique talent/skill or combination of actions that will compensate for the lack of an action or skill on your list. The advantage of developing this kind of profile, however, is that you start with a clear, unambiguous, and realistic picture of the person you want for your position.

PROJECT COORDINATOR
DESIRED PROFILE—*ACCOUNTANT/MANAGER*

▲ Review on the phone   ■ Review in person   ● Review Faxed Résumé

Ideal Traits
___ ASK—3 or lower with good verbal skills
___ CONTROL—about 2 or 3
___ PREDICTABLE—3 or higher
___ CONFIDENT—3 or higher

Continued Next Page

Communication Actions/Skills

___ ▲ ■ ● Detailed

___ ▲ ■   Easygoing

___ ▲   Excellent phone voice

___ ▲ ■   Likes to work on the phone

___ ▲ ■   Upbeat

___ ▲   Won't mind not having a lot of outside contact w/ others

___ ■   Professional appearance

___ ▲ ■   Inquisitive

___ ■   Discreet

Performance Actions/Skills

___ ▲ ■   Goal-oriented

___ ▲ ■ ● Precise

___ ■   Thrifty

___ ●   Computer literate

___ ●   Typing skills: 60 WPM, three errors per minute

3. Identify When You Can Make Reads—You will note that next to each item is a notation that indicates when you might be able to make a read: on the phone, in person, or reviewing a faxed résumé. Identifying possible opportunities for making reads can be a significant time-saver for you and prospective employees. The notations don't mandate that reads be made only as indicated, rather they are reminders of possible opportunities for making reads. For example, one might be able to make a read of the communication action *detailed* by reviewing how the résumé is constructed.

4. Format Ad So That It Appeals to the Profile You Are Seeking—If you are advertising for your position in a local newspaper, use language that will appeal to the profile of the person you hope to hire. Some examples: if you are looking for an INNOVATOR, use language that is idea driven; if you are looking for a MANAGER, use bottom-line language. Finally, it is recommended that prospects fax or mail you a résumé, which provides an opportunity to review qualifications and make reads.

5. Review Résumé—Two of the desired actions in the sample profile are *detailed* and *precise*. Hunches can be developed about these two actions from the way the résumé itself is constructed, previous work responsibilities, and the degree of success the candidate had in positions which required that one be *detailed* and *precise*. Obviously, one shouldn't rely solely upon a résumé for a read as someone else or a software program may have prepared the résumé or the person intentionally or unintentionally misrepresented themselves. A résumé, however, can provide initial reads that you can test during an interview. For example, if you are looking for an ACCOUNTANT type, but a past work history suggests that a person might be a SALESMAN type, you would want to carefully test your ASK-TELL and CONTROL-EXPRESS reads.

6. Contact by Phone and Make First Read—Since we know that unobtrusive reads are often the best, let's put it to use here. Once you have received the résumé, you can make a confirmation call, confirming that:

1. The résumé was sent by the candidate (sometimes friends will send in résumés and forget to tell their friends).
2. The candidate understands the basic responsibilities of the position and necessary qualifications.
3. The salary range, hours, and so on are in line with what the candidate is seeking (sometimes people don't read carefully).

Use open-ended questions to give candidates the opportunity to respond in a way that will reflect their type. While the candidate perceives this as a facilitation call, often you can make valuable unobtrusive reads, which you can test during your interviews, as well as save valuable time when there is an obvious mismatch. As with each of the suggestions, please consult with your legal counsel to be sure that you are faithfully complying with local, state, and federal laws and guidelines.

7. Select Who Will Do Interviews and Where—When possible, incorporate different environments to create more opportunities to make accurate reads, and involve more than one person in the interviewing process. The collective idea here is to capitalize on those who can make the most accurate reads, while providing more than one environment so that a prospective employee's traits and range can be efficiently identified. One group does this as follows: First, the key players who will conduct the interviews identify which person is the most adept at reading which trait. For example, in an engineering group, Elizabeth might be more adept at reading PREDICTABLE-UNPREDICTABLE, while Chris might be more adept at reading

COMMUNICATION types. For a change of environments, Elizabeth interviews a prospect in her office, but Chris conducts his interview over lunch at a nearby cafe.

Resist Diagonal Accommodation—There is always a possibility that a candidate may not fit your profile, but he may still be able to carry out the responsibilities of the position. For example, you might ideally be seeking a SALESMAN type, but you find a SERGEANT who is low TELL who can do the job. Rarely, however, will you find someone who is the *opposite* of the type that you were seeking who will be able to fill the position, unless you miscast the position. That is, someone whose type is positioned *diagonally* from your target type. An example of *diagonally* positioned types is an ACCOUNTANT and a SALESMAN. When you look at the graphic representation of these types in Chapter 5, they are diagonally positioned from each other. This is because they do not share a common trait.

When hiring, resist making diagonal accommodations, unless both traits are about 1 and a person's range allows him to move to the opposite trait. This is an uncommon individual, so choose carefully and test your reads.

When grooming a present staff member for a future position, it may be possible for someone who is a SALESMAN to learn a couple of the actions of the SERGEANT, because both share a TELL trait. Don't, however, ask or expect someone who is a SALESMAN to adopt more than one action, if any, of an ACCOUNTANT type—its diagonal opposite—because they don't share any common traits.

CROSS-CULTURE PROFILING

Profiling is an indispensable skill when traveling abroad. My observation is from firsthand experience having travelled to over a dozen countries during the last five years.

I've have given presentations to such diverse groups as university students in Belgrade, Serbia, during the middle of a war, law enforcement officers in Switzerland trying to combat gangs, and business leaders in Warsaw, Poland, struggling to develop a sound work ethic.

For books and documentaries, I've interviewed Polish skinhead youths explaining why they hate, mothers in Kiev, Ukraine, telling of transitions in their daily lives brought on by the fall of communism, and I even helped a friend, Monika Brunschwiler, a Swiss police officer, tackle a thief in a public square in a quaint Swiss town right after I gave a crime prevention talk to Swiss business leaders. While Monika manacled the unfortunate fellow, who happened to steam past us with a stolen valise in his clutches, I had to keep the gathering crowd at bay, even though I couldn't speak Swiss German. Snapshot reads came in handy as some of the crowd became hostile. They thought we were mugging the thief as Monika was in plain clothes!

What makes it possible to profile people from cultures that are significantly different from ours is that the core traits of human behavior are consistent cross-culturally. Stripped of our cultural facades, we are all made of the same stuff.

The ability to successfully profile in cross-cultural environments requires that we acknowledge what we have in common with others and identify our differences. The latter involves three important steps.

1. Identify cultural expressions and customs—actions—which might be mistaken for a trait. Preferably, this is done before going abroad by doing some homework.

2. When first entering a culture, allow yourself time to actually observe people in social and professional environments so that you can take in the nuances of the expressions and customs that you identified in Step 1.

3. Make unobtrusive reads whenever possible.

There are two types of cross-cultural environments in which you will use these questions to profile. The first environment is one in which people speak your language, but have a distinct culture. In the second environment you are unable to speak or understand the language. Before reviewing these three steps, let's first consider profiling people in cultures in which your language is spoken. And, let's assume that you are American and your native tongue is English.

In the US, distinctive cultures in which people speak English, but with additional phrases and expressions from their native languages and cultures, include: Cajun, Chinese, Hispanic, Polish, etc. In these communities people speak English, but, because they have a unique cultural/language background, there will be unique turns-of-phrase, pronunciations, and customs that may confuse us.

This can also occur in other English-speaking countries, sometimes with a bit of embarrassment.

When in England giving a speech to a group of professionals, I spoke about a nearby *affluent* community. I pronounced the word, as do many Americans, as *e-fluent*, with the accent on the second syllable. Everyone started chuckling. Later, I was informed that *effluence*, which sounded nearly the same as my American pronunciation of *affluent*, is a word that is used in England to describe that which comes out of a sewer. I was embarrassed. They were entertained.

Strangely, it is in England that I have observed Americans having more communication snafus than in countries in which English isn't the native tongue. People mistakenly and complacently assume that clear dialogue is taking place because English is being spoken. In countries where they don't speak the language, however, they know they must pay close attention, and they usually do.

Therefore, the most important rule when in a unique culture in which English is spoken is: Don't assume that you understand all that is being communicated. It's easy to be lulled into complacency when speaking in or listening to your native tongue. Stay alert and be sure that everyone is tracking with the same level of understanding. Be curious and vigilant. Be curious about unique expressions and pronunciations. Be vigilant in your efforts to thwart miscommunication.

Now let us look at the three important steps that will help you profile in cultures where your language *isn't* commonly spoken.

Step #1—The first step for identifying someone's profile is to identify specific cultural expressions/customs which might be confused for an action which might reveal a trait. Here are two examples:

Japan—A Japanese manager is asked by a salesman: *Would you like to purchase this machinery?* In response, the manager politely bows low at the waist and says, *Yes*. In fact, what he means is: *Yes, I will consider your request*. It is simply a courteous response. To the uninitiated, one might mistakenly believe that this potential Japanese customer is ASK, because of his agreeable style of communicating, when in fact the manager might be strong TELL, who is simply displaying a cultural custom.

Hungary—It is common for many Hungarians to use broad sweeps and slashes of their hands when they communicate. Even those with a strong CONTROL trait often communicate in this manner. It is the cultural facade. To the uninitiated, this might lead one to conclude that most Hungarians are EXPRESS.

Ideally, one should identify cultural expressions and facades which can be confused for traits *before* entering a new culture. Many companies offer training for staff members who travel internationally. Additionally, independent workshops are taught on this subject. Other places to find recommendations for source information are the major international airlines, embassy offices, and the Internet (be careful here as there is also a lot of misinformation).

To help you organize cultural actions/customs which might be misinterpreted for a personality trait, list all the traits on a small note card. You can carry this card in your meeting planner, a passport pouch, or a foreign pocket dictionary. Next to each trait, list the specific cultural actions which might be confused with a trait. As per the Japanese example, you would note that the response to a request could be misinterpreted as ASK. In Hungary you would note that the free use of hands can be confused for EXPRESS or TELL.

When possible, review your list with someone from that culture who is observant and fluently speaks your language. In this way you can sharpen your awareness list. This effort on your part will also be appreciated by your guests as it says that you care about them as individuals.

Let your list serve as a safety check, acting as a reminder to take more than one read and to make your reads with cultural sensitivity.

Finally, identifying cultural expressions that can be confused for traits is different than identifying other kinds of customs, such as whether you should or shouldn't cross your legs when seated or which hand expressions to avoid. In some Arab countries, for example, it is an insult to cross your legs and let the sole of your shoe be seen, while in some Latin American countries making the "A-OK" sign with your thumb and index finger joined in a circle is a severely insulting gesture. These kinds of customs, while important to observe, will not help you identify someone's profile.

Step #2—After having identified some cultural trip wires, spend some time in the culture actually observing people in various types of interactions—both social and professional. Don't just rely on the homework you did before entering the culture. Observe and become familiar with the nuances of each culture's expression.

It is recommended that you allow yourself at least two or three days before attempting to identify profiles. Then, as you observe actions which might be misinterpreted for a trait, record any nuances that you see on your list. Finally, review your refinements with someone from that culture as you did in Step 1 to be sure that your observations are accurate.

Step #3—Unobtrusive reads will often be your window into the heart of a culture, enabling you to read people without your "foreign influence" artificially affecting their actions. The following are some suggestions for when and how to make unobtrusive reads.

Observe response during translation—When using a translator, first identify your translator's profile. This will provide you with a cultural reference point, enabling you to gauge how other profiles are likely to react or respond to him as he translates. Then, after you have spoken a phrase that he must translate, watch how the person to whom your comments are directed reacts during the translation. There is often transparency when this person is listening to your foreign words being translated, especially if he asks your translator to clarify a thought. The reason people are often more transparent than normal is that, out of a courtesy to you, they are trying to insure that the nuances of their thoughts are clearly communicated to you, or that your thoughts are fully understood. (Believe it or not, when giving a speech, you will often find that your delivery in a foreign culture will be better than in the US. Why? First, because you have a chance to think about your next thought during the translation. Second, you are able to read your audience unobtrusively and modify your thoughts during the translation, resulting in a more focused and sensitively delivered presentation.)

Learn how people respond to you—Before entering a culture, consider the context in which you will be interacting with people. If you will be making presentations, consider how people with different profiles in your city or town typically respond to a particular story, proposal, or joke. Surprisingly, you will find that people with similar profiles in another country may respond similarly. This can provide an excellent opportunity for making unobtrusive reads.

Observe people engaged in commerce—Much can be learned by just strolling the streets surrounding an open-air square (often called a platz in Europe), observing people at ticket counters, watching someone discover a parking ticket on a windshield (a source of stress), observing clerks in a bank, or watching people haggle over the prices of goods. Be creative with the time you have and observe people in as many types of situations as possible.

Tone of speech—In cultures in which you can't understand the language, it is possible to make reads based upon the *tone* of someone's speech and the *reaction* others have to someone's dialogue. This is primarily useful when watching others communicate, and not when someone is communicating with you.

A Helpful Exercise—Most television cable companies now have stations that are broadcast from foreign countries, such as Japan and Mexico. Watch one of these stations and try to profile the characters of a weekly show, those interviewed in news broadcasts, game show contestants, and so on. You will be surprised how quickly you will catch on to nuances that will enable you to read traits.

When possible, enlist the help of a colleague or student at a local university who can point out examples of people who might represent the extreme ends of each gauge. It's best if your examples are from television programs you have recorded or video clips you have shot on a previous trip, so that you can easily review them. Reviewing tapes is especially helpful when preparing for a return trip to a culture.

Some Confusing Traits—When you are interacting with someone directly, there are traits which are commonly confused for others. This often occurs when people are listening to you, or to your translator. This is especially pronounced if someone is only partially fluent in your language. One of the reasons that people may temporarily operate outside of their actual traits is that they aren't quite as confident when interacting with you, which can manifest itself as uncertainty and hesitancy. The tendency is to be a bit more courteous and reserved than usual. Together, these two tendencies can create some of the following mistaken reads.

- **TELL misread as ASK**—When people aren't fluent in a language, they often take on a more ASK persona. This occurs because a person is inquiring about what you are communicating. Therefore, people who are TELL can be misread as ASK, or people who are low ASK misread as high ASK.

- **EXPRESS misread as CONTROL**—People tend to tilt toward the CONTROL end of their range when intently trying to process what you are saying. Therefore, people who are EXPRESS can be misread as CONTROL, or people who are low CONTROL misread as high CONTROL.

- **CONFIDENT misread as low FEARFUL**—This is due to the hesitancy that people display when taking longer than customary to process the content of a conversation before responding, making a decision, or taking action. Therefore, people who are CONFIDENT can be misread as FEARFUL, or people who are low FEARFUL misread as high FEARFUL.

The remedy for each of these sources for misreads is to make more than one read and use unobtrusive reads, such as observing how someone interacts with his colleagues or family. Also, the above misreads usually won't apply when people are solely interacting between themselves, because you are not a factor affecting their dialogue.

RANDOM ACTORS: ADDITIONAL OBSERVATIONS

It is my observation that the number of RANDOM ACTORS has increased steadily and in significant numbers in the US and Europe due to 30 years of prolonged social upheaval—high rates of divorce, addiction, etc.

Presently, there are over 30 million youths in the US alone who come from homes in which one or more of the following are present: divorce, separation, physical or sexual abuse, or one of the parents is *severely* dysfunctional, because of alcoholism or other problems. My experience is that the roots of an exaggerated and high FEARFUL trait can often be traced back to these kinds of trauma in a person's youth, similar to most members of youth gangs. When there is a severe rupture in family life, such as divorce or abuse, this often directly impacts the willingness of many youths to trust others. This can then drive those who have a FEARFUL trait further to the extreme, or for those who are CONFIDENT to FEARFUL. And, when a youth already possesses an UNPREDICTABLE trait, another RANDOM ACTOR is produced.

What seems to make the US particularly vulnerable to producing RANDOM ACTORS is the fact that *innovation, free-spiritedness, risk-taking,* and *cre-*

ativity have been some of the finer hallmarks of our country. Actions driven by a national UNPREDICTABLE trait, if you will. A trait that can thrive and be nurtured in a free society. But, when the fabric of the culture is shredded, instead of finding people operating out of *confidence,* more operate with a FEARFUL trait. And, as the deterioration extends over decades, the more extreme the fear. And, the more massive the threat.

This alarming increase of RANDOM ACTORS has manifested itself in diverse arenas such as workplace violence in unlikely work environments and new, unprecedented juvenile gang variants, exemplified by the appearance of leftist youth gangs—youths as young as thirteen-years-old building bombs. Some of these trends are addressed in this section as well as observations that can be helpful when interacting with RANDOM ACTORS in either a professional and personal situation. Consider and apply each observation with caution as what follows, although based upon many years of observations, appeals to a need for more quantitative research.

Dealing with RANDOM ACTORS Based Upon Communication Type—RANDOM ACTORS by nature, when their traits are extreme, are troublesome. Therefore, whatever advantage we can harness we should do so when we must interact with them. One of the most powerful strategies is to operate with a RANDOM ACTOR based upon his COMMUNICATION type. While RANDOM ACTORS may be UNPREDICTABLE, and therefore their actions seemingly random, we can get a bead on how they will operate because of their COMMUNICATION type. Even though they are UNPREDICTABLE, they can even be methodical and detailed because of their COMMUNICATION type.

Here are some examples in which the RANDOM ACTOR's COMMUNICATION type visibly affected their criminal behavior.

- Ted Kaczynski (ACCOUNTANT/RANDOM ACTOR), dubbed the Unabomber, carried out a bombing spree for seventeen years, until his arrest in 1996, during which he sent meticulously constructed letter bombs to numerous people, killing three people and injuring twenty-three. Due to his ACCOUNTANT type, it was predictable that he would most likely use an *indirect* method to carry out an assault—a letter bomb sent in the mail. He also claimed that if his *written* manifesto (an indirect method of communicating) was published that he would stop his activity.

His paper was published in the *New York Times*, but when arrested in his reclusive hideout in Montana, another bomb was found under his bed without an address.

- David Koresh (SALESMAN/RANDOM ACTOR) chose a more "in your face" approach, pointing weapons directly in the face of federal agents and *telling* his followers what to do through perversely constructed and crazed teachings. Koresh, similar to Kaczynski, promised to surrender if his "message" was proclaimed. A TELL person, he chose a tape recording in which he *told* the world his views. Predictably, Koresh the RANDOM ACTOR lied. He refused to come out of his compound after a local radio station broadcast the tape.

- Dr. William Swicegood II (ARTIST/RANDOM ACTOR) seduced a Dallas suburban teen through the use of his sensitive, confiding communication style. The headlines of the *Dallas Morning News* on December 16, 1996, read: *Doctor recalled as loving; others say he was 'deeply troubled.'* Even the headline helped identify his COMMUNICATION type by describing him as "loving," which is often attributed to an ARTIST/RANDOM ACTOR who uses his EXPRESS trait to snare victims.

Many extreme RANDOM ACTORS are either sexually deviant or perversely promiscuous. This is often driven by an extreme FEARFUL trait. They are afraid to enter into a noncontrolling relationship. Thus, it is common, for example, for extreme RANDOM ACTORS to molest children, whom they can control. What is different is the manner in which they will carry out their misdeeds, which will typically be tipped off by their COMMUNICATION type. Dr. Swicegood, for example, used his ASK and EXPRESS traits to quietly get in close to a youth, while Koresh used his TELL trait to convince his followers through his oral teachings that he had a right to "marry" young teens.

By separately identifying the COMMUNICATION type, one can better predict the specific actions of a RANDOM ACTOR. Additionally, in a confrontational environment, by identifying the COMMUNICATION type, one can attempt to operate with this person based upon his *positive* COMMUNICATION actions. For example, if one encounters a "loner," who is probably ASK, one should appeal to positive ASK actions when engaging this person. If, however, the individual displays a "grandiose sense of self-worth" through twisted oral teachings, one might appeal to positive TELL actions.

Addressing a RANDOM ACTOR based upon individually read COMMU-NICATION and PERFORMANCE actions could be a significant step forward in those situations in which a nonbehavioral science expert is forced into interacting with these individuals in a crisis situation.

Numerous experts, including hostage-rescue team (HRT) experts, believe that the ability to uniquely interact with a RANDOM ACTOR, separating communication from performance actions, could also be a valuable tool for trained professionals in crisis environments in which decisions must be made quickly. If one only has to identify four traits to develop a profile, this would shorten the time for tactical response, while increasing the odds for successful resolutions to a crisis. Even experienced professionals can use a simple grid to separate a person's *walk* from his *talk*.

Perpetrators of Workplace Violence—It appears that a majority of those who commit extreme acts of violence in the workplace—such as those who shoot their colleagues—are extreme RANDOM ACTORS (those whose plots points are about 5). Additionally, there seems to be a pattern of where violence committed by a RANDOM ACTOR is most likely to strike. While what follows is still a theory, and should be approached and applied with great caution, a number of experts believe that there is enough substance here so that it should be considered carefully by managers, law enforcement, and others.

Surprisingly, over the past ten years a large number of US postal workers have either seriously assaulted or killed their colleagues. The question is: why the post office and not florist shops or advertising firms? The fact that extreme violence has found its way into what appears to be a sedate environment raises some questions.

Is there something about the postal environment that might act as a triggering device in some people? Why haven't we seen perceivable numbers of UPS workers—those engaged in a similar type of commerce—do the same? What is different about the UPS environment or the UPS worker that might restrain similar acts of violence?

I believe the key triggering component for the postal worker who is a RANDOM ACTOR is the severe predictability of his environment—both colleagues and work responsibilities—when compared to his extreme RANDOM ACTOR profile, which is extreme UNPREDICTABLE.

Here are some clues which I think help solve the mystery.

1. The postal system and its employees, when profiled as a group, are extreme PREDICTABLE, when compared with UPS, which is a private enterprise and not as severely predictable. For example, UPS workers have more direct input in UPS's less bureaucratic environment.

2. The postal system attracts more PREDICTABLE people than other industries, such as education, and it is this trait that acts as the source of agitation for *extreme* RANDOM ACTORS. For example, let us assume that Murray is an *extreme* RANDOM ACTOR. Murray's colleagues, however, are usually at least 3 PREDICTABLE, while he is 5 UNPREDICTABLE. When Murray has a problem—loses his girlfriend, job, wife, or faces major rejection—the extreme predictability of his job *and* that of his colleagues only fuels his anger. In his mind, he can't talk to his colleagues about his woes because he can't relate to them and they can't relate to him. In a deteriorating situation, Murray views his colleagues with a paranoiac "us against them" mentality, fueling his anger. Irrationally, he thinks of his colleagues as an uncaring threat— that they don't care who he is or what goes on in his life. When he goes over the top in his personal life and rage erupts, Murray takes out his anger on those who "never cared about him." His actions cannot be excused, but the PREDICTABLE-UNPREDICTABLE connection should not be minimized.

3. The majority of the perpetrators of the over 400-plus incidents of postal violence during the last several years involved workers who worked "inside" jobs (260), versus those who worked "outside" jobs (150), such as a mail carrier. This variance isn't surprising because the *inside* job is more PREDICTABLE. There are fewer opportunities for change, new interactions, etc. The opportunities for variety, which appeal to someone who is UNPREDICTABLE, are more likely *outside* the shop. A worker's FEARFUL trait is also less likely to be triggered as a carrier, due to fewer opportunities for interactions which can cause stress and confrontations. The outside job is also less confining. A RANDOM ACTOR doesn't have to be reminded daily that his colleagues don't understand or want to listen to or empathize with him.

Consider the following list of individuals who were involved in workplace shootings detailed in Michael Mantell's book, *Ticking Bombs, Defusing Violence in the Workplace* (Irwin 1994). As noted in the US Postal Service example, the majority of those in Mantell's list worked in extremely predictable environments or had jobs that were extremely predictable. There were few on Mantell's list who had jobs or who worked in environments that would allow for more unpredictability/spontaneity, such as a researcher, interior decorator, teacher, and so on which might ease the irritation of a disgruntled RANDOM ACTOR.

- A fired San Diego, California, General Dynamics plant worker.
- A disgruntled supermarket employee.
- Upset female worker at a battery plant.
- An 18-year employee of a print shop, who was put on disability leave for "mental instability."
- A former IBM lab worker.
- A Dallas, Texas, car-rental employee.
- Terminated Woodlawn, Maryland, car mechanic.

Recipe for Violence—The three components that work together to create an environment for these kinds of volatile incidents committed by RANDOM ACTORS are:

1. An extreme RANDOM ACTOR.
2. An extremely PREDICTABLE work environment or job responsibility.
3. Some event in the personal or professional life of the RANDOM ACTOR that triggers rage.

The above three factors should be considered in an organization as follows: *The more PREDICTABLE the environment or work responsibility, the greater the risk that a RANDOM ACTOR might commit a volatile act if confronted with significant personal trauma.*

Practically, this means that one should screen carefully for extreme RANDOM ACTORS, particularly in organizations in which the environment and the specific job responsibilities are high PREDICTABLE. The more predictable your work environment, the closer you should monitor those who are mid to extreme RANDOM ACTORS (about 3 or higher on both gauges). Remember, people can operate within a range. This means that someone who is exposed to a life-changing trauma and who is 3 FEARFUL, can move to 5.

Defusing the Detonator—If one has an employee who is an extreme RANDOM ACTOR in the type of environment noted, the following three suggestions can help prevent explosive, violent behavior.

1. Initiate preventive measures by providing this employee with responsibilities and an environment that incorporate change and variety, accommodating his UNPREDICTABLE actions.

2. Place this person in a group in which there are some people with UNPREDICTABLE traits, to promote a friendly and understanding climate in which this person can relate to others.

3. While there is little one can do that will drive down the narcissistic bent of RANDOM ACTORS, develop a team management approach that promotes individual trust, one of the most important factors that will help drive down the fear or paranoia of a RANDOM ACTOR.

It must be reemphasized that what is presented here is anecdotal, although based upon many observations, and should be considered carefully before applying.

Finally, organizations may be approaching a dilemma that may force a rewriting of existing laws. It goes something like this: 1. Workplace violence is increasing, forcing organizational liability issues. 2. It appears that most acts of extreme workplace violence are committed by RANDOM ACTORS. 3. We also know that past behavior is one of the best predictors of future behavior. Logically, this means that at some point organizations may be pressed to ask questions about an individual's past in order to assess risk factors, such as the presence of extreme RANDOM ACTOR traits. This would require asking questions about a person's past that presently cannot be asked, due to existing laws. I am not advocating that intrusive questions into a person's past be required, but this could happen if social conditions don't reverse themselves, violence increases, and organizational liability issues fuel pressure to rewrite current laws.

The Bunker Response—Hitler, cult leaders Jim Jones and David Koresh, and Dr. Swicegood, the affluent Dallas doctor, were all RANDOM ACTORS and all had something in common. They each committed suicide when cornered. Some even chose to take others with them, as did Hitler, Jones, and Koresh, as noted in the examples that follow.

- Hitler (SERGEANT/RANDOM ACTOR) committed suicide in his bunker with Eva Braun and other Nazi leaders when Berlin was captured by the Soviet army.
- Jim Jones (SERGEANT/RANDOM ACTOR) induced over 900 followers to drink poison-laden fruit drink and commit suicide with him as authorities began to close the net on his compound in Guyana in 1978.
- When David Koresh (SALESMAN/RANDOM ACTOR) and his followers, who had illegally amassed a huge cache of weapons, were surrounded in their compound by federal agents, I was asked by news teams what I thought would happen. My response: the longer the siege, the greater the likelihood for a bloody conclusion. Unfortunately, my prediction came true. Two months later, under Koresh's direction, the compound was torched, killing over eighty men, women, and children.
- Dr. William Roy Swicegood II (ARTIST/RANDOM ACTOR), a Plano, Texas, physician known for weekend stints in jazz and blues religious music concerts, committed suicide the day after charges of sexual misconduct with a teenage patient were brought against him. According to published accounts, he told the young girl he loved her, wanted to marry her, and would commit suicide if she told anyone of his advances. He apparently made good on his word, killing himself in December of 1996.

Regardless of the COMMUNICATION type of an *extreme* RANDOM ACTOR, if you corner them without a way out, the chances of suicide escalate. What I call the *Bunker Response.*

I first encountered this in 1981, when investigating James Hydrick, the Salt Lake City cult-like leader, who was alleged to be a psychic. When police considered arresting him on an assault charge, he threatened to kill himself and anyone else who approached. Hydrick's arms were testament to this mentality, which bore over 50 self-inflicted razor blade slashes from previous confrontations and stints in jail.

The extreme RANDOM ACTOR's unwillingness to trust others and extreme self-absorption can drive other actions to the extreme, such as self-pity, self-concern, selfishness, etc. Any profile can display these actions, but the FEARFUL trait can exaggerate selfish and manipulative actions out of a desire to protect "what I want." When this is carried to the extreme, this means taking everything, including life itself. Regularly, RANDOM ACTORS from child molesters to embezzlers to maniacal leaders of groups attempt sui-cide—sometimes killing others in the process or encouraging others to also take their lives.

What can we learn from this?

If confronting a RANDOM ACTOR whose PERFORMANCE traits are 3 or higher, approach with caution and follow the suggestions in Chapter 8. (Of the two traits, the FEARFUL trait should be monitored the most closely. As already noted, the reason a plot point of 3 is recommended as a cautionary line, is that in some cases when a person is confronted with trauma, the per-son's range can extend a plot point of 3 up to 5.) Find ways to confront, arrest, etc. that do not create a no-way-out situation. This applies to virtually any kind of environment.

Youth Subculture Trend—Another expression of the increase of RANDOM ACTORS in the US is the appearance of new gang variants. I have researched and written extensively on why youths from affluent communities are forming gangs in their neighborhoods for the first time in US and European history. This resulted in my book, *Suburban Gangs—The Affluent Rebels* (International Focus Press, 1994). One gang variant which I predicted in 1994 would appear in the US, and later did in 1995, is what might be labeled a leftist-anarchist gang. If you can imagine the extremist types of protest groups which committed terrorist acts in the 1960s translated into a present day junior high and high school setting, you can get a picture of the type of gang I predicted would appear. Almost every week in the US in 1995 and 1996, somewhere a youth from an affluent community detonated or planted an explosive device, who fit the profile that I developed.

I compiled a predictive behavioral profile as well as a background profile of these youths. The profile was as follows: (1) Bright student (2) At-risk home environment, such as abuse, divorce, and so on (3) Lives in an affluent neighborhood (4) RANDOM ACTOR PERFORMANCE type (5) Any of the COMMUNICATION types.

Additionally, it appears that there is a significant surge in youths who are attracted to this type of gang who are ARTIST or ACCOUNTANT RANDOM ACTORS. Typically, ARTISTS and ACCOUNTANTS avoid confrontations—especially those on the street—due to their ASK trait. Today, however, many of these youths have more mobility and the means to engage in crimes which are indirect in nature, such as computer hacking and planting bombs. This is a troubling trend as many of these youths might be INNOVATORS rather than RANDOM ACTORS, if not for the troubled homes in which they are growing up. If this trend continues, look for more RANDOM ACTORS with ASK traits in the adult population as these and other non-gang youths grow older.

I developed the profile of this new type of gang member with two goals in mind. First, juvenile officers, teachers, and others who work with youths might be able to identify these youths before they commit crimes. Second, if RANDOM ACTOR youths with a leftist bent can be identified before a crime is committed, by an adult who can gain their *trust,* then perhaps some can be dissuaded from committing crimes and acts of terrorism. Presently, this profile has helped law enforcement accomplish the first goal, and hopefully, if the trend persists, accomplish the second goal.

Are Extreme RANDOM ACTORS Sociopaths?—In one profiling workshop, a profiler for the FBI asked me the following question: *Do you think that an extreme RANDOM ACTOR is a sociopath?* The term *sociopath* is often used interchangeably with *psychopath.* Robert D. Hare, one of the foremost experts on psychopathic behavior, explains the confusion over the two terms:

> In many cases the choice of term reflects the user's views on the *origins and determinants* of the clinical syndrome or disorder . . . some clinicians and researchers—as well as most sociologists and criminologists—who believe that the syndrome is forged entirely by social forces and early experiences prefer the term *socio*path, whereas those—including, this writer—who feel that psychological, biological, and genetic factors also contribute to development of the syndrome generally use the term *psycho*path. The same individual therefore could be diagnosed as a sociopath by one expert and as a psychopath by another.[1]

I personally fall somewhere between these two camps, as I believe that social and psychological factors work together to shape this individual coupled with *choices* that this person makes. For the purposes of discussion here, I have opted for the term *sociopath.*

I had never considered the FBI agent's connection between a sociopath and an *extreme* RANDOM ACTOR (those operating at a plot point of 5 on each

PERFORMANCE gauge). There does seem to be some linkage, though, in many cases, and this knowledge might be useful as follows:

If the characteristics of a sociopath are the same or nearly the same then many, if not a majority, of those who are *extreme* RANDOM ACTORS can be identified as a sociopath by just answering two questions: *Is the person extreme UNPREDICTABLE and FEARFUL?* This can be a significant strategic advantage in a fast-developing crisis situation. One wouldn't have to review a checklist of a dozen or more sociopathic indicators to profile someone and determine the best course of action. Only two traits would have to be identified. And considering that there are, conservatively, over 2 million sociopaths in the US,[2] this can be an invaluable tool for a nonbehavioral science expert who must quickly respond to the threats of a sociopath in a crisis. While one would prefer to call a forensic psychologist or a crisis management expert for help in a crisis, this is often not possible, hence the need for a "down and dirty" method to begin to operate in a volatile situation.

To investigate the possibility of the sociopath/RANDOM ACTOR connection, I called my colleague, Dr. Margaret Singer, who is an expert in sociopathic behavior. Years before, Dr. Singer provided me with a layman's definition of a sociopath. She said: "Sociopaths are people who know the difference between right and wrong, but they just don't think it applies to them. It's like being morally insane, although the person is in complete touch with reality. A sociopath is someone with a virtually seared conscience. A supreme manipulator."

To evaluate the answer to the agent's question, we reviewed several quantitative assessment lists associated with sociopathic behavior. One well-accepted list, provided below, was developed by Hare.[3]

1. Glib and superficial
2. Egocentric and grandiose
3. *Lack of remorse or guilt*
4. Lack of empathy
5. *Deceitful and manipulative*
6. Shallow emotions
7. *Impulsive*

8. *Poor behavior controls*
9. *Need for excitement*
10. *Lack of responsibility*
11. *Early behavior problems*
12. *Adult antisocial behavior*

The highlighted actions are those that are either identical (such as *impulsivity* and *irresponsibility*) or very similar to the actions of a RANDOM ACTOR (such as the *need for excitement,* which can be reflective of someone who is UNPREDICTABLE). In effect, these actions are PERFORMANCE actions.

A review of Hare's and other similar lists seems to indicate that many, if not most, *extreme* RANDOM ACTORS might qualify as sociopaths. (As previously noted, if someone has plot points of 3 on both PERFORMANCE gauges, his plot points could extend to 5 in a crisis due to his *range* of actions. Hence, an *extreme* RANDOM ACTOR, although one might not want to type this person as a sociopath as their behavior is not extreme on a daily basis.)

Please note, however, that the other behaviors, such as *glib, egocentric, grandiose,* and *shallow emotions* are more reflective of COMMUNICATION actions associated with TELL, CONTROL, etc. This is important as I have investigated and observed numerous sociopaths who are *not* glib, egocentric, or possessing shallow emotions when they *communicate* (although they don't have emotional empathy for those whom they harm). One individual was an ACCOUNTANT/RANDOM ACTOR who had threatened to bomb abortion clinics. He was not glib, or grandiose, but he certainly operated from a seared conscience, was impulsive, deceitful, and so on.

Presently, it is assumed, and perhaps rightfully so, that most sociopaths possess communications actions such as *glib* and *lack of empathy.* I believe that this perception may change in the future, however, as more RANDOM ACTORS with ASK traits become more common—something that I have observed in the youth subculture in the US and Europe. This is not a good trend as criminals who are RANDOM ACTORS with ASK traits are often more difficult to investigate and apprehend as they prefer to be *indirect* in their assaults, such as sending letter bombs, and more covert in how they operate. They don't leave open, visible trails, thus frustrating investigators.

Of the different types that the Korem Profiling System identifies, the RANDOM ACTOR is the one type that will be of continued personal interest and research for a number of years. As noted at the beginning of this section, what I have presented here is based upon personal observations over a period of fifteen years, but it has not been quantified, although it has been thoughtfully reviewed by a number of behavioral science experts. Hopefully, quantifiable research might be done in the future. Until then, the reader is urged to apply this information with the utmost caution.

CHAPTER 14

Accurate Reads and Clue Sources

Now that you have been profiling for a number of weeks, you are ready for this final lesson—refining *where* to focus your reads so you can increase your profiling speed and accuracy. You have learned how to plot people on the gauges by observing their actions and comparing their personas to those at the extreme ends of each gauge. Now you will be introduced to the five categories for observing clues which will help you increase your accuracy as well as speed when profiling. How? By knowing where to look for clues. At the end of the chapter is a checklist that will remind you of the components for making accurate reads.

ORGANIZING CLUES

In grade school science classes, teachers use a recall game in which a cloth-covered tray of objects is brought out. When the cloth is removed, everyone looks closely at the objects on the tray for 30 seconds, trying to remember as many as possible. Then the teacher replaces the cover, and the students list all the items they can recall seeing on the tray.

Usually there are one or two people in the class who can list everything accurately, while the rest wonder how one person can absorb so much information in such a short period of time.

How do they learn to make such quick and thorough observations?

The answer is that they are able to see patterns or "common elements" in the items on the tray or in the arrangement of items that allow them to focus their memory on a smaller set of facts. For example, they may "see" that the tray is arranged in four sections or corners and then memorize the key items in each corner. Or they may make quick associations between certain objects on the tray. In either case, they see similarities or find common features that allow them to remember several items by remembering only one or two common characteristics. Using this strategy, they don't have to remember each and every item. They simply let one item or relationship trigger their recall of another item.

The same principle of "seeing patterns" applies to profiling and making accurate reads. The best profilers are people who can quickly see patterns in another person's actions. This is one of the reasons why the Korem Profiling System was constructed using just four gauges. You can quickly organize the actions that you see in others by simply answering four questions, which will then reveal a profile.

In this chapter we will look at five categories of clue sources that will help you organize *where* to focus your reads so that you can reduce the time necessary to profile someone. These categories will help you quickly remember *where* to look in order to identify a *specific* trait. When in a critical meeting, working on a deadline, or in a confrontation, this knowledge is invaluable. Some additional suggestions for making accurate reads is also provided at the end of the chapter.

CLUE SOURCES

As stated in Chapter 2, we profile people based upon our reads of *actions*, which can range from speech to a memo to past actions. Expanding the idea of reading specific actions, we will break down the *sources* for making our observations into five categories which can quickly point you toward a specific trait. These categories are:

- Attire and grooming
- Speech
- Actions
- Nonverbal actions and reactions
- Background information

(Attire and grooming are regarded as *actions* because people *choose* what they will wear in most situations.)

The purpose of this section is not to add to the flood of "helpful hints," common sense, and even some nonsense found in the popular and business press about how to interpret the hidden meaning of people's actions, "body language," attire, conversation, etc. The idea here is to help you better identify common patterns that often reveal traits, reinforcing the first part of Rule #1 that promotes systematic accuracy: *People typically act in consistent, similar ways called traits.*

For example, if you must identify someone's ASK trait, you will learn which clue categories are most likely to reveal an ASK action.

The emphasis will be on observations that come more naturally, so you won't have to worry about looking for an obscure set of clues. Insights for each observation/clue category will include:

- The usefulness of the category.
- How traits relate to the category, including the traits each category is most likely to reveal.
- Common relationships between observed expressions of specific actions and the trait(s) often revealed. (Example: People who forcefully use their hands when they communicate are often TELL and/or EXPRESS.)

Before beginning, it must be reemphasized that none of the relationships between specific clue sources and traits will apply in every situation. The relationships are only *suggested* possibilities. Resist stereotyping, such as assuming that people who wear loud ties are always EXPRESS. Someone may wear a loud tie, which he doesn't like, because it was given to him by his daughter and he doesn't want to offend her.

Remember and practice Rule #3 that promotes systematic accuracy: *Anything that is worth measuring is worth measuring at least twice.* Be sure to test your reads. Resist simply looking for additional clues that will confirm your first hunch.

Lastly, the guidance and suggestions in this section are designed to promote understanding of how observations can help identify specific traits. The lists of observation-trait relationships are not intended to represent the full scope of possibilities; this would require another complete text. Rather, they are intended to promote insight into which clue source categories are more likely to help you identify specific traits when using the Korem Profiling System.

ATTIRE AND GROOMING

Attire and grooming (appearance) can be a good source of reads for identifying the following two traits:

- CONTROL-EXPRESS
- PREDICTABLE-UNPREDICTABLE

When making reads in this category, be certain that you are familiar with the culture in which you are operating. In some cultures, for example, bright colors are indicators of EXPRESS, while in others, bright colors are normative, and not necessarily related to a trait. Alternately, in Paris, a majority of the population currently wear black, which in the US is often associated with adults who are CONTROL. In Paris, however, it is a cultural fashion.

In some situations it may be helpful to read attire and grooming separately. For example, Judith, who is UNPREDICTABLE, may have to wear conservative attire because of the conformity requirements of her professional environment. Judith may choose to exhibit her individuality, however, through her grooming, such as subtleties in makeup or hairstyle.

Controlled v. Individual Appearance—Appearance is one of the easiest observations to make. Controlled attire and grooming often indicate CONTROL and/or PREDICTABLE, while those who adopt an individualistic persona are often EXPRESS and/or UNPREDICTABLE.

But be careful.

Volumes have been written about how to alter attire and grooming to convey an impression.

Identifying targeted impressions, however, can be useful because it can tell us something about who a person is trying to impress. A simple example is when an ARTIST, who is normally casually attired in pastels or black, puts on a pin-striped suit to make a favorable and PREDICTABLE impression for a banker.

To avoid stereotyping or being fooled by an altered appearance, make reads from the other categories as a cross-check and test your reads.

Corporate Uniform—When someone wears a corporate "uniform" (any standard business attire for a specific type of work), there is a tendency to assume that this person is PREDICTABLE. This may or may not be true. The continuity of attire and grooming dress may be a requirement, thus sending a false clue. For example, some advertising executives, who are

UNPREDICTABLE, wear attire that presents a more PREDICTABLE facade when meeting with clients.

Elements of individuality added to one's attire and grooming, however, can reveal traits, such as ties, jewelry, scarves, interpretations of the "uniform," hairstyle, condition of nails. They can be the subtle or not-so-subtle layer that reveals culturally suppressed traits.

Specific Action-Trait Relationships—For each clue category, a list is provided of *specific* actions that can reveal a trait. For example, someone who is FEARFUL might display the action of being *insecure*. Insecurity, however, can be displayed in many ways. As noted in the list below, a person who is FEARFUL might display his insecurity through the *specific* action of poor grooming, which can be reflective of a poor self-image.

The purpose of each list is to give you an idea of some of the ways that a *specific* action can be expressed that can reveal a specific trait. The following list details common relationships between observable attire/grooming choices people make and the traits those specific actions can illuminate.

Poor Grooming
- FEARFUL or low CONFIDENT—reflective of a diminished self-image.
- ASK—nonassertive, not concerned with one's representation to others.

Meticulous Grooming
- CONTROL—every hair must be in place.
- FEARFUL—afraid if things not in their place.

Individualized Attire
- Low CONFIDENT—desire to be noticed.
- High TELL—desire to make a statement.

Nonindividualized Attire
- PREDICTABLE—desires uniformity.
- CONTROL—prefers not to express oneself visually.
- FEARFUL—especially for CONFORMIST type.

SPEECH

Speech, which includes content, voice quality, and tone, can be a source of reads for any of the four traits, but they can be especially helpful for identifying the following three traits:
- ASK-TELL
- CONTROL-EXPRESS

- CONFIDENT-FEARFUL

In many situations speech will obviously help you read a person's COM-MUNICATION type. (Physical actions, as noted later, are usually more helpful when identifying PERFORMANCE traits.) When listening to a person's speech to develop hunches, we are specifically listening for:

- Patterns and content of speech
- Voice quality and tone

Patterns and Content of Speech—Listening to people dialogue can be one of the most *unobtrusive* ways to make reads. By being a "fly on the wall" and just listening, much can be learned about someone. (This also applies if one is able to review audiotaped or videotaped footage of a person.)

One way to read speech patterns and content is to listen to what is said *over time* and identify patterns of consistency or breaks in consistencies—leakage (discussed in Chapter 6). Consistencies and breaks in consistency can indicate expressiveness, interpersonal control, and confidence. For example, a stiff or monotonous speech pattern can indicate higher predictability or CONTROL, while an erratic or constantly changing pattern can indicate higher UNPREDICTABLE, EXPRESS, or a person who is FEARFUL.

Additionally, different types break their speech pattern in different ways when confronted with stress. As noted in Chapter 6, under pressure, people typically rely upon their actual traits. This can result in an exaggeration effect as they move to the extreme end of their range, enabling you to make an accurate read. For example, people who are TELL, typically "tell" or use their verbal trait even more, moving to the high end of their range, while those who are ASK tend to become more quiet and reserved. The same is true for the three other traits. Those who are EXPRESS, for example, may become more expressive, and so forth.

Finally, open-ended questions and comments, as noted in Chapter 6, is an effective method for allowing people to communicate in a way that more naturally reveals their traits, as it is nonrestrictive.

Voice Quality and Tone—The basic quality of a person's voice has little to do with personality, except when that quality may be artificial or affected. The *consistency* of the voice quality when *compared* with other reads, however, can help reveal a trait. The key question is: Does the voice quality match the situation, the words being used, or any of your other reads?

If there is a match, your read might be confirmed.

If there isn't a match, you test your reads.

For example, let's assume that you are EXPRESS. You meet with Terry, who in the past appeared to be CONTROL. She has a proposal for a new project. In your present meeting, Terry's voice quality and tone seem to be artificially EXPRESS.

In this situation there isn't a match between what you are presently observing and what you observed in the past, so test your read. Perhaps she intuitively knows that you express your emotions, and she is trying to enhance rapport. What is important is that you don't let her well-intentioned effort confuse you when profiling. Take another read.

The more "uncontrolled" aspects of a person's voice, such as tone, are also a good source of reads. Breaks in pattern, and changes in loudness, hoarseness, or vibrato can all be indicators of a person's current state.

Specific Action-Trait Relationships—The following are common relationships between observable speech content, voice quality, and tone and the traits which may be revealed. (The first two categories specify that *both* content and tone or tone *and* language be present simultaneously to achieve a more affirmative read of the traits suggested.)

Reserved Speech Content *and* Tone

- ASK—prefers to be in the background.
- CONTROL—indicates lack of expressiveness.
- PREDICTABLE—desires uniformity, resists change.
- CONFIDENT—doesn't feel he has to make his point with words.
- FEARFUL—doesn't say much because of fear.

Inquiring Tone *and* Language

- ASK—indirect approach preferred when seeking a response.
- FEARFUL—questions used to avert making decisions or taking action.

Forceful

- TELL—desires to be directive using language, set of the jaw, etc.
- EXPRESS—can aid TELL person's ability to sell an idea.
- CONFIDENT—reveals commitment to carrying out an agenda.

Monotone

- CONTROL—lack of expressiveness.
- PREDICTABLE—resistant to change.
- ASK—desire to be indirect, not noticed.
- FEARFUL—afraid to reveal oneself.

Effusive

- TELL—prefers to drive across one's point.
- EXPRESS—expressive nature is a part of how he communicates.

Reminder—Each observation-trait relationship list is intended to provide insight into common associations between observable actions and traits that might be revealed. Not every category should be relied upon to reveal each of the four traits. For example, under "Effusive," PREDICTABLE and UNPREDICTABLE are not suggested because a person who is effusive can possess either trait. The traits noted are those for which there is a greater possibility of connecting a specifically observed action with a trait.

ACTIONS

Beginning in Chapter 3, you learned how to plot people on the four gauges by observing actions. In this clue category, we are looking for *physically observable actions*. Some examples:

- Patricia confidently moving forward on a high-risk project.
- Marvin working to create a predictable environment.
- Richard's rebellious attitude.
- Jacqueline stubbornly not yielding ground during negotiations.

We are not looking at a person's speech. That is another category. Nor are we looking at how a person uses his hands when he communicates. That, too, is another category.

In the "Actions" category we are looking for *observable* actions that will reveal PERFORMANCE traits—the *walk*. As noted in Chapter 13, observing how a person handles *situations* or tasks can reveal PERFORMANCE traits. In most situations, the kind of actions in the examples above will reveal these traits. The manner or *flair* in which an action is performed and how someone handles people can reveal COMMUNICATION traits—the *talk*. Most actions you will observe in this category, however, will point to PERFORMANCE traits.

Therefore, actions in this category can help identify any of the four traits, but the order of usefulness is as follows:

- PREDICTABLE-UNPREDICTABLE
- CONFIDENT-FEARFUL
- CONTROL-EXPRESS
- ASK-TELL

Suggestions for Observing Actions—When observing actions, such as someone making and carrying out a decision, remember to apply the two ideas that were addressed in Chapter 6:

- *Look for clear consistencies or sharp breaks from consistency (leakage).*
- *Unobtrusive observations are usually the most reliable.*

For example, expanding on the military example in Chapter 10, let's say we are trying to profile a private in the army. Privates are taught to consistently appear CONFIDENT, follow orders (be PREDICTABLE), not give orders (ASK), and CONTROL emotions. If one only observed a private during a heavily supervised drill, it's unlikely that we'd obtain many reliable reads when looking at his pattern of actions. However, if someone angered the private (an infusion of stress), we might see a break in the pattern and get insight into one of his traits. Or, if we unobtrusively observed the private off duty with other soldiers, we would be more likely to make accurate reads.

As previously suggested, be sure to do your homework about cultural variations so that you don't misinterpret what you read, regardless if the culture is in a foreign country or an unfamiliar local professional environment.

Always continue to make observations and learn to interpret what you find. You can never make enough reads of someone's actions. Ask yourself: Is what I am observing consistent with the situation at hand? For example, if a company is booming, yet a particular employee's actions reveal that he is afraid to make a decision—even when a safety net is in place—then it's a safe bet that this person makes decisions out of fear.

Another suggestion is to make observations whenever possible of *unguarded* or *unplanned* actions, such as a person's reaction to unanticipated events, questions, or circumstances. These *reactions* typically provide reliable reads about emotional control and predictability. For example, if a person has an animated out-of-the box reaction, we can test hunches that the person is EXPRESS and UNPREDICTABLE. Alternately, a subdued response should lead us to test hunches about CONTROL and PREDICTABLE.

Perhaps you are thinking: *But I am not skilled when it comes to interpreting people's actions.* Don't panic.

Remember, your first job is simply to plot someone on each gauge between the two *extremes* of each gauge. As you have already experienced in the previous assignments, by taking more than one observation you can plot most people. If, however, you find that you are consistently off when interpreting people's actions, get some help. Take someone along with you to help you interpret or review what you have seen. Also, do some homework. Research a person's background (a category we will address shortly). Obtain information about the cultural idiosyncrasies. By following these suggestions, even those who initially struggle to accurately profile others, with practice, will begin to significantly improve their skills.

Specific Action-Trait Relationships—The following list of relationships is short, focusing on PERFORMANCE traits, because observable physical actions are usually the most helpful when identifying these traits.

Decisive When Taking Action
- CONFIDENT—decision to take action based in confidence.

Wavers When Taking Action
- FEARFUL or low CONFIDENT—lacks sufficient confidence to take action.

Resistant to Change
- PREDICTABLE—prefers predictability, uniformity.
- FEARFUL—afraid of unknown.

Welcomes Change
- UNPREDICTABLE—comfortable with ambiguity.
- CONFIDENT—although some people may be PREDICTABLE, their CONFIDENT trait enables them to move past their desire for predictability when a specific opportunity is presented or change is needed.

NONVERBAL ACTIONS AND REACTIONS

The popular term for nonverbal actions and reactions is "body language." Nonverbal actions and reactions, or *nonverbals* as they will be collectively referenced, are a moderately good source for identifying the following three COMMUNICATION traits:
- ASK-TELL
- CONTROL-EXPRESS
- CONFIDENT-FEARFUL

As already noted, speech can be helpful for identifying COMMUNICATION traits, while actions are more helpful for identifying PERFORMANCE traits. Nonverbals are like "silent" speech, which is why they are more helpful for identifying COMMUNICATION traits. However, because nonverbal reactions are tied to a person's actions, they can also be of some help, though more limited, when identifying PERFORMANCE traits. The difference between a nonverbal action and a nonverbal reaction is that the former is an action that is *not* prompted by some external influence.

For example, some people who are TELL or EXPRESS will point their finger or wave their hand like a baton when communicating. These nonverbal actions can be an extension of one of their traits which they will present regardless of whether or not an external pressure or influence is present. Or, they can be driven by a cultural custom, such as the Hungarian example in Chapter 13.

Nonverbal *reactions*, however, are actions that appear because someone is reacting to a situation—an external influence. This includes a reaction to a question or statement, a response from an audience during a presentation, a response to a pleasant or stressful situation, and so on.

For example, a person with a strong TELL might use a hard gaze in response to being affronted. Or a grandmother, who is EXPRESS, might display an open, expressive smile that extends to her eyes and forehead when she is asked to retell the moment her granddaughter was honored during a graduation ceremony.

This means that nonverbal *reactions* are more likely to reveal a trait than nonverbal *actions* because *reactions* are a response to some kind of positive or negative influence or pressure. Thus, when looking for and evaluating nonverbal, focus on nonverbal *reactions*.

Some typical sources to make reads of both types of nonverbals are: eye contact, facial expression, use of hands when talking, and body movements and posture.

Questions that can be helpful when observing nonverbals are:

- Is the nonverbal action or reaction consistent with the situation?
- What are the person's nonverbal patterns and consistencies?
- When do breaks occur in the nonverbal patterns?

Specific Action-Trait Relationships—The following will list common nonverbals and the traits they can reveal. As already suggested, compare your reads with those from the other categories.

Forceful Use of Hands

- TELL—used to drive home one's position.
- EXPRESS—extension of expressiveness.

Retreating Use of Hands (Example: If Henry is asked, "Did you do this?" a retreating action would be Henry bringing his open-palmed hand against his chest, as he responds, "You mean me?")

- ASK—a nonassertive response.
- FEARFUL—an insecure reaction to being asked a question.

Hard Gaze (More than just staring back.)

- TELL—used to increase forcefulness.
- CONFIDENT—unwilling to move on a position.

Empathetic Expression (Example: When the inside of the eyebrows move upward, causing the eyebrows to form an upside-down "V." This involuntary action usually indicates sadness—only about 10% of the population can do this at will.)

- EXPRESS—expressively relating to someone or a situation.
- ASK—an agreeable-curious response.

Stiff Posture (Be careful that someone doesn't just have back problems!)

- TELL—means of being forceful, directive.
- CONTROL—an expression of emotional control.
- PREDICTABLE—not as common, but can indicate need for predictability.

Casual, Open Posture

- EXPRESS—venue for displaying expressiveness.
- ASK—can indicate desire to be indirect, laid back.
- UNPREDICTABLE—not confined to convention.

BACKGROUND INFORMATION

Background information—past actions—is a compilation of the four previous clue categories, which means that any of the four traits can be revealed. The only difference is that the actions occurred in the *past*.

As noted in Chapter 6, developing background information about someone will increase the accuracy of our reads because past behavior is the best predictor of future behavior. The exception to this principle is when a person is undergoing some kind of significant, life-changing event or experience. Because large portions of the population in the US and other countries are experiencing these kinds of events, it is wise to inquire if a person's past actions were due to a life-changing event. Additionally, it can be helpful to identify if *present* actions are being influenced by a life-altering situation.

Sources for Information—Developing background information is also one of the best ways to make reliable unobtrusive reads. For professional relationships, this information can be collected from present and past:

- Professional associates—Employers, employees, persons with whom the individual has done business
- Friends and acquaintances
- Adversaries
- Media—professional journals, electronic and print news accounts, etc.
- Résumés, memos, correspondence, etc.

While it might seem difficult to develop reads from media accounts, memos, and so on, consider these three examples that clearly reveal the traits of both individuals and a group.

- In the aftermath of an on-line computer service's access going down in the early days of on-line services, during which its members could not access it, a news report quoted one source as follows: "Many subscribers are pioneers. . . . These are the kind of people who are more accepting of growing pains."[1] The source noted that the subscribers would be understanding with the temporary halt in service. Describing many subscribers as *pioneers* and *accepting of growing pains*, clearly points to those who are more likely UNPREDICTABLE, a common trait for many on-line computer users in the early days of this kind of service.

- When Bill Moyers, noted American journalist and former press secretary to President Lyndon B. Johnson in the 1960s, was interviewed for a light background piece, he made several remarks which revealed his ASK trait. First, in 1965, at the age of 31, he was featured on the cover of *Time* and *Newsweek* magazines for his intellectual wizardry. Here is his remark about this high-visibility coverage: "This is the truth. I didn't want to go on the covers. LBJ wanted me to go on the covers. It didn't go to my head. I had a contrary response to it, and regretted the visibility I was gaining. It limited my capacity to do good work for him."[2] When Moyers was asked to identify his "trademark expression" when responding to others with whom he was conversing, he replied, "Is that right?" A characteristic, open-ended response by an ASK person who is conducting an interview.

- Unabomber Ted Kaczynski, referenced in Chapter 13, while living like a misfit hermit in Montana, wrote a series of letters to his family over a period of several years prior to his arrest. Kaczynski's brother, David, said this about his brother that clearly illuminates his ACCOUNTANT/RANDOM

ACTOR profile: "Through the years, the letters have shown sudden and unpredictable mood swings [UNPREDICTABLE], a preoccupation with disease, extreme phobias [FEARFUL], compulsive thinking and an inability to let go of minutiae [ACCOUNTANT type absorbed with details].[3]

- This is an excerpt from an American missionary's letter to supporters who sent him on a missions trip to a small town in Russia. Note the clearly EXPRESS tone: "Well, I made it back alive. Not only alive, but changed from the inside out!!! I have so many stories to share that glorify God, but before I share them, I will explode if I don't first thank you (*spaceeba*, in Russian). I thank you from the bottom of my heart for your exceeding generosity."

A fun and stimulating exercise is to read a number of articles and practice identifying traits. Not every read will, of course, be accurate, due to the bias of a reporter, the accuracy of the report, or the image someone is trying to project to the media. But articles and correspondence can provide a starting point for identifying traits or for confirming reads from other clue sources.

When you must be discreet and avoid any possibility of direct contact with the person you are profiling, consider having someone else gather information, such as a colleague or trusted friend. Being discreet will not only aid your reads, but it also protects the person whom you are reading from needlessly feeling threatened. In a professional context, profiling someone before direct interaction, as described in Chapter 13, can enhance effective communication and interaction. For those who have investigative/security responsibilities, it is the backbone of the job.

A Strategy for Gathering Background Information—The following is a simple and direct strategy for developing background information that can reveal someone's profile:

1. Prioritize which trait(s) or type(s) is the most important to identify.
2. Identify the likely places where you can obtain reads of each trait.
   - To identify PERFORMANCE type, concentrate on how someone handles *tasks.*
   - To identify COMMUNICATION type, concentrate on how someone handles *people.*
   - Example: To identify PERFORMANCE traits, you will need sources that can shed light on a person's predictability and how someone follows through on decisions. Ideally, this means getting input from people

who have worked with or observed this person. Social contacts, however, might be a better source in some instances to identify COMMU-NICATION traits.

3. Organize your file of information so that it is broken down by traits.

4. Remember that you are getting filtered information. Friends and adversaries will each have their own spin, which may or may not be an accurate read. Always get more than one opinion. Test your reads.

5. Look for patterns that emerge from people who are supportive of the person you are profiling and from those who may have had confrontations with this person.

6. Inquire about actions and reactions in stressful situations.

Short List of Common Relationships between Clue Categories and Traits—A long list of common action-trait relationships is not included for the background category because background information can reveal any of the traits covered in the previous categories. Thus, the action-trait relationships are the same. Instead, the following list points out the clue categories that are more likely to reveal a trait when you are reviewing *past history*. For example, if you must identify PREDICTABLE-UNPREDICTABLE, consider looking at attire and grooming and actions that reveal how someone handled past situations.

ASK-TELL

- Speech
- Nonverbals
- Actions (not as likely to be helpful)

CONTROL-EXPRESS

- Attire and grooming
- Speech
- Nonverbals
- Actions (only moderately helpful)

PREDICTABLE-UNPREDICTABLE

- Actions
- Attire and grooming

CONFIDENT-FEARFUL

- Actions
- Speech
- Nonverbals (only moderately helpful)

CHECKLIST FOR ACCURATE PROFILING

The following is a summary checklist to help you remember the key ingredients for accurate profiling. The chapters in which each concept was covered have been included for easy reference.

- Read people by comparing them to the examples at the extreme ends of each gauge (Chapter 3).
- Take more than one read and test reads (Chapter 2).
- Make unobtrusive reads (Chapter 6).
- Make opposite assumptions and test reads (Chapter 6).
- Consider someone's range (Chapters 3 and 10).
- Past behavior is the best predictor of future behavior (Chapter 6).
- Under pressure, actual traits are usually revealed (Chapter 6).
- Review COMPREHENSIVE PROFILE to see if it matches the cumulative effect of your reads (Chapter 11).
- Consider cross-cultural idiosyncrasies (Chapter 13).
- Consider suppression of traits by culture or choice (Chapter 10).
- Consider if someone has learned a specific action (Chapter 10).
- Consider if you have confused one trait for another (Chapter 10).
- When you need to identify COMMUNICATION traits, observe how a person handles people (Chapter 13).
- When you need to identify PERFORMANCE traits, observe how a person handles situations and tasks (Chapter 13).

CHAPTER 15

The Long Haul

You've finished the first pass. Now what are you going to do?

Are you going to retire to a distant corner in a room, watching and cataloging every action you see in others? Looking for a silent, covert edge.

Are you going to continue to read people as you have in the past, but with a couple of added insights under your belt?

Or have you made a commitment to read people with wise and clear eyes, seizing opportunities to use the philosophy promoted in this book? *I know who you are. Good for me, better for you.*

They were frightened, but vicious. Even more frightened than their hostages.

Talladega prison. Alabama. The summer of 1991.

The prison population had taken over everything but their own fears, which jackknifed in the minds of angry inmates.

Clint, what did you do before you went in?

Clint Van Zandt was one of the original members of the FBI's esteemed Behavioral Sciences Unit. One of the world's foremost profilers, he developed and confirmed the profile of the "Unabomber," Ted Kaczynski in 1996.

In 1985, as the FBI's chief hostage negotiator, Clint led negotiations for four-and-a-half days and nights when a militaristic group of families, who called themselves The Covenant, the Sword, and the Arm of the Lord, threatened violent action from their compound in Arkansas.

Clint brilliantly suggested that the men come out first "so that you can see that your women and children are treated with respect." Clint didn't want to risk the men changing their mind after their families were safe and then hunkering down for a firefight.

You always look for closure after this kind of incident. Something to help put the hammer of stress behind you.

Everyone came out. No one was hurt. But Clint never found closure.

As the special agents were looking for holdouts in the compound, Clint offered his hand to a young, ten-year-old boy in fatigues. The boy swatted away Clint's warm handshake, and glared, "We could have beaten you. We could have killed you. If Jim Ellison [the leader] hadn't heard from the Lord, you'd be dead. I'll get you when I'm older."

Looking at the youngster, he thought, "I've seen the face of the future. Here is the next generation. And he has already learned to beat, kill, and hate the government."

Clint was also in Waco, Texas, in 1993 when Koresh followers torched their compound and eighty men, women, and children perished in the blaze. There was nothing that Clint or his colleagues could have done that would have altered the outcome. Another law enforcement agency made the regrettable mistake of assaulting Koresh's compound while he was with his group. Clint and his group simply tangled with an inevitable outcome plotted in Koresh's twisted mind.

As a hostage negotiator, Clint had experienced liberating victory and life-ending defeat.

I met Clint during the fall of 1993 when I was invited by his unit to lecture for two days at the FBI National Academy. We spent half a day together. I dubbed Clint and his colleagues "the boys of the bunker." I told Jana Monroe, the lone female profiler in the unit, about the nickname. She good-naturedly smiled and said, "Yea. That's about right."

When the first FBI director, Edgar J. Hoover, built the FBI National Academy on the county-sized grounds of the Marine base in Quantico, Virginia, he wanted his brightest to be able to survive a nuclear attack. So he encased the two basement floors of the Academy in steel. There are no windows. Office walls are painted cinder blocks. The offices of Clint's unit were ten feet further underground than people are buried.

I'll never forget Special Agent Al Brantley showing me pictures of a logger who used a chainsaw to take his own life. The case set off a panic in Washington State. As I looked at the photos of the nearly decapitated man lying next to a pickup, I kept thinking, They deal with all this and they don't even get a window!

It was from this sparse command post that Clint and the rest of his colleagues operated.

At Talladega Prison there were eleven hostages. Ten days deep into the siege, they just wanted a chance to go home.

Clint wanted the same. So he met the inmates face to face. No flak jacket. No concealed weapon. Just a refined understanding of people and how they respond under pressure. Some colleagues thought it was too risky—foolish to go in without at least minimal protection.

"Look, these guys are armed with swords and knives. They're afraid. I have to face them equally stripped down to show them that I am not afraid."

So Clint, what did you do before you went in?

I asked the question hoping to get a nugget of insight. Hostage negotiators don't write textbooks. They can't. Information is typically shared in closed-door conferences and in cubicles.

"I prayed," was his simple reply.

We looked at each other and both nodded.

That is what you do when you get ready to apply your knowledge for the benefit of others in an extreme situation—labeled a critical incident by those in law enforcement. Nothing cavalier. You acknowledge that you can't control all situations, predict everyone's behavior, or that you have all of the needed insight.

People are precious. So you study. You observe. You share ideas. You care. And, you pray.

The best profilers are people who care about others when it's really important. Their eyes are clear. Motives are others driven.

When it comes to profiling, there are two kinds of selfish people.

There are people who don't care enough about those around them to take the time to develop their skills—even when given the opportunity. They don't care about seeing who is really in front of them. They make snap judgments and stick with them. Their "I" dominates—the treacherous vertical pronoun. A little extra heart-driven effort for them is only for the "weak."

The second group only become profilers for personal gain. Cynical eyes and cloaked hearts are their badge of honor, caring only about capturing their own edge. Beloved is not a description that people use to characterize the meat of their lives. They watch you, but never give anything away. Their demise is usually a shallow, lingering dance. Their partner is a shadow of their own expectations.

I hope you, however, choose to develop your profiling skills for the benefit of others—both those you like and dislike. But no one can do it for you. Not your colleagues, your boss, or your friends. Not even a cherished mate or relative. It is an act of your will. A choice.

Forty years ago, people generally had a better sense of who they were in relationship to everyone else. Families were more stable. For most of us there was at least one person who helped instill in us our internal and external bearings. That's changed. It's almost like we are starting all over again—rediscovering who we are and how we are put together. Durable homespun wisdom is now uncommon. We can no longer draw upon the resident memories that previous generations have been able to draw from.

Recently, my sixteen-year-old son, Erik, was selected by his classmates to be a "peer helper" at his high school of over 1,500 students. The twenty-five peer helpers, who are carefully interviewed and screened by counselors, offer an alternative for troubled youths who want help. They can go to a responsible peer for guidance. And the training for the peer helpers is rigorous, combining students from four high schools at a weekend retreat.

During one exercise, Erik and his new friends experienced what it is like to be stereotyped. For the demonstration, Erik and four other students were selected from the one hundred trainees and given a headband to wear. On the headband was a label and a command. Erik nor his four colleagues were allowed to look at what was printed on their own headbands.

For the next fifteen minutes, the five teens treated one another as per the label and command on their headbands. Their ninety-plus peers observed the five youths interact. Then the five students sat down in chairs in front of the rest of the group. They were asked to guess what was written on their head-bands.

Erik said, "I think my label is *Nerd* and the command is *Make fun of me.*" In fact, Erik quoted the label and command verbatim. He didn't even miss a word. His peers were amazed and they cheered at his insight. But the cheering was short-lived.

The counselor pointed out how Erik, a six-foot-two, two-hundred-and-thirty-five-pound football player, appeared confident before the exercise. His body was erect. His head and gaze were steady. As he was derided, however, he changed. When Erik was asked to take a seat in his chair, he was slightly slumped forward. The ever-present smile gone from his face.

When asked how he knew what was on his headband, he said, "When I was ten, I was overweight and kids made fun of me. I hadn't grown yet. It did-n't take much to remember how people used to treat me."

No one likes to be treated based upon callously applied labels. Shallow stereotyping.

Erik was fortunate. He grew and the derision faded. But what about other people we know on whom someone has placed a label that we insensitively read and react to? People whom we don't take the time to profile and treat them based upon who they really are.

In the future, I hope that profiling becomes a part of course curriculums to equip all young people and university students, not just peer helpers.

As your skills develop, you might even consider keeping a journal of your insights. And, perhaps, send one or two to be shared with others to the Internet website, mentioned in Chapter 1, at IFPINC.COM. I will continue to post new insights, refinements, and helpful tools on the webpage, so be sure to check it from time to time.

And finally, I hope that the time that you have spent with this text will continue to reward you and aid those whom you care about.

Source Notes

CHAPTER 2

[1]Lewis R. Goldberg and others, such as Michael K. Mount, Murray R. Barrick, and J. Perkins Strauss, have done extensive research regarding the five core personality factors. These five elements of personality are: Extroversion v. Introversion; Agreeableness v. Disagreeableness; Conscientiousness/ Dependability v. Undependability; Emotional Stability v. Neuroticism; Intellectual Ability. The Korem Profiling System was adapted from the first four, thus providing the four gauges/questions used in the system. A principle reason that the Korem Profiling System can be used cross-culturally is because human behavior internationally is comprised of the same core traits.

CHAPTER 3

[1]As noted in Chapter 2, the four gauges used in the Korem Profiling System were derived from the "Big-Five" personality traits. The CONTROL-EXPRESS gauge in this chapter and the ASK-TELL gauge in Chapter 4 are similar to the Agreeableness v. Disagreeableness and the Extroversion v. Introversion gauges noted in the source note in Chapter 2. These two gauges are also similar to those proposed by David Merrill and Roger Reid in their book, *Personal Styles and Effective Performance* (Chilton, 1981) which was derived from the research of Dr. James W. Taylor. (The labels used to represent the ends of the ASK-TELL and CONTROL-EXPRESS gauges are the same as the Merrill and Reid model as they have received common acceptance.) Merrill and Reid presented techniques for reading interpersonal style as a way to improve management interactions. These earlier and highly recommended works were some of the first to describe the use of interpersonal style management as a tool for managerial and business success. However, it is the understanding of the author that the present work is the first to combine a modified application of these two gauges with the two gauges

discussed in Chapter 7 in order to provide a comprehensive personality profile that can be used in an impromptu, non-self-assessment test environment that is consistent with current psychological research regarding the basic structure of human personality.

CHAPTER 5

[1]The combining of these two gauges is similar to two of the "Big Five" gauges extensively researched by Goldberg and others as well as the Merrill and Reid model. Regarding the Merrill and Reid model, while the labels used for the ends of each gauge are the same, the descriptors for each type are significantly different as the actions identified in the Korem Profiling System focus on communication actions.

CHAPTER 7

[1]The two *performance* gauges, CONFIDENT-FEARFUL and PREDICTABLE-UNPREDICTABLE are similar to two of the "Big Five" gauges tested by Lewis R. Goldberg. The dependability dimension, Conscientiousness/Dependability v. Undependability, allows us to categorize peoples' behavior as predictable/dependable v. unpredictable/undependable. The stability dimension adds a measure of motivation. The stability dimension, Emotional Stability v. Neuroticism, separates people who operate in ways that express a balance and confidence (emotional stability) from those motivated by fear (neuroticism).

CHAPTER 13

[1]Robert D. Hare, *Without Conscience* (New York: Pocket Books, 1993), pp. 23–24.

[2]Hare, p. 2.

[3]Robert Hare, "Comparison of Procedures for the Assessment of Psychopathy," *Journal of Consulting and Clinical Psychology* 53 (1985):7–16. In J. Reid Meloy, Ph.D., *The Psychopathic Mind* (Northvale, NJ: Jason Aronson, Inc., 1988).

CHAPTER 14

[1]Bruce Horowitz, "AOL takes right approach offering mea culpa, rebate, *USA Today*, 9 August 1996.

[2]As quoted in the *Dallas Morning News*, 12 January 1997.

[3]*Associated Press Wire Service.*

Additional
Resources

PROFILING ADDENDUM ON THE WEB

A website on the Internet is provided by International Focus Press (IFP) that updates this text. IFP is the first publisher to use the web to act as a live addendum for a book in print without additional cost to the reader. If you develop new application ideas, refinements, etc., please send them, and IFP will post many of them. The E-mail address is provided at the website and the website can be accessed without cost at IFPINC.COM.

PROFILE SEMINARS

Professional interactive profiling seminars are available through Korem Productions. Each workshop is designed to shorten the learning curve so that participants can accurately profile others in just one day. The typical participant is able to move from 25% accuracy at the beginning of the seminar to 75% by the end of the seminar. Two-day workshop formats address specific applications for various professions, which presently include: human resource, healthcare, education, audit, law enforcement, security, and sales. Workshops are conducted in both open and in-house forums.

Throughout the workshop, your profiling skills will be tested as you view fascinating and carefully selected video clips of real people in real situations. As you learn the Korem Profiling System, you will be asked to profile each person you see by entering your responses on your *own* interactive touch-key pad. The interactive system immediately tracks your comprehension of each critical point. Collective class responses are then projected at the front of the class so that you can see how you are progressing in comparison to your colleagues. This also enables the faculty member (Dan Korem or another internationally respected faculty member) to immediately determine which concepts need further clarification. This powerful interactive dimension is not only engaging and keeps everyone involved, but studies also demonstrate that learning retention is increased by up to 30%.

For information contact: Korem Productions, P.O. Box 1587, Richardson, TX 75083. Telephone: (972) 234-2924.

THE ART OF PROFILING INTERACTIVE CD-ROM

It is anticipated that IFP will release a CD-ROM companion to the text, *The Art of Profiling—Reading People Right the First Time,* that you can use to sharpen your profiling skills. Video clips of real people in numerous environments will be provided to test your profiling skills. Additionally, Dan Korem will provide narrative explaining the nuances of each read and guidance when you inaccurately profile any of the video clips. Please consult the IFP website for the release date or write IFP at the address provided.

STREETWISE PARENTS, FOOLPROOF KIDS (2d ed.)

Written for parents, educators, law enforcement officers, and other professionals who interact with youths (ages 4-17). Includes the following:

- Profile of the youth who is the easiest to deceive and how to instruct a youth to resist becoming that person.
- A simple method for teaching a youth how to discern whether someone is lying or telling the truth.
- How to recognize who is potentially violent and appropriate responses.
- How to distinguish between illusion and reality.
- When it is and isn't appropriate to use deception—i.e., trick play in football versus cheating.
- Guidelines for distinguishing when fantasy and imagination can turn harmful.
- Good versus bad secrets—when it is and isn't appropriate to keep a secret and what to do with harmful secrets.
- Guidelines for healthy decision making and the parent's role.
- Additional chapters that affect the youth culture, including: entertainment and news media, drugs, gangs, and cults.

285 Pages Hardbound ISBN: 0-9639103-2-9 $19.95 postage paid.

SUBURBAN GANGS—THE AFFLUENT REBELS

In the mid-1980s, Dan Korem predicted that gangs would appear in affluent communities for the first time in US history. By the late 1980s his prediction became fact. Presently, the typical suburb of 50,000 has 250–500 gang members. Based upon seven years of research in eleven countries, Dan Korem, an internationally recognized gang expert and lecturer and consultant for the FBI, has produced the first hard-hitting guide to counterattack this unprecedented trend.

Laced with riveting accounts and lucidly written for professionals and laymen, *Suburban Gangs* answers the whys while giving real solutions and identifying the following critical information:
- The only proven gang prevention strategy that stops gangs from forming in affluent and inner-city communities. (Korem applied this strategy to over 400 inner-city youths, and not one joined a gang in six years.)
- The Missing Protector Factor: The most important factor that puts a youth at risk of gang recruitment.
- The profile of the youth most likely to be recruited into an affluent gang.
- Gang types and activities found in affluent communities.
- Disengagement strategy and the eleven reasons why youths disengage from gangs.
- Why skinhead and occultic gangs mysteriously appeared simultaneously in the US and Europe.
- Unique survey of skinhead gang members.
- European parallels that foreshadow gang trends in the US.
- Photographic pictorial—Over 70 photographs show how youth gang cultures in the US and Europe now influence each other for the first time in modern history.

285 Pages Hardbound ISBN: 0-9639103-1-0 $19.95 postage paid.

PSYCHIC CONFESSION
Forty-eight-minute videotape presentation in which the psychic demonstrations of cult-like leader James Hydrick are exposed as trickery, and Hydrick provides history's first recorded confession of a noted psychic. Critically acclaimed by the *Los Angeles Times* and suitable for both adults and youths. **$20.00 postage paid.**

CULTS IN OUR MIDST
Margaret Singer, Ph.D., with Janja Lalich
Although not published by IFP, Dr. Singer's text is regarded as the definitive text on cult behavior. Over twenty million people have joined cults during the past two decades, and Dr. Singer, a clinical psychologist and emeritus adjunct professor at U. C. Berkeley, has interviewed over 3,000 current and former cult members and their relatives and friends. Recognized internationally as the leading authority on cults and thought reform, Dr. Singer's text thoughtfully addresses the following issues:
- Why don't people just leave cults?

• What characteristics do cults have in common?
• Why aren't the US Marines or Alcoholics Anonymous considered a cult?
• Who are the people most likely to join cults?
• Where can I go for help if someone I love is living in a cult?
• What actions can we take to prevent the spread of cults' influence?
381 Pages Hardbound ISBN: 0-7879-0051-6 $27.50 postage paid.

WORLDS AT WAR, MINDS AT PEACE
James T. Reese, Ph.D.

Each of the five members of a midwest family were shot in the face with a shotgun while asleep. James T. Reese of the FBI's Behavioral Sciences Unit was assigned the case. Although a seasoned veteran, for months afterwards, whenever Reese put his daughter to bed, he returned to her bedroom and looked at her face to assure himself that she was all right.

This is what is called a "critical incident"—an event which can severely traumatize anyone, producing reactions that interfere with our ability to function. Reese had seen others on his unit lose control of their lives as they dealt with grisly crimes. Now he was struggling to cope. Traditional "stress management" training doesn't work in these kinds of environments. Reese knew it. So he asked the director of the FBI for permission to develop a strategy that would allow people to face life's most hellish moments and retain or recapture control of their emotions and regain balance in their lives.

Reese's teaching is recognized as the finest in the world, having taught at the FBI's National Academy for many years. Laced with powerful anecdotes of his experiences in the "mind hunter" unit, Reese shares what he has taught to tens of thousands in law enforcement and Fortune 500 organizations . . . An attitude and regimen that works even under the most severe conditions.
225 Pages Hardbound ISBN: 0-9639103-4-5 $21.95 postage paid. Available: April 1, 1998

TO OBTAIN MATERIALS
To obtain any of the materials listed or to receive a list of other books and materials distributed by International Focus Press, please consult IFP's website at www.IFPINC.COM or write:

INTERNATIONAL FOCUS PRESS
P.O. BOX 1587
RICHARDSON, TEXAS 75083

Author

Dan Korem is an independent investigative journalist, author, documentary producer, and keynote speaker. He is the president of two Dallas-based communication companies that research various international issues and communicate through live forums and electronic and print media. Korem is a keynote speaker and seminar leader for corporate, professional, law enforcement, and university groups in the US and abroad. Issues addressed include: deception as it affects business, ethical, and social trends; profiling in corporate as well as confrontational environments; formation of aberrant groups; international youth trends; youth gangs and gang prevention; and methods of paranormal power fakers.

In 1983, Korem produced the documentary, *Psychic Confession*, the first exposé and confession of a cult-like figure who claimed to have paranormal powers. He is also the author of several critically acclaimed books, including *Suburban Gangs—The Affluent Rebels* and *Streetwise Parents, Foolproof Kids* (2d ed.).